Context, Cognition, and Deafness

CONTEXT, COGNITION, AND DEAFNESS

M. Diane Clark

Marc Marschark

Michael Karchmer

Editors

Gallaudet University Press
Washington, D.C.

Gallaudet University Press
Washington, DC 20002

Library of Congress Cataloging-in-Publication Data

Context, cognition, and deafness / M. Diane Clark, Marc Marschark, Michael Karchmer,
editors.
    p. cm.
  Includes bibliographical references and index.
  ISBN 1-56368-105-6 (alk. paper)
   1. Deaf children. 2. Child development. 3. Cognition in children. I. Clark, M. Diane.
  II. Marschark, Marc. III. Karchmer, Michael A.

HV2391 .C66 2001
155.45′12—dc21

                                                                    2001023017

⊛ The paper used in this publication meets the minimum requirements of American National Standard for Information Sciences—Permanence of Paper for Printed Library Materials, ANSI Z39.48–1984.

For William C. Stokoe—
scholar, teacher, and a great man

CONTENTS

Acknowledgments   ix

Contributors   xi

1. Interdisciplinary Perspectives on Context, Cognition,   1
   and Deafness: An Introduction
   M. Diane Clark

2. Deafness, Cognition, and Language   6
   William C. Stokoe

3. The Clinical Assessment of Deaf People's Cognitive Abilities   14
   Jeffery P. Braden

4. The Impact of Sign Language Expertise on Visual Perception   38
   Margaret Wilson

5. Cognition and Language in Italian Deaf Preschoolers   49
   of Deaf and Hearing Families
   Elena Pizzuto, Barbara Ardito, Maria Cristina Caselli, and
   Virginia Volterra

6. Understanding Language and Learning in Deaf Children   71
   Marc Marschark and Jennifer Lukomski

7. Vocabulary Development of Deaf and Hard of Hearing   88
   Children
   Amy R. Lederberg and Patricia E. Spencer

8. Theory of Mind Development in Deaf Children   113
   Ethan Remmel, Jeffrey G. Bettger, and Amy M. Weinberg

9. Emotional Development in Deaf Children: Facial Expressions,   135
   Display Rules, and Theory of Mind
   Colin D. Gray, Judith A. Hosie, Phil A. Russell, and Ellen A. Ormel

10. Social Change and Conflict: Context for Research on Deafness   161
Kathryn P. Meadow-Orlans

11. Context, Cognition, and Deafness: Planning the Research   179
Agenda
Marc Marschark

Index   199

ACKNOWLEDGMENTS

The editors gratefully acknowledge individuals and institutions that provided support for this volume. First, support for a related preliminary conference titled "The Impact of Deafness on Cognition," was provided by the National Institutes of Health–National Information Center on Deafness and Communication Disorders (#1R13DC03145–01A1). *The Journal of Deaf Studies and Deaf Education* provided partial support during this conference and the American Educational Research Association provided space for the meeting. Special appreciation goes to Dr. Kathryn P. Meadow-Orlans for her keynote address during the meeting, a presentation that challenged all of us to better understand the development of deaf children. This volume was prepared while the first editor was on a National Institutes of Mental Health training fellowship in prevention research at Johns Hopkins University Prevention Research Center (5 T32 MH 18834–12).

CONTRIBUTORS

Barbara Ardito
Institute of Psychology
Division of Neuropsychology of
Language and Deafness
National Research Council
Rome, Italy

Jeffery P. Braden
Department of Educational
Psychology
University of Wisconsin, Madison
Madison, Wisconsin

Jeffrey G. Bettger
Department of Special Education
San Francisco State University
San Francisco, California

Maria Cristina Caselli
Institute of Psychology
Division of Neuropsychology of
Language and Deafness
National Research Council
Rome, Italy

M. Diane Clark
Department of Psychology
Shippensburg University
Shippensburg, Pennsylvania

Colin D. Gray
Department of Psychology
University of Aberdeen
Aberdeen, Scotland

Judith A. Hosie
Department of Psychology
University of Aberdeen
Aberdeen, Scotland

Amy R. Lederberg
Department of Education Psychology
and Special Education
Georgia State University
Atlanta, Georgia

Jennifer Lukomski
Department of School Psychology
Rochester Institute of Technology
Rochester, New York

Marc Marschark
Department of Research
National Technical Institute
for the Deaf
Rochester, New York

Kathryn P. Meadow-Orlans
Professor Emerita
Gallaudet University
Washington, D.C.

Ellen A. Ormel
Department of Psychology
University of Aberdeen
Aberdeen, Scotland

Elena Pizzuto
Institute of Psychology
Division of Neuropsychology of
Language and Deafness
National Research Council
Rome, Italy

Ethan Remmel
Department of Psychology
Stanford University
Stanford, California

Phil A. Russell
Department of Psychology
University of Aberdeen
Aberdeen, Scotland

Patricia E. Spencer
Department of Social Work
Gallaudet University
Washington, D.C.

William C. Stokoe
Professor Emeritus
Gallaudet University
Washington, D.C.

Virginia Volterra
Institute of Psychology
Division of Neuropsychology of
Language and Deafness
National Research Council
Rome, Italy

Amy M. Weinberg
Graduate School of Education
University of California
Berkeley, California

Margaret Wilson
Department of Psychology
North Dakota University
Fargo, North Dakota

Context, Cognition, and Deafness

1

INTERDISCIPLINARY PERSPECTIVES ON CONTEXT, COGNITION, AND DEAFNESS: AN INTRODUCTION

M. Diane Clark

Webster defines context as "the interrelated conditions in which something exists or occurs: environment, setting." *Context, Cognition, and Deafness* employs this definitional sense to explore the effects of person-environment outcomes that occur during the cognitive development of individuals with varying levels of hearing loss (Clark 1993). These outcomes are interrelated and depend on the fit between individuals and their environments or social settings such as family, peers, and schools. *Context, Cognition, and Deafness* examines these interactions in order to explain successful developmental and educational outcomes within these social fields.

An interdisciplinary approach is vital to an understanding of cognitive development, cognitive strategies, and educational attainments within these layered contexts. Here, the strength of many methodologies works together to disambiguate the sometimes conflicting and often confusing research findings related to the cognitive development of individuals with different degrees of hearing loss. Current research is providing information helpful for understanding earlier findings that concluded the educational performances of deaf children of deaf parents were at levels equal to or higher than those of hearing children with hearing parents (Brasel and Quigley 1977; Meadow 1967, 1968, 1969; Stuckless and Birch 1966; Vernon and Koh 1970. See also Marschark 1993 and Meadow-Orlans, this volume.) Recent work on the use of ABC stories (Rutherford 1993) and the focus on connecting written English with signs through fingerspelling play (Erting, Thumann-Prezioso, and Benedict 2000) point out tools that culturally Deaf children possess that can be used when they enter school and begin formal instruction in reading English. The early parent–child focus on preliteracy skills provides the connection between ASL and written English, which in turn fosters reading readiness. These types of interdisciplinary connections between anthropology, education, psycholinguistics, and early parent–child socialization allow research discrepancies to be synthesized and integrated into current and expanded theoretical frameworks.

Integrating a wide range of research paradigms and their focuses provides a challenge to this approach. Differences in analysis levels employed across disciplines can be compared to the story of three blind men trying to describe and understand an elephant. One explores the elephant's trunk and exclaims that the animal is like a snake; another, after feeling the tail, exclaims that it is a rope; while the third, after running his hands up and down one of the elephant's legs, believes that it must be a tree. A dialogue integrating their experiences would have been more descriptive of this multifaceted animal. An example more central to this field is the difference between clinical and cultural paradigms. This dichotomy is often related to an emic-etic point of view (Clark 1998). The clinical paradigm is often characterized as hearing-centered (Lane 1988) or an etic (e.g., outsider) perspective, and the cultural paradigm is characterized as a deaf-centered (Paul and Jackson 1993) or emic (e.g., insider) perspective.

Within this dichotomy, the clinical framework understands "deafness as a disease or disability . . . [to be either] prevented or cured" (Paul and Jackson 1993, xiv). This clinical framework assumes that research on hearing individuals will apply directly to individuals with hearing losses. In contrast, the cultural view focuses on broader effects such as sociology and anthropology, which "depathologize deafness" (ibid.). This culture paradigm "has called into question the indiscriminate application of mainstream developmental theories" (ibid.) to the development of those with hearing losses. Both frameworks can be useful when fit within conceptual frameworks that "explore the interaction of hearing children of hearing parents as well as those of deaf children of both hearing and deaf parents" (ibid.). This type of conceptual framework has been called a "developmental-interactive" model. Comparisons now are made not only in regard to deaf children found within different family contexts (deaf versus hearing parents) but with hearing children found within these same contexts. The strength of each framework now complements the other in explaining person-environment interactions through more interdisciplinary modeling.

Interested Disciplines and Some Concerns

Disciplines related to the intersection of cognition and deafness include anthropology, education, psychology, linguistics, sociology, communication disorders, and neuroscience. Each of these disciplines has overlapping subspecialties that if integrated could inform a broad view of context, cognition, and deafness. Several issues have hindered this type of integration. Diverse research paradigms are used within these related disciplines. The different methodologies make interdisciplinary dialogue and cross-study comparisons problematic. Research is spread widely across different settings and published within discipline-specific journals, making broad access to the information more "hit or miss."

Concern about the lack of interdisciplinary integration is not new (e.g., Clark and Hoemann 1991). However, interdisciplinary discussion has occurred, if only at specialty meetings. These discussions encouraged researchers to be clearer when defining variables, such as "deaf participants" or "fluent in American Sign Language" (ASL), and recent publications reflect more precise definitions. In addition, methodological issues such as how control groups are defined and chosen and which statistical analyses are most appropriate have received attention. Lederberg and Spencer have combined sequential designs (including both cross-sectional and longitudinal data collection) in their ongoing project focusing on vocabulary learning. Future analysis can now include more person-centered views, exploring individual differences in background factors such as early detection, family characteristics, linguistic backgrounds, and educational settings.

Thorny and emotional questions remain for truly interdisciplinary endeavors. They include:

- What topics are important within the field?
- How can researchers from divergent backgrounds utilizing different methodologies benefit from ongoing research programs?
- What types of training programs are available to encourage interdisciplinary research?
- How can theory inform practice?

Marschark and Lukomski have integrated two areas of research—school psychology and cognitive development—as one example of the intersection of theory and practice.

A common lament when discussing interdisciplinary issues is the lack of dialogue between teachers and researchers. Teacher/practitioners tend to find basic research questions "irrelevant" to their daily experiences. At the same time, basic researchers rarely stop to ask how their findings affect the daily experiences of practitioners (see Marschark, this volume). Current projects are bridging this gap by utilizing mutual self-interests between these groups. Basic researchers require access to participants and teacher/practitioners desire curricula to improve the educational outcomes for their students. Through dialogue and partnerships, both of these goals can be met for the mutual benefit of all constituents.

Content, Cognition, and Deafness Defined Interdisciplinarily

Johnson, Liddell, and Erting's (1989) *Unlocking the Curriculum: Principles for Achieving Access in Deaf Education* highlighted the differences of philosophy regarding whether deaf children should be taught ASL as their first language and precisely how to establish the most supportive context for deaf children within school systems. Regardless of people's opinions on these polarizing issues, many people realized that the current status quo was not working. Since that time, more networks have been established among researchers, and the dialogue has begun to effect the successful adaptation of children with hearing losses. Interdisciplinary research will benefit from these dialogues.

Researchers have met face-to-face, some for the first time, over the last several years at preconference workshops designed for sharing methodologies and research concerns. Many of these researchers had not had the opportunity to share research ideas cross-disciplinarily up until this point. Such meetings have provided opportunities to integrate research ideas and to engage in collaborative exchanges.

The goal of an interdisciplinary program of research should be to continue networking in order to determine how and under what conditions successful development occurs given specific background conditions. Individual outcomes can then be evaluated by determining how well individuals with hearing losses adapt to their context. Person-centered analyses in conjunction with variable-centered analyses of these outcomes can then begin to delineate what works, when, and for whom.

In Sum

The 1990s provided many challenges and changes for the field, which is sometimes referred to as "psychology of deafness." Networks have been established, dialogues have begun, and theorizing has increased. Publication rates have jumped with the addition of the *Journal of Deaf Studies and Deaf Education,* which has also fostered international collaboration. In addition, many deaf researchers have joined the field. Knowledge in related fields, such as the linguistics and psycholinguistics of ASL, have stimulated creative new questions related to ASL literacy and bilingual/bicultural education.

I believe the development of networks at conferences and the resulting dialogues have changed the ways in which business is conducted in this field. Dialogue at these meetings is always exciting, if at times heated. The opportunities to discuss how research findings can be integrated and moved forward has been eagerly seized. Researchers want to continue networking in order to be able to benefit from the synergy created during these brief meetings.

The advantage of moving to a more inclusive, interdisciplinary framework is that it addresses critical research issues while building theory. In addition, the move out of individual disciplines to more interdisciplinary exchange allows for synergistic exchanges to challenge and evaluate our current state of affairs. These changes have positioned the field to make a qualitative jump in knowledge during this decade. This volume begins to bridge the gap between the many disciplines focusing on the intersection of cognition and deafness. Snapshots from the "bigger picture" are included as we increase efforts to network among the diverse researchers investigating aspects of cognition and development among those with varying degrees of hearing loss. The goal is to develop strong connections, both formally and informally, and to understand the impact of deafness on cognition.

References

Brasel, K. E., and S. P. Quigley. 1977. Influence of certain language and communication environments in early childhood on the development of language in deaf individuals. *Journal of Speech and Hearing Research* 20:81–94.

Clark, M. D. 1993. A contextual/interactionist model and its relationship to deafness research. In *Psychological perspectives on deafness,* ed. M. Marschark and M. D. Clark, 353–62. Hillsdale, N.J.: Lawrence Erlbaum.

Clark, M. D. 1998. A hitchhiker's guide to holes and dark spots: Some missing perspectives in the psychology of deafness. In *Psychological perspectives on deafness,* vol. 2, ed. M. Marschark and M. D. Clark, 331–42. Mahwah, N.J.: Lawrence Erlbaum.

Clark, M. D., and H. W. Hoemann. 1991. Methodological issues in deafness research. In *Advances in cognition, education, and deafness,* ed. D. S. Martin, 423–26. Washington, D.C.: Gallaudet University Press.

Erting, C. J., C. Thumann-Prezioso, and B. S. Benedict. 2000. Bilingualism in a deaf family: Fingerspelling in early childhood. In *The deaf child in the family and at school: Essays in honor of Kathryn P. Meadow-Orlans,* ed. P. E. Spencer, C. J. Erting, and M. Marschark, 41–54. Mahwah N.J.: Lawrence Erlbaum.

Johnson, R. E., S. K. Liddell, and C. J. Erting. 1989. *Unlocking the curriculum: Principles for achieving access in deaf education.* Gallaudet Research Institute Working Paper 89–3, Washington, D.C.: Gallaudet University.

Lane, H. 1988. Is there a "psychology of Deaf"? *Exceptional Children* 55:7–19.

Marschark, M. 1993. *Psychological development of deaf children.* New York: Oxford University Press.

Meadow, K. P. 1967. The effect of early manual communication and family climate on the deaf child's development. Ph.D. diss., University of California, Berkeley.

———. 1968. Early manual communication in relation to the deaf child's intellectual, social, and communicative functioning. *American Annals of the Deaf* 113:29–41.

———. 1969. Self-image, family climate, and deafness. *Social Forces* 47:428–38.

Paul, P. V., and D. W. Jackson. 1993. *Toward a psychology of deafness.* Boston: Allyn and Bacon.

Rutherford, S. 1993. *A study of American Deaf folklore.* Washington, D.C.: Linstok Press Dissertation Series.

Stuckless, E. R., and J. W. Birch. 1966. The influence of early manual communication on the linguistic development of deaf children. *American Annals of the Deaf* 111:452–60.

Vernon, M., and S. D. Koh. 1970. Early manual communication and deaf children's achievement. *American Annals of the Deaf* 115:527–36.

2

DEAFNESS, COGNITION, AND LANGUAGE

William C. Stokoe

Inability to hear or hear well is an individual physical condition, but deafness is a socially constructed abstraction. Historian Nicholas Mirzoeff dates its origin early:

> Prior to the eighteenth century, deaf people did not constitute a category for social intervention by the state, and it may be said that although people were born deaf, no one was born with deafness. The constitution of deafness as a medicalized category of the body politic, and hence a social question, was the direct outcome of the Enlightenment sensualist philosophy in general and the politics of the French Revolution in particular. (1995, 6)

We have come far since the French Revolution, but we still have a long way to go. Twentieth-century textbooks on the psychology of deafness for the most part have maintained the medical categorization; deafness is still generally understood as a pathology demanding intervention, diagnosis, treatment, and description. And yet, a person who cannot hear is an individual, unique, as are we all. Whatever specialists and the public may say and think and do about deafness does not necessarily apply to an individual who cannot hear. Deafness, as Mirzoeff points out, is a label for a social, medicalized categorization that itself is flawed. To put it plainly, people who cannot hear are not all the same. Setting up deafness as a category does not make them identical. It may be hoped that in the current century, science—if not whole societies—will take more notice of human variation, of individual differences. One hopeful sign is the recent appearance of books by Oliver Sacks and others pointing out how important it is to treat patients, not diseases, and how differently individuals with the same diagnosis may react to an illness and its treatment.

A child who cannot hear well enough to decode speech may develop language and social sophistication at the same rate as a hearing child—provided the deaf child is reared in a signing milieu. Children with defective hearing may still hear well enough to acquire workable speech and to understand speakers when they can see their faces; yet it is still true that deaf children are much more likely to face difficulties in acquiring language and mental and social skills. I conclude therefore that *the difference in outcome has less to do with being deaf than with what others do about it.*

Cognitive science of the present and future will be at fault as long as one very basic fact is overlooked or its truth denied: A sign language environment for deaf children is as important to their cognitive development as a spoken language environment is for hearing children. Through interaction with sign language users, a deaf child's cognitive development can be every bit as normal as that of a hearing child. However, such an environment is available to fewer than 5 percent of deaf children—those who have deaf, signing parents and the still smaller number in genuinely bilingual programs.

Cognition is inevitably affected when a child who cannot hear lives in a spoken language environment and can neither understand what is said nor respond appropriately. What family, society, and specialists think and do have more effect on the child's cognitive development than not hearing. Interacting with the deaf child in a language that can be seen—real language, not someone's would-be ingenious code—promotes mental growth, as attested to by the life stories of hundreds of deaf people who grew up in deaf, signing families.

Inability to understand and produce normal speech is not the first effect of a child's early inability to hear. Children are far from cognitively inactive during the many months before they speak their first words and make two-word utterances. From birth, all their working senses are furiously busy taking in the world around them and using all their motor ability to interact with those bigger, active, and generally benevolent creatures who come near them. A great many developmental studies done in deaf, hearing, monolingual, and multilingual homes, including those by Volterra and Iverson (1995), reach one conclusion: All children, hearing and deaf, communicate with gestures for several months before beginning to use the language of those around them.

The findings by Volterra and Iverson should prompt us to look more closely at what is going on cognitively in children from birth onward, for it shows that infants are attending to the world around them and making sense of it—and that they express their understanding through gestures. When children communicate using gestures, before they use what we call a language, they are using their uniquely human perceptual-action system to make sense of the physical and social world in which they find themselves. At first all the senses work to bond infant to caregiver, but soon the infant becomes aware that the caregiver is not always present, and vision and movement lead it to conceptualize the distinction between self and other.

Vision takes the lead in this cognitive advance, but soon the infant's own actions are put to use. *Up* is a most important conception. Before being able to sit or stand or crawl, the infant shows a wish to be picked up and held by raising the arms. And so starts a whole unfolding of prelinguistic cognitive advances that have received much less attention from caretakers and scientists than the child's first attempts at speaking. Nevertheless, there is evidence that children's gestural interaction and the brain structures controlling and interpreting it build a foundation without which language would not exist—either in the infant or in the species.

The biological foundations of language are usually considered the modern (ca. 50,000-year-old) human vocal mechanism and the auditory system, which must be able to discriminate vocal output, treating it sometimes as different and sometimes as the same. But these are the biological components of speech, not of language. Language is cognition connected to sensory input and perceptible output. Speech is mere noise until a community of users share a convention connecting certain patterns—made by voices and detected by hearing—to meanings. There is precedent, however, for seeking cognitive precursors of language. For example, see Armstrong, Stokoe, and Wilcox (1995), Armstrong (1999), and Stokoe (forthcoming).

PERCEPTION, CONCEPTION, AND LANGUAGE

Herb Clark (1973) examines the fit between perceptual space and the terms that an individual's language has for this knowledge—that is, what everyone needs to know and does know about the three-dimensional world we live in and the workings of gravity. Logic and nature agree here: Our experience and perception of space must precede any ability we acquire to talk about it. Clark calls that basic knowledge *perceptual space* ("*P*-space"). When we talk about it, however, we use what Clark terms *language space* (*L*-space). He proposes a necessary relationship: "the concept of space underlying the English spatial terms, to be called *L*-space, should coincide with *P*-space: any property found in *L*-space should also be found in *P*-space" (28).

Clark also presents two hypotheses about the relationship of *L*-space to *P*-space. The first he calls the "correlation hypothesis, [which] claims that the structure of *P*-space will be preserved in *L*-space—that is, there will always be a close correlation between *P*-space and *L*-space" (28). He examines the biological bases of *P*-space and notes that it is asymmetrical or unequally valued. *Up* is positive and *down* negative because although gravity pulls downward, the human "canonical position" is upright. Likewise, *forward* is positive, *backward* negative. As Clark says, "there appears to be no reason, at least perceptually, to choose either leftward or rightward as being the positive direction" (33). I would suggest that brain laterality and hand preference may tend toward asymmetry here also.

Human *P*-space is entirely cognitive, not so much nonverbal as preverbal. It is contact with the physical features of terrestrial space that produces the psychophysiological features of a human infant's *P*-space. Thus conceived, *P*-space is by no means neutral or valueless. As Clark points out, in this respect it differs sharply from space described by the geometer or physicist. To *get up* is superior to lying supine if a human creature is to *get on* with the business of living. To move forward, to get on, is natural and positive as well. Forward is the direction human anatomy and physiology favor and the direction in which the human binocular visual system is directed. There is in all this a bias imposed not just by life and animal nature but additionally by human anatomy and function. *Up* to quadrupeds must be much like *behind* to us bipeds; it is a direction they are not adapted to seeing or moving in directly and easily. As Clark says, "Man is an inhabitant of a world consisting of objects, people, and time. And because of his biological makeup, he perceives these objects, people, space and time, and their interrelations in a particular way" (1973, 30).

Once again, all these experiences—perceiving and conceiving—are preverbal, or cognitive. Gestural representation of these concepts is, however, almost certainly part of the process of knowing them. It is incorrect to call such gestures (for *up, here,* etc.) preverbal because months before verbal expression begins (using the caretakers' spoken or signed language), the child has been seeing, feeling, and experiencing these features of space, getting them, as Clark (1973) puts it, into *P*-space—and, as Volterra and Iverson (1995) point out, representing and understanding them as gestures.

After explaining the properties of space and the "canonical encounter" (the face-to-face situation natural for exchange of messages, both verbal and nonverbal)[1] Clark summarizes thus,

> When man is in canonical position, P-space consists of three reference planes and three associated directions: (1) ground level is reference plane and upward is positive; (2) the vertical left-to-right plane through the body is another reference plane and forward from the body is positive; and (3) the vertical front-to-back plane is the third reference plane and leftward and rightward are both positive directions. (1973, 35)

Herb Clark's first hypothesis, "that the structure of P-space will be preserved in L-space," strongly implies that the spatial terms of a given language are originally represented and understood in gestures. Gestures that point up, down, forward, back, left, and right do more than represent P-space; they provide an externalization of our perceptions to help the perceptions become conceptions. They permit humans to internalize what is out there.

Clark states his complexity hypothesis thus: "Given two terms A and B, where B requires all the rules of application of A plus one or more in addition, A will normally be acquired before B. . . . In antonymous pairs, the positive member should be acquired before the negative member" (54–55). He illustrates this concept by pointing out that the meaning and proper use of *in* are normally acquired before the meaning and use of *into*. *Into* includes all that *in* means and adds to that the implication of movement. This addition is made dynamically visible by common gestures as well as sign languages: All or part of one hand enclosed in the other plainly signifies *in*. To signify *into*, one hand is moved into the waiting curve formed by the other. This hypothesis about spatial terms also fits well with linguistic hypotheses about marked and unmarked forms. As Clark notes, "Two of the first spatial terms to be noted are the simple deictic expressions *there* and *here*, which have been reported in most children with two-word utterances . . . with perhaps the positive term *there* predominating" (1973, 60).

The probability that perception and gestural representation of *there* does come before *here* as a handle on P-space might be empirically tested. The test would require observing the vocal and gestural activity of children for evidence that they understand the meaning of *there* and *here*. To negate this hypothesis one would need to find children who used the spoken words (or their equivalents in other languages) correctly and never used gestures for the concepts.

Observation might also test a further corollary of Herb Clark's complexity

---

1. Here, the application of the term "nonverbal" becomes questionable. Once messages are being exchanged and understood, those exchanging them may not be using spoken words; but if there is any structure at all in the expression of the messages, whether the expression is in vocal sounds, manual gestures, or simply understanding looks, the parties to the exchange have experiences something much more like the use of language than the negative term nonverbal implies. The common usage of verbal and nonverbal is doubtless too deeply ingrained to be changed by an appeal to logic and evidence, but those who continue to use the terms with their popular meanings would do well to consider the damage this practice has done and is doing to deaf children.

hypothesis: that in *P*-space as well as in *L*-space the simpler precedes the more complex. One might discover whether infants point *there* while still at a stage when getting "there" themselves or obtaining something from "there" requires the intervention of another. It may be that gestures meaning *go there* or *bring some thing here from there* are later to emerge.

It should be noted that the term *gesture* is being used here in a special sense. Infants' gestures are not all such simple matters as pointing a hand or index finger at something; they include the infant's whole aspect: eye gaze, facial expression, body posture, and more. We have no way to talk about these matters, which are indeed preverbal, without using the lexicon of *L*-space, but it should be apparent that some of the following pairs of terms are linguistic realizations of *P*-space, and others stand for cognitive operations on *P*-space: *up, down; there, here; that way* (left), *this way* (right); *come nearer, go away;* and *in, out, go in,* and *come out.*

This early phase of orienting oneself to space by perception-action may have a greater influence on a child's cognitive development than whether the child can or cannot hear speech. And this too might be tested. Once the possibility is entertained that language in a child may not begin with spoken or signed words (nor spring full grown from a genetically bestowed instinct or language organ) but may develop as a result of perceptual-motor (gestural) interaction with the world and other humans, it is possible to use Clark's approach to examine the visual–gestural means by which not only space but time, another essential feature of human existence, is internalized.

FROM SPACE TO TIME

Our earliest conception of time derives from our still earlier knowledge of space and activity: We learn at an early age that it takes more walking to get to a far place than to a near one and that running reaches both faster. Naturally, having gestural representations for *far off* and *nearby* makes it easier (not only for today's infant but also as it must have done for very early humans) to think about time by using gestures for *there* and *here* metaphorically, that is, using them to mean *later on* and *right now.*

Let us coin a term on Herb Clark's model and consider *P*-time as the cognitive grasp of such matters as *now, earlier, later,* and so on. *P*-time must be acquired later in life than *P*-space if for no other reason than that the human conception of time seems to be unique; many other animals have a very keen and well-developed sense of three-dimensional space and gravity (e.g., hunting cats, tree-top dwelling primates). But nonhuman animals have nothing like our sense and understanding of time, which comes later in human development than understanding of space. Thus, another conjecture, which might be tested and related to Clark's, is that the human conception of *P*-time depends on the earlier acquisition of *P*-space and perhaps even its transformation into gestural, and later spoken, *L*-space. One might suppose there exists a cognitive as well as a metaphysical relationship between space and time and if so that the relationship is an analogy:

P-space : *L*-space :: *P*-time : *L*-time

But this expression does not correctly represent the relationship. The linguistically expressed items that compose the *L*-space of any language map precisely onto the details of *P*-space, as Herb Clark's essay demonstrates. (Whether *P*-space "carves nature at the joints" as science is supposed to do, *L*-space does follow the cuts made by the human perceptual-action system.) For example, the *P*-space concepts of *up* and *down, forward* and *back,* and so on when translated into any language's *L*-space must be exactly translatable into any other language's *L*-space. It would be absurd to suppose that Language X has words that all other languages lack for some special space relationships—the very idea suggests the realm of science fiction.

L-space depends on *P*-space; that is, the human ability to talk about space had to follow on experiencing the basic features of space as one passes through infancy. But it may be argued that *P*-time, sorting present from past and future time, also depends on *P*-space. Not only does perceptual time figure later in the evolution of (hominid and infant) cognition than perceptual space, but also perception of space and its gestural representation (well before *L*-space is mastered) serves as an avenue to conceiving of time. Here our own *L*-time, our language, creates a complexity. Time, whether mundane or Einsteinian, cannot be directly perceived; it has to be cognitively constructed. Conceptual time (*C*-time) is a more descriptive term than *P*-time because we conceive of time and cannot perceive it with any sensory system.

Of course, making or using metaphors is clearly part of cognitive development. Gestures themselves are metaphors; pointing forward and down to mean *there* is understood to designate a point or area of space, but the gesture is a metaphor; it is not the place itself. A mental or neural network that was correlating gestures with visual perceptions-conceptions would need little adjustment to correlate the same gestures or modifications of them with a more complex conceptual construction—a moment (of whatever duration) in time.

The section before this is entitled "Perception, conception, and language" because, as Andy Clark (1998) points out, the spatial concepts and the words our languages use for them occur in that order; but perception and conception do not sufficiently mark the cognitive path to language. My argument here is that a fourth process, representation, must be recognized: perception, conception, (visible) representation, and language. Indeed, it is probably more accurate to say that concepts of the kind needed for language are formed by the interaction of perception and representation. Andy Clark puts it this way:

> It increasingly appears that the simple image of a general-purpose perceptual system delivering input to a distinct and fully independent action system is biologically distortive. Instead, perceptual and action systems work together, in the context of specific tasks, so as to promote adaptive success. Perception and action, on this view, form a deeply interanimated unity. (1998, 262)

What Andy Clark points out rings true, but it is not the whole truth. We do experience space before we can put our experience into words. However, between *P*-space and *L*-space (with *L*-space understood as the spatial terms of a language) there is *M*-space, that is, *manual* or *manifested* space (the latter adjective derives from Latin *manus* and *fecit,* "handmade").

All of us reach an understanding of the elements of space before using appropriate language for them, but as Andy Clark (1998) points out, current brain science has found that we form our conceptions of space with perception and action working together. By being picked up as infants and later by standing up and falling down and still later by looking and pointing up and down, we form our cognitive *P*-space. Without the action component of perception-and-action (called *M*-space in this context), it seems doubtful that there would be any *L*-space—or language either. No other animals possess, as far as we know, our perception of the world because no other animals have hands and arms just like ours.

This discussion of the developmental path from experience, perception, action, gesture, and word has a direct bearing on what happens when a child is unable to hear. For many months before they use language, deaf and hearing children alike are building the cognitive foundation on which language is built. By paying attention to this early stage of development, by interacting visibly and gesturally, not just vocally, caregivers can ensure that a child's cognitive development will be optimal. In the months before children begin to use the language of their human environment, their brains are growing at their fastest rate. Again, this is true whether the children can hear or not. Children are surrounded by people using terms for *L*-space as well as *L*-time, but the deaf child cannot hear these. Were it recognized that before the adult terminology for space and time are acquired, were we to surround both hearing and deaf children with people attuned to gestural representation of space and time, both might benefit. It is in the early months that the brain circuits necessary for cognition and language are being formed and connected (or selected, as Nobel neuroscientist Gerald Edelman [1987, 1989] suggests). Although some linguists think that all children are born with a brain hard-wired for language, brain science has no evidence to bear that out.

Deafness per se has little to do with this engagement of the infant's perception-action system with the world of space and time, but the development of cognition and language in the individual who cannot hear is an individual matter. Deafness is a category into which society lumps a population that, like all populations, is full of variation. However, evidence abounds that infants and young children who cannot hear will develop cognitively and acquire language, with all that entails—if others interact with them in a sign language or even use gestures with them and are attuned to the children's own gestural representations. Parents of hearing children naturally and without conscious attention use gestures, but parents of deaf children are often told to suppress gesturing because it will interfere with the child's acquisition of speech—nothing could be more pernicious and further from the truth. Moreover, infants and children who can hear stand to benefit also from early visual, gestural interaction with elders as their brains and minds are being formed in the months when communication leads to language.

Realization that perception, conception, and visible representation precede competent use of language terms for basic concepts could lead to better opportunities for deaf children and help them acquire full language competence. Bilingual programs in schools for the deaf (which supply clearly visible terms for time and space) are still not very numerous, but their results are positive and impressive. The children acquire linguistic competence in a natural process: first *P*-space and *P*-time, then the sign language representation of these, and almost at the same time, spoken *L*-space and *L*-time.

In his book *The Hand: How Its Use Shapes the Brain, Language, and Human Culture*, Wilson (1998) presents case histories of experts in diverse occupations: puppeteers, jugglers, mountain climbers, musicians, sculptors, and mechanics. What they have in common besides preeminence in their particular fields is a history of using their hands creatively from an early age and following their hands' lead into successful and satisfying life work. Except for mountain climbing and repairing and rebuilding machinery, most of these people use their hands in the arts or entertainment. This suggests that it matters little whether the hands are used instrumentally, to climb a cliff or balance a crankshaft, or symbolically—to perform music, present a drama with marionettes as characters, shape clay or marble, or create intricate patterns of movement with falling objects. The important factor seems to be that using hands has a profound effect; it can shape an individual's life. Hands and brains coevolved, as Wilson, a neuroscientist, cogently explains.

It seems likely that creative and symbolic use of human hands would have had from the outset at least as much effect as their instrumental use, as in tool making. Our growing knowledge about hands and brains and sign languages strongly suggests that there were sign languages long before there were spoken languages (see, for example, Armstrong 1999). Heeding what hands and their movements can signify naturally and directly to eye and mind could also help us give all children, including deaf children, the best possible chance to reach their full potential. Hands are real—not abstractions—and they are so thoroughly connected to brains that their use literally makes impact after impact on cognition.

References

Armstrong, D. F. 1999. *Original signs: Gesture, sign, and the sources of language.* Washington, D.C.: Gallaudet University Press.

Armstrong, D. F., W. C. Stokoe, and S. E. Wilcox. 1995. *Gesture and the nature of language.* New York: Cambridge University Press.

Clark, A. 1998. Where brain, body, and world collide. *Dædalus* 127(2):257–81.

Clark, H. 1973. Space, time, semantics, and the child. In *Cognitive development and the acquisition of language,* ed. T. Moore, 27–63. New York: Academic Press.

Edelman, G. 1987. *Neural Darwinism: The remembered present.* New York: Basic Books.

Mirzoeff, N. 1995. *Silent poetry: Deafness, sign, and visual culture in modern France.* Princeton, N.J.: Princeton University Press.

Stokoe, W. C. Forthcoming. *Language in hand: Why sign came before speech.* Washington, D.C.: Gallaudet University Press.

Volterra, V., and J. Iverson. 1995. When do modality factors affect the course of language acquisition? In *Language, gesture, and space,* ed. K. Emmorey and J. S. Reilley, 371–90. Hillsdale, N.J.: Lawrence Erlbaum.

Wilson, F. 1998. *The hand: How its use shapes the brain, language, and human culture.* New York: Pantheon Books.

3

THE CLINICAL ASSESSMENT OF DEAF
PEOPLE'S COGNITIVE ABILITIES

Jeffery P. Braden

Clinical assessment differs from other forms of assessment because it has a direct social purpose for the person being evaluated. That is, clinical assessment typically seeks information to help make decisions that will influence the person's social disposition. Examples of such decision making include assignment to educational programs, eligibility for vocational rehabilitation services, sentencing in criminal proceedings, or allocation of health insurance benefits. Knowledge of a deaf person's cognitive abilities may be important in making these and other decisions. This chapter reviews the common contexts in which clinical assessments of deaf people's cognitive abilities are conducted. It also looks at the methods used for clinical assessment, issues and controversies related to clinical assessment, and guidelines for effective clinical assessment practices.

CONTEXTS FOR CLINICAL ASSESSMENT

Clinical assessment of cognitive abilities is a relatively recent practice. The first practical test of intelligence was developed in the early 1900s by Binet and Simon (1914) to help Parisian educators decide which students were most likely to profit from academic instruction and which students were most likely to profit from vocational instruction.[1] These clinical tests were quickly translated into other languages and applied to other purposes, including eligibility for immigration, identification of gifted and mentally retarded individuals in schools, and drawing distinctions between thought disorders (such as schizophrenia) and diminished cognitive ability (such as mental retardation or dementia) to guide social competency and criminal proceedings. Individually administered tests were quickly adapted for group administration and applied to military selection and assignment, employment selection, and college admissions. The significant life impacts associated with these decisions, such as immigration, employment, or college entry, continue to prompt questions regarding the value and purpose of clinical cognitive assessment (e.g., Gould 1996).

Clinical assessment differs from other forms of assessment in its purpose. The technologies and methods of assessment that clinicians use may be identical to

---

1. Many who are familiar with Binet and Simon's seminal work in intellectual assessment are not aware that these researchers also had early interest in oral and manual methods of teaching deaf children (Binet and Simon 1910).

those that researchers use. Unlike research, which seeks to better understand the nature of cognitive abilities and processes among deaf people, the clinical assessment of deaf people's intelligence is an effort to better serve them. Despite the clinician's desire to meet the needs of deaf people, it is not always clear whose needs are truly met in clinical assessments of cognitive abilities. That is, social systems may demand information about the deaf person in order to make decisions. Social agencies want to know "Is this person eligible for a program or service?" But it is not clear that this information has intrinsic value to the person. That is, if the service was available without restrictions, would it be necessary to assess the deaf person's cognitive abilities? Consequently, when one considers the social contexts for clinical assessment, one should always consider whether the social system or the deaf person is the primary beneficiary of clinical cognitive assessment.

The importance of appropriate clinical assessment is best illustrated by the example of what can happen when clinicians fail to appropriately assess deaf people's cognitive abilities. Vernon and Andrews (1990, 203) describe the case of Susan, a deaf girl whose developmental delays and extremely low IQ from a language-loaded intelligence test[2] led her to be placed in a residential institution serving severely mentally retarded children. The clinician based the assessment of Susan's cognitive abilities in part on characteristics associated with mental retardation in hearing children, such as delayed or absent speech, limited social skills, and significant academic deficits. Unfortunately, the clinician did not recognize these characteristics as common to deaf children of average cognitive abilities. Seven years later, Susan was given a language-reduced intelligence test, which yielded an above average IQ. She was moved to a school serving deaf children, from which she graduated, earned a college degree, married, and pursued a professional career. Had there not been a second assessment, it is possible that Susan would have experienced a substantially different life. Thus, the decision whether developmental delays are due to deafness, mental retardation, or other factors is essential for accurate differential diagnosis and appropriate social responses to deaf people's needs.

Educational Contexts

Clinical assessment of a deaf child's cognitive abilities may be useful in determining eligibility for and placement within educational programs. The most common question addressed in this context is whether the deaf child has educationally relevant cognitive impairments (e.g., Bradley-Johnson and Evans 1991; Heller 1990; Mullen 1999) or exceptional cognitive abilities (e.g., Gamble 1985; Yewchuk and Bibby 1989) in addition to hearing loss.

Differential diagnosis attempts to identify the likely causes of observed behavior (e.g., Sattler 1992). An inability to communicate with peers may be due to

---

2. By language-loaded, I mean tests whose content or directions require substantial language competency to understand and complete. The language in which competency is required is assumed to be oral English unless otherwise specified.

social-emotional factors, cognitive delays, or hearing loss. Clinicians differentially diagnose by "ruling out" and "ruling in" causes for an observed behavior. For example, if a child has normal attachment to family members and familiar peers and an average score on a cognitive test, the clinician "rules out" the possibility of social-emotional or cognitive impairments as a source of social isolation. The concomitant finding of a severe hearing loss may lead the clinician to "rule in" deafness as the cause of social isolation. Differentially diagnosing the cause of the observed behavior has implications for the educational and social responses to the behavior. For example, a child with normal social-emotional and cognitive development, along with deafness, may be best placed in a program serving deaf children. Conversely, a child with severe social-emotional delays, concomitant cognitive impairments, and deafness may be more appropriately placed in a program serving children with severe to profound mental retardation. In other situations, the child's needs may be met in an inclusive setting so that separate programmatic placement is unnecessary. However, cognitive assessment may generate hypotheses regarding the underlying causes of academic delays or maladaptive behaviors, which in turn may be useful in suggesting environmental supports for inclusive settings. Identifying the causes underlying maladaptive or atypical behavior can guide the social response to meeting the child's educational needs.

The assessment of cognitive abilities is essential for differential diagnosis in educational settings. Federal legislation, such as the Individuals with Disabilities Education Act (IDEA 1993, 1997), identifies eligibility for special education programs in large part on the basis of cognitive abilities. Cognitive abilities may be used as a positive indicator of a condition; for example, mental retardation requires evidence of substantial and pervasive cognitive delay. Cognitive abilities may also be a negative indicator. For example, social-emotional disturbance requires that the observed educational problems not be due to cognitive delays. Finally, cognitive abilities may be used for both positive and negative indicators of a condition. For instance, a learning disability diagnosis requires evidence of a deficit in one or more basic psychological processes, yet also requires that the student's overall cognitive ability or aptitude be substantially higher than current achievement levels. Other diagnostic systems, such as the *Diagnostic and Statistical Manual-Fourth Edition* (DSM-IV) (American Psychiatric Association 1994), adopt similar definitions of disability relative to cognition.

Clinical cognitive assessment is often essential for guiding decisions regarding eligibility for special education services. Furthermore, these eligibility categories are often associated with specific educational programs and services. However, this need not be the case; recent trends in special education have sought to sever the link between eligibility category and services provided (Prasse and Schrag forthcoming), so that educational placement and services are provided based on the child's response to instruction and services rather than diagnostic category. However, the special education tradition to identify diagnostic category with a service or program is still strong, and so eligibility decisions may also drive service and placement decisions. For most deaf children, the primary decision for special education eligibility is made independently of cognitive ability—that is, on the basis of hearing loss. However, cognitive assessment is nearly always included in educational assessments to help rule out or rule in the presence of additional cognitive disabilities that may render the child eligible for additional or different educational services (e.g., Sikora and Plapinger 1997).

Social Services Contexts

Clinical cognitive assessment in social services contexts helps determine eligibility for services. For example, deaf children who have cognitive disabilities may qualify for additional services, such as respite care, that are not available to deaf children without cognitive disabilities. Clinical cognitive assessment may also help social service agencies select appropriate assistance. For example, a vocational rehabilitation counselor serving a deaf adult who qualifies for services on the basis of hearing loss may use cognitive assessment data to help determine whether support for a postsecondary educational program, job training, or sheltered workshop setting might best meet the person's needs (e.g., Fry 1986). Social service agencies that demand cognitive assessment data to determine eligibility or placement include health insurance agencies, vocational rehabilitation services, and social welfare and support agencies. In some contexts, agencies may demand cognitive assessment results for deaf people to determine additional services or to recommend program/treatment options.

The use of cognitive assessment in determining eligibility for, and guiding decisions about, social services is sometimes controversial. Of course, decisions are made on the basis of many factors—not just cognitive test scores—but cognitive abilities may influence a person's eligibility for and selection of social services. Labeling is a controversial practice; on the one hand, the label of cognitive disability may enable a child or family to receive additional support from social agencies. Yet, on the other hand, being labeled as cognitively disabled may elicit negative expectations from teachers, peers, or others in the community, which can damage the child's development. Likewise, the costs of program or treatment selection differ markedly for the person versus the agency. Agencies typically seek to minimize errors and avoid costly programs, especially those that are unlikely to succeed. People typically seek the most services regardless of cost. For example, a deaf adult may want to try college, but the vocational rehabilitation agency may be reluctant to support this effort, especially if cognitive assessment data suggest the person has cognitive abilities lower than other college-bound students. Appropriately and accurately assessing the cognitive abilities of deaf people presumably helps both agencies and people by maximizing the person–program match. But critics argue that making such decisions with cognitive assessment results may "track" people into options that may limit or deny social, psychological, or economic benefits.

Finally, clinical assessment may be performed to help deaf people better understand their abilities and characteristics, so that they can make informed decisions about career, vocational, and other life choices (see Fry 1986; Sattler 1992). Assessment of general intelligence may be useful in this regard, but more commonly, clinicians seek to describe people's cognitive styles and preferences to help them make informed and appropriate life choices. Relatively few adults seek such information on their own, and probably even fewer deaf adults seek clinical assessment for personal development and planning purposes, but it is a common goal of most vocational counselors and vocational agencies to provide such information.

Medical Contexts

Occasionally, deaf people have medical conditions for which assessment of cognitive abilities is relevant. For example, closed head injury or other brain trauma, stroke, or degenerative conditions associated with disease or aging may elicit concerns about cognitive functioning. In most cases, the primary concern is with the degree to which cognitive function has changed as a result of a medical condition or trauma. In some instances, the outcome of the assessment may drive eligibility for continued medical services. For example, a cognitive assessment may suggest a diagnosis that is covered by a medical insurance program. In other instances, the information is of more value to the person and physician in serving the deaf person. For example, knowing whether and how a deaf person's abilities have changed may be useful in tracking response to stroke and in treating conditions associated with dementia (Paist and Martin 1996).

Two aspects of these assessments are particularly challenging. First, the assessment of cognitive abilities is compounded by the linguistic, cultural, and sensory differences presented by deaf people—a feature that is common to all assessments in this chapter. The second challenge is that formal assessments of cognitive abilities prior to onset of the condition are rare and typically are not available. For example, it is rare that a deaf person suffering a closed head injury in an automobile accident will have had a complete, formal assessment of cognitive abilities shortly before the accident occurred. Thus, clinicians in medical contexts must often make retrospective judgments of cognitive ability, and compare these judgments to postmorbid (i.e., after the trauma or condition) assessments of cognitive functioning.

Assessment of cognitive functioning in medical contexts is usually not a contentious issue because these assessments lead to better treatment or additional services. However, some situations are controversial. For example, a diagnosis of cognitive dementia such as Alzheimer's disease could lead to an involuntary change in an elderly deaf adult's living situation; likewise, assessment of cognitive change or stability in a coma victim may influence the decision to continue or withdraw life-support systems. The clinician's ability to reliably and accurately separate issues related to deafness, such as a lack of responsiveness to spoken language, from cognitive impairment is essential for accurate identification and treatment of some medical conditions.

Forensic Contexts

The primary use of cognitive assessment in forensic contexts is to determine an individual's competence. In criminal proceedings, cognitive assessment helps address the question "Can the defendant understand the criminal charges and participate in the legal defense?" The answer to this question determines whether the defendant will stand trial, be placed in a treatment setting such as a psychiatric hospital until competent to stand trial, or be appointed a guardian to represent his or her interests. Note that this decision is not the same as deciding whether the defendant was sane at the time of the crime; temporary insanity typically depends on assessment of emotional, not cognitive, characteristics.

In civil proceedings, competency issues generally relate to questions of custody or accommodation. Cognitive assessment may help inform these decisions by providing a sense of the cognitive capabilities (and disabilities) of the person involved. For example, a deaf parent may be accused of being incompetent to care for a child in a divorce proceeding, and findings of cognitive ability may help answer the charge. Likewise, average cognitive abilities may help demonstrate that a deaf applicant is "otherwise qualified" for a position, and thus the employer may be obligated to hire and accommodate the deaf employee's needs.

Tidyman (1974) describes a criminal case addressing a deaf person's competence. The defendant, a deaf man, was accused of murder. However, the judge ruled—in part on the basis of a psychological assessment that suggested significant cognitive deficiencies in addition to deafness—that he was not competent to stand trial. The defendant was ordered to stay in a psychiatric hospital until a (deaf) lawyer reopened the case, arguing that the defendant had been denied the right to trial. The argument depended on demonstrating to the court that the defendant's first psychological evaluation was inappropriate and inaccurate, in part because it underestimated the accused man's cognitive ability to understand the charges and participate in his own defense. The lawyer won a retrial and the defendant was acquitted—but was later arrested and convicted for a different murder.

Summary

Clinical context provides a purpose for assessment that differs from research. Research uses clinical and experimental assessment techniques to understand the development and nature of cognitive abilities in deaf people. However, clinical context uses assessment to provide information that influences a person's disposition and welfare. Most often agencies initiate or demand clinical cognitive assessment results to determine the person's disposition, but in some cases the person may seek the information to treat a problem or to enhance self-awareness and appropriate life planning. Ultimately, the value of cognitive assessment in a clinical context is determined by how effectively it helps agencies and people to make appropriate decisions.

METHODS FOR ASSESSING DEAF PEOPLE'S COGNITIVE ABILITIES

The primary challenge confronting clinicians' assessment of deaf people's cognitive abilities is discriminating language deficits resulting from cognitive deficits. Most deaf people experience substantial language deficits because they are isolated from consistent exposure to oral language. Clinicians respond to this challenge by using multiple forms of assessment and then seeking consistency of evidence across such methods. Assessment comprises many methods or tools for gathering information. Typically these tools can be divided into four major categories:

- observations
- interviews
- informal assessments, and
- formal assessment procedures.

These categories are not mutually exclusive; for example, there are some standardized, formal interview techniques. However, most clinicians typically use observations, interviews, reviews of records, informal assessments devised for specific purposes, and formal tests of intelligence to assess deaf clients' cognitive abilities.

Observations

Direct observation of behavior in cognitive assessment is rare, with the exception of observing responses to test and interview questions. Clinicians may draw inferences about a person's cognitive abilities from informal observations during assessment sessions. Atypical behaviors such as perseveration, smelling materials, or lack of responsiveness to context changes may suggest limited cognitive abilities, whereas atypical insight, use of sophisticated vocabulary, or uncommon knowledge about many topics may indicate advanced cognitive abilities. However, clinicians typically test the hypotheses developed from informal observations with more formal, structured assessment methods. Few behaviors are sufficiently frequent and reliable to differentiate cognitive abilities within the normal range. However, observation scales, such as the Glasgow Coma Scale (Lowry 1999), for measuring abnormally low cognitive abilities, and the Glasgow Outcome Scale, for measuring improvements in cognitive functioning following trauma, have been developed (Teasdale et al. 1998). As their titles imply, direct observations of cognitive behaviors are typically employed in medical settings.

Observations are valuable for developing hypotheses regarding cognitive abilities, but they may also be misleading. For example, inarticulate speech, nonlinguistic vocalizations, limited vocabulary, and a lack of responsiveness to environmental sounds may indicate depressed cognitive abilities in hearing people but are often exhibited by deaf people with normal cognitive abilities. Although direct observation of behavior can be very helpful in developing hypotheses and guiding subsequent assessment, clinicians must be cautious about the inferences they draw from observations.

Interviews and Record Reviews

Clinicians frequently use interviews and record reviews to obtain information about cognitive abilities. There are three issues commonly addressed through interviews:

1.   immediate cognitive functioning,

2. habitual levels of cognitive function, which is known as "adaptive behavior," and

3. historical development of cognitive functions.

Each of these issues is critical to assessing cognitive function and dysfunction.

Immediate Cognitive Functioning

Clinicians often interview a person seeking services to obtain a broad estimate of the person's cognitive abilities. These interviews are termed "mental status exams" and either follow a formal protocol or compose an informal set of questions and procedures (Brackley 1997). Mental status exams often include questions to measure people's ability to orient themselves in time, space, and social settings. Individuals whose representations of time, space, and social setting are distorted or incomplete may experience cognitive impairments.

Habitual Levels of Cognitive Function (Adaptive Behavior)

Clinicians often interview others, such as a spouse, parent, or family member, to obtain information about a person's typical functioning in home, community, or school settings. The goal of such an interview is generally to measure adaptive behavior or the individual's capacity to adapt to environments (see Schalock 1999). Formal interview protocols exist for measuring adaptive behavior (e.g., Sparrow, Balla, and Cicchetti 1984), although some take the form of rating scales that may be completed by a respondent (e.g., Lambert, Nahira, and Leeland 1993). Adaptive behavior interviews solicit information about an individual's ability to adapt to normal environmental demands, including the ability to communicate, provide independent self-care, and engage in socially sanctioned behaviors such as driving or obeying laws. Whether assessed via interview or a checklist that the respondent completes, the responses allow the clinician to compare the deaf client's adaptive behavior to the adaptive behavior of other individuals, often in the form of a scale score similar to an IQ.

Assessment of adaptive behavior is necessary for diagnosing general cognitive impairment—that is, mental retardation. A low score on an intelligence test is insufficient for a diagnosis of mental retardation. To make such a diagnosis, the clinician must also provide evidence of delayed or substantially below-average functioning on a measure of adaptive behavior (American Association of Mental Retardation 1992). Thus, clinicians must assess adaptive behavior to develop a comprehensive estimate of cognitive abilities, and the primary technology for measuring adaptive behavior is to interrogate knowledgeable respondents via interviews and checklists (Schalock 1999).

Adaptations to structured interview protocols for deaf clients are limited. The Vineland Adaptive Behavior Scale (Sparrow, Balla, and Cicchetti 1984) provides special norms based on deaf children in residential schools. These norms allow clinicians to compare the adaptive behavior score of a deaf child to those of deaf children selected from a residential school population. This type of alternate norms is discussed later with respect to intelligence tests; it is a controversial but occasionally useful tool in the clinician's assessment repertoire. However, clinicians must be sensitive to the validity of certain question types contained in adaptive behavior scales. For example, one of the questions appearing on many adaptive behavior scales is whether the client can use a telephone independently. Given deaf people's hearing loss, many do not use a telephone independently and thus might be rated as failing this item unless the clinician explores the use of the telephone through assistive technologies.

Historical Development of Cognitive Functioning

Clinicians interview caregivers, such as parents, and review available records from schools, work settings, or other agencies to help understand prior cognitive functioning and history. These records frequently include observations, test scores, and the like and help provide a historical record of behaviors related to adjustment and cognitive functioning. Clinicians seek to identify the developmental history of the person's cognitive functioning to determine whether problems have been pervasive, chronic, or acute, and whether problems are manifest in multiple settings. For example, mental retardation is likely if developmental milestones such as sitting up, walking, or talking are delayed and pervasive across home, school/work, and community settings. Also, mental retardation must be evident during the developmental period, whereas later general loss of cognitive functioning indicates dementia or brain injury (American Psychiatric Association 1994). Conversely, specific cognitive dysfunctions such as learning disabilities are typically manifest only in specific situations, although they too must be first evident prior to adulthood.

Of particular concern for deaf people is the issue of appropriate development. For example, delayed speech is a salient symptom of mental retardation in hearing infants and toddlers, but delayed speech is common among bright deaf children. However, such adjustments may be overgeneralized; there is no reason that deaf children should not acquire other developmental milestones, such as sitting up, walking, or toilet training, within developmental ranges normal for hearing children. Thus, clinicians should isolate those milestones that may reflect lack of hearing from those reflecting delayed cognitive development. This can make diagnosis difficult, especially when the suspected disorder closely parallels the difficulties shared by hearing loss. For example, delayed academic achievement, especially in reading and written language, is common to children who are deaf and children who have a learning disability, rendering it extremely difficult to differentially diagnose learning disability from general language and achievement delays in deaf students (Samar, Parasnis, and Berent 1998).

Informal Tests

Clinicians may use assessment devices whose parameters are not formally described. For example, clinicians may assess a client's ability to solve certain kinds of problems or respond to various items, teach the clients some strategies for responding to these items, and then test the client again to determine whether the client learned and applied these strategies. This type of test-teach-test assessment protocol is often characterized as dynamic testing (Grigorenko and Sternberg

1998). Clinicians commonly use informal assessment protocols in neuropsychological assessment to develop hypotheses about brain-behavior relationships and in psychoeducational assessment to understand specific educational deficits.

Because informal tasks are by definition informal, little formal research has been conducted regarding the application of information assessment methods to deaf people. Dynamic testing, using groups of deaf children, has been recommended (Braden 1985a; Keane 1987) and studied (Tzuriel and Caspi 1992), although the clinical value of dynamic testing is yet unproven (Frisby and Braden 1992; Grigorenko and Sternberg 1998). Neuropsychological assessment frequently employs informal tests but is not well developed for use with deaf clients (Mayberry 1992), despite some research suggesting some nonverbal neuropsychological techniques may be useful clinical tools (Kelly 1995). Curriculum-based measurement has been recommended for use with deaf students (Roth 1991), although its technical adequacy is questionable (Allinder and Eccarius 1999). Consequently, clinicians who use informal tests with deaf people often trade off the unknown reliability of these informal measurements against the hope that they will illuminate specific features of cognitive functions of value for diagnosis and treatment. Given the lack of reliability for most of these procedures, this practice is questionable.

FORMAL TESTS OF COGNITIVE ABILITIES

Formal tests of cognitive abilities, often known as intelligence tests, are the most evolved and studied tool in the clinician's repertoire. As with other forms of assessment, clinicians seek to isolate problems of cognitive functioning from problems associated with deafness. However, tests strongly influence diagnoses, and they are—by definition—formal and constrained in their procedures. Therefore, I describe the philosophy and practice of assessment accommodations and then review research findings on the use of formal cognitive tests with deaf people.

Assessment Accommodations

Historically, accommodations have been driven by clinical intuition regarding appropriate and fair assessment practices. Initially, psychologists did little to accommodate deaf people. When deaf people scored low on language-loaded tests of cognitive ability, the results were interpreted as evidence of the deaf person's limited cognitive abilities (Braden 1994; Marschark 1993, chapter 7). However, the field gradually recognized that language-loaded tests confused language exposure and fluency with cognitive abilities, rendering low scores ambiguous. That is, does a low score on a language-loaded test reflect limited cognitive abilities, or does it reflect limited language exposure? Consequently, psychologists began to use reduced-language test content such as nonverbal tests with directions that minimized oral language comprehension (e.g., written directions) or language comprehension (e.g., gestural administration). Additional examples or practice items, removal of extra items to reduce fatigue (Garrison and Coggiola 1980), extra time, or removal of time limits on speeded tests are also used.

Next to using language-reduced assessments, the most common evaluation accommodations are translation of directions and test items into other presentation modes such as printed directions or English signs, and translation of directions and items into American Sign Language (ASL). Altering the mode in which directions or items are given, such as printing or fingerspelling oral directions or test items, may retain the original content of the test and its directions but still confound comprehension and exposure to the content with cognitive ability. For example, simply printing the words "In what way are music and humming alike?" is unlikely to tap cognitive ability in deaf people who are unfamiliar with the English words or concepts of music or humming. Conversely, translating a question from English into ASL may also introduce construct-irrelevant variance by inadvertently making the item easier or harder. For example, the question "How many are in a dozen?" translated into ASL is "How many are 12?" thus rendering the query easier than in its original form. Other effective accommodations include translating directions to ensure that deaf people understand directions and task demands (e.g., Braden and Kostrubala 1995; Maller 1996), providing additional practice items (Neuhaus 1967; Ray 1979), and offering corrective feedback on selected items (e.g., Bracken and McCallum 1998).

There are many assessment accommodations recommended for deaf people (e.g., Botterbusch and Michael 1985; Heller 1990; Heller and Harris 1987; Vernon and Andrews 1990, chapter 10); however, these recommended accommodations are driven largely by clinical intuition. In some cases, recommendations presume "higher is better" with respect to scores. That is, researchers presume that tests or practices that yield lower scores for deaf people, even nonverbal ones, are assumed to be biased (e.g., Vonderhaar and Chambers 1975). This approach is flawed because the decision that an accommodation is appropriate must be independent of its score. If not, clinicians risk a self-fulfilling prophecy—that is, accommodations that produce scores that match prior expectations are good, and those that do not are bad. Jensen (1980, chapter 9) has identified this type of reasoning as the "egalitarian fallacy." Clinicians need a framework for determining appropriate accommodations on clinical tests of cognitive abilities independent of the scores achieved by deaf people if they are to result in accurate, valid assessments.

A Framework for Accommodations

As suggested elsewhere (e.g., Braden 1999), Messick's (1995) work on assessment validity provides a framework for guiding appropriate cognitive assessment accommodations for deaf people. Messick proposes that there are two sources of error that invalidate test results: (a) construct-irrelevant variance and (b) construct underrepresentation. Construct-irrelevant variance reflects the degree to which a test measures something that it is not supposed to measure. For example, a test intended to measure cognitive abilities may presume knowledge of English, such as defining vocabulary words, explaining how two words are alike or different, or knowledge of mainstream culture, such as what individuals should do in social situations. In these situations, individuals without prior exposure to English or mainstream cultural norms may do poorly on the test due to construct-irrelevant

factors. For example, deaf people may be unable to explain the relationship between two words not because they do not understand the concept involved but
because they do not understand the English words.

Construct underrepresentation is the second source of invalidity clinicians
must avoid. Construct underrepresentation occurs when tests do not adequately
sample the construct intended. For example, a test of intelligence that included
only the ability to recall digits would be less valid than a test of intelligence that
sampled reasoning—verbal and quantitative—as well as other cognitive factors
that compose intelligence. Most clinical tests of intelligence address this problem
by including a variety of tasks to estimate cognitive ability. For this reason, most
clinical tests of intelligence are called "batteries" because they include multiple
means to sample cognitive abilities. By using multiple indicators, clinicians are
more likely to represent intelligence in their assessment and thus provide more
valid assessment of cognitive abilities.

Fortunately, most clinicians attempt to reduce or eliminate construct-irrelevant variance when assessing deaf people's cognitive abilities, most often by eliminating language-loaded directions and content items (e.g., Vernon and Andrews
1990). Unfortunately, clinicians have not considered construct underrepresentation as a threat to validity when designing assessment accommodations (but see
Marschark 1993, chapter 7). Eliminating language-loaded test items may reduce
construct-irrelevant variance, but it may also reduce construct representation. For
example, verbal reasoning and general fund of knowledge may be important aspects of cognitive ability that are not measured if verbal tests are eliminated. This
problem is not trivial; language-related knowledge and cognitive skills are far better predictors of academic achievement in deaf students (Kelly and Braden 1990;
Maller and Braden 1993; Osberger 1986) and vocational training outcomes in deaf
adults (Falberg 1983) than are language-reduced assessments.

There are many reasons why construct underrepresentation is ignored, including:

- the lack of consensus regarding the essential cognitive abilities comprising intelligence (Neisser et al. 1996)
- the presumption that general intelligence is manifest in all cognitive tasks and
  thus can be sampled with equal accuracy across verbal and nonverbal domains (see Jensen 1998), and
- the general schism between contemporary psychological research and clinical
  practices with deaf people (Braden 1994).

Regardless of the reason, it is important for clinicians to balance the need to
eliminate construct-irrelevant variance, such as language proficiency, with the
need to retain construct representation, such as adequate sampling of verbal
knowledge and reasoning (see Braden 1999).

Clinicians should seek to eliminate construct-irrelevant variance and retain
construct representation when selecting accommodations. Thurlow, Yssledyke,
and Silverstein (1995) have proposed a taxonomy for creating and describing accommodations. Essentially, accommodations affect one or more of the following
four aspects of assessment:

1. Setting (e.g., isolated room, customized furniture to fit a wheelchair)

2. Timing (e.g., breaks, extra time)

3. Presentation (e.g., large print, sign language, oral versus written directions, content)

4. Response (e.g., oral, written, signed)

Table 1 classifies commonly recommended assessment accommodations for deaf people within this taxonomy. Note that the most popular accommodations recommended for use with deaf people, such as deletion of language-loaded directions, tests, and items, are not regarded as acceptable accommodations in Thurlow et al.'s framework. Because changes to test content change what is being tested, such changes are termed "modifications" rather than "accommodations" (Tindal 1998). Thus, accommodations seek to reduce construct-irrelevant variance while retaining construct representation, whereas modifications alter construct representation by altering the construct assessed or the level at which it is assessed.

Table 1. Recommended Assessment Accommodations by Accommodation Type

Accommodation	Setting	Timing	Presentation	Response
Additional examples			✔	
Avoid examiner nonverbal cues			✔	
Eliminate language-loaded tests*			✔	✔
Eliminate speeded tests*			✔	
Eliminate time limits		✔		
Extra time		✔		
Gestural administration			✔	
Practice items			✔	
Remove "extra" items to reduce fatigue*		✔	✔	
Sign language administration**			✔	
Sign language interpreter**	✔	✔	✔	✔
Sign language response**				✔
Use reduced-language tests			✔	

*Invalid accommodation—alters test content.
**Valid only if translation is accurate.

Clinical Assessment Methods

By far the most popular accommodation clinicians use to assess deaf peoples' cognitive abilities is language-reduced tests (Braden 1994). For example, the Wechsler Performance Scales (Wechsler 1989, 1991, 1997) are the most widely used method to assess cognitive abilities in deaf people. Available research supports the use of these tests, in that reliability and validity indexes for these tests tend to be similar for groups of deaf and hearing people (e.g., Braden 1994; Braden and Hannah 1998; Bradley-Johnson and Evans 1991; Maller and Braden 1993). However, not all language-reduced tests yield comparable results. Those emphasizing manipulation of objects, such as performance batteries, produce higher scores than nonverbal tests that provide little or no motor involvement in samples of deaf people (Braden, Kostrubala, and Reed 1994). Newer nonverbal tests to measure cognitive abilities include the Universal Nonverbal Intelligence Test (Bracken and McCallum 1998), which has the added advantage of providing standardized, nonverbal, gestural administration directions, and clinical data supporting the use of the test with deaf people. Other language-reduced tests recommended for use with deaf people (see Botterbusch and Michael 1985; Osberger 1986; Vernon and Andrews 1990) include the Matrix Analogies Test (Naglieri 1985), draw-a-human-figure tests (e.g., Naglieri 1988), and the Ravens Progressive Matrices tests (e.g., Ravens 1960, 1965).

Some cognitive tests are developed specifically for deaf people, including the Snidjers-Ooman Nonverbal Intelligence Tests (Tellegen and Laros 1993), the Hiskey-Nebraska Test of Learning Aptitude (Hiskey 1966), and the Central Institute for the Deaf Preschool Performance Scale (Geers and Lane 1984). These tests typically provide gestural administration directions, nonverbal content, and norms based on deaf people. Some tests developed for hearing people have been especially adapted for use with deaf people. These include administrative modifications to the Wechsler Intelligence Scale for Children-Revised (WISC-R, Wechsler 1974) (e.g., Courtney, Hayes, Couch, and Frick 1984; Jenkinsen 1989; Ray 1979, 1982). Standardized, formal ASL translations are available for the Wechsler Intelligence Scale for Children-Third Edition (WISC-III, Wechsler 1991) (e.g., Maller 1996) and the Wechsler Adult Intelligence Scale-Third Edition (WAIS-III, Wechsler 1997) (e.g., Braden and Kostrubala 1995). Also, special norms based on deaf people are available for the WISC-R (Anderson and Sisco 1977) and the Raven's Progressive Matrices (Chatterji, Mukerjee, and Gupta 1987).

These special and adapted tests have little conceptual or empirical support. That is, despite the pervasive presumption that norms and tests developed specifically for deaf people are superior to those normed and developed on hearing people, there is little supporting evidence. There are no studies examining incremental validity, classification accuracy, or other outcomes that would support or refute the value for deaf people of special tests or special test adaptations and norms. Simply showing that special tests, administration, or norm sets produce higher scores than another method is not sufficient to demonstrate utility. Rather, evidence showing greater accuracy, prediction, or other forms of utility, such as the selection of treatments or programs, must be presented to demonstrate the value of clinical accommodations, modifications, and special norms. Given the poor technical adequacy of many special tests (e.g., Kamphaus 1985), clinicians should be cautious about using special procedures, tests, or norms when assessing deaf people.

CONTROVERSIES IN THE COGNITIVE ASSESSMENT OF DEAF PEOPLE

The clinical assessment of deaf people's cognitive abilities can be controversial. That is, some recommendations conflict, and specialists draw differing conclusions, sometimes on the basis of the same research. Four controversies surrounding clinical assessment of intelligence in deaf people deserve particular attention:

1. Deficit versus difference

2. Special versus general norms

3. Verbal versus nonverbal tests, and

4. Signed versus interpreted test administration.

Each of these controversies is described in the following sections. These sections also describe and evaluate the evidence bearing on each area of disagreement.

Deficit versus Difference

One of the longest-running controversies in the clinical assessment of deaf people's intelligence is whether lower test scores represent a deficit or a difference in cognitive abilities. Deaf people often get lower scores on tests of intelligence even when those tests reduce or eliminate language skills as a factor (Braden 1994; Braden, Kostrubala, and Reed 1994). Historically, psychologists (e.g., Pintner 1928) have suggested that deaf people may experience somewhat delayed or retarded cognitive skills, in part because of the linguistic deprivation or environmental deprivation associated with nonstandard educational settings (e.g., Raviv, Sharan, and Strauss 1973). Other psychologists (e.g., Tomlinson-Keasey and Kelly 1978; Zwiebel 1987; Zwiebel and Mertens 1985) have suggested that low scores mask qualitative differences in the way deaf people organize and process information (see Marschark 1993). This "difference" position implies that, because deaf people approach cognitive tasks differently than their hearing peers, lower scores reflect cultural and personal differences in cognitive processing styles, rather than deficits in intellectual abilities.

With respect to clinical tests of intelligence, the evidence on this point is mixed. The primary form of evidence offered to test the "deficit versus difference" position is factor analysis of cognitive test batteries. That is, if the factor structures extracted from a given test battery are similar when samples of deaf and hearing participants are analyzed independently, researchers infer that the test is tapping the same underlying cognitive traits (see Jensen 1998). However, if the factor structure for a sample of deaf participants is different from the factor structure extracted for a sample of hearing participants, then researchers infer the test may be measuring different things within the two groups. Although some factor analyses claim to provide evidence of factor differences between deaf and hearing samples (e.g., Bolton 1978; Zwiebel 1987; Zwiebel and Mertens 1985), others have found factor similarity (e.g., Braden 1985b; Sullivan and Montoya 1997; Sullivan and Schulte 1992).

Resolution of these contradictory findings is elusive, as different studies may use different methods or tests for factor analysis (Marschark 1993). However, reanalysis of multiple published data sets suggests that the age of the deaf people may explain the contradictory findings (Braden and Zweibel 1992). That is, younger samples of deaf children tend to yield substantially different factor structures than same-aged hearing peers, whereas older (12 years and older) samples show virtually identical factor structures for deaf and hearing samples. Thus, it may be that the experiential differences between deaf and hearing children affect the nature of intellectual development relatively early in the developmental span, but these differences in intellectual development gradually dissipate. This implies that deaf and hearing children become more similar in the ways they perform intellectual and cognitive processes. Such a position would be consistent with recent advances in behavioral genetics, which commonly finds fairly large environmental influences on intelligence for young children, followed by a virtual "washing out" of environmental effects—that is, strong genetic effects—for individuals as they approach adult status (e.g., Brody 1997). However, there may be other plausible accounts of this phenomenon that require investigation.

Special (Deaf) versus General (Hearing) Norms

Some tests of intelligence provide special norms based on samples of deaf participants. Clinicians can use these norms to derive IQs for deaf people if they choose. Although many clinicians presume these norms are more useful than norms based on hearing normative samples (e.g., Bradley-Johnson and Evans 1991; Vernon and Andrews 1990), this assumption is rarely justified. Apparently those who presume special norms are superior to general norms believe that special norms are more fair because they compare an individual's score to the scores of other similar individuals. Such a comparison might lead to more appropriate assessment practices and test content. Fairness appears to be the primary argument in favor of special norms, in part because most norms are based on postpublication versions of tests. That is, test content cannot be altered to accommodate deaf people because the content is fixed at publication. Special norms development may change administration procedures in specified ways (e.g., Hiskey 1966; Ray 1979), but some special norms do not and may even fail to specify standardized administration procedures (e.g., Anderson and Sisco 1977).

Two primary arguments may be advanced for special norms. The first argument is conceptual. The argument that people should be compared only to norms based on individuals similar to the person (e.g., Vernon and Andrews 1990) has been shown to be fallacious (Jensen 1980). The second argument is practical. That is, when a clinical population differs from the normal population, it may be useful to know how a person compares to an atypical clinical population. The irony is that because deaf people's IQ distributions on nonverbal or language-reduced tests are very similar to hearing people's IQ distributions on the same test (see Braden 1994), there is little clinical value in using special norms developed for language-reduced tests (Braden 1985c). A further irony is that special norms might attenuate unusual clinical test profiles, making it more difficult to diagnose specific cognitive deficits.

In contrast, deaf people's score distributions on language-loaded intelligence tests and tests of academic achievement are markedly lower than hearing people's score distributions (Braden 1994). I defer the issue of language-loaded tests of intelligence to the next section; however, there are some good reasons to consider special norms for academic achievement tests. These norms are available for the Stanford Achievement Test-9th edition, and the special norms may allow more effective interpretation of student performance. For example, special norms allow people to understand that a deaf person's achievement might be low compared to normal hearing peers but at or above average relative to deaf peers. Special achievement test norms may also provide a more sensitive and appropriate scale for linking cognitive test scores to academic achievement (Braden, Wollack, and Allen 1995; cf. Kishor 1995a, 1995b).

Verbal versus Nonverbal Tests

Recommendations to use only nonverbal or language-reduced tests with deaf people (e.g., Vernon and Andrews 1990) fail to consider the problem of construct underrepresentation. Thus, as psychologists develop consensus regarding the domain of cognitive abilities comprised in the term "intelligence" (e.g., Neisser et al. 1996), the omission of language-loaded tests may underrepresent the construct of intelligence (Braden and Hannah 1998). A practical argument favoring the use of language-loaded tests is that they predict academic achievement better than nonverbal tests (Maller and Braden 1993).

However, there are two reasons to oppose the use of language-loaded tests with deaf people. The first is that language-loaded tests do not measure the same constructs in deaf and hearing people (Maller 1996). That is, even those clinicians who want to assess language-related cognitive abilities may be unable to do so with current language-loaded tests, perhaps in part because of different language experiences that affect measurement of language-related cognitive skills. The second argument against the use of language-loaded tests with deaf people is that low verbal test scores may lead to inappropriate consequences for deaf people. That is, the consequential validity (Messick 1995) of language-loaded test scores argues against their use with deaf people because it might lead to inappropriate diagnoses of limited cognitive abilities (e.g., Vernon and Andrews 1990). The arguments for and against the use of language-loaded tests are compelling on both sides. The decision to use or avoid language-loaded tests should depend on the clinician's weighing of benefits against risks. Benefits for using language-loaded tests might include more accurate prediction or more comprehensive description of cognitive abilities. Conversely, the risks for using language-loaded tests include more error-prone scores and the possibility that scores may be interpreted inappropriately.

Signed versus Interpreted Test Administration

There is general agreement in research (e.g., Braden 1994) and law (e.g., the Individuals with Disabilities Act 1994) that deaf people must be assessed using their primary mode of communication. Most deaf people communicate primarily via sign systems, either in isolation or with concurrent signs and speech (Schildroth and Karchmer 1986). Because many mental health service providers are not proficient in sign language systems (Steinberg, Sullivan, and Loew 1998), many clinicians will seek the services of a sign language interpreter when assessing deaf people. It is important to note two caveats to this practice. First, interpreters are not bound by standardized, uniform interpreting practices and so may deviate substantially when translating directions. Second, communication through interpretation alone may be necessary but is not sufficient to guarantee successful assessment and delivery of mental health services (see Leigh et al. 1996; Raifman and Vernon 1996).

Research that examines interpreter use in intellectual assessment is limited to use of the Wechsler Performance Scales with deaf people (Osberger 1986; Sullivan 1982). These studies show that interpreted administrations yield higher Performance IQs (PIQs) than oral or written administrations, yet yield lower PIQs than when the clinician signs directly with the person. Unfortunately, this research confounds administration status with individual clinicians (Osberger 1986), so it is not clear whether direct sign communication is superior to administration via an interpreter. It is clear that either direct or interpreted administration is preferable to oral, written, or gestural administration modifications (Braden 1994).

The controversies of deficit versus difference, special versus general norms, verbal versus nonverbal tests, and signed versus interpreted test administration have yet to be resolved by direct, controlled studies. Whereas the controversies of deficit versus difference and verbal versus nonverbal tests require substantial elaboration of conceptual and empiric investigation, the use of special versus general norms and signed versus interpreted administration are much more amenable to direct study. The important point is that, despite claims to the contrary, these controversies are not resolved. Clinicians should be aware of these controversies and their lack of resolution, so that they make informed decisions during clinical assessments of deaf people.

CONCLUSIONS

Clinical assessment of deaf people's cognitive abilities is a challenging practice. Clinicians must reconcile the needs of the person, the desires of the social systems that consume clinical assessments, and the challenges for best practice in psychological assessment. Best practices are occasionally easy to identify, if difficult to execute. For example, there is consensus that expertise in sign language, knowledge of deaf culture, and competence in psychological aspects of deafness are all desirable clinical qualifications—yet there are few clinicians with these skills. Conversely, some practices, such as the use of special norms and tests, avoidance of language-loaded tests, and interpreters, are controversial. Clinicians must know and apply available research and practice to enhance the person's well-being.

At the outset of this chapter I distinguished clinical from experimental assessment of cognitive abilities in deaf people. The primary distinction between these enterprises is intent; that is, clinical assessment seeks to enhance knowledge of the person to promote the person's welfare, whereas experimental assessment seeks to better understand the nature and function of deaf people's cognitive abilities. Because of this distinction, clinical assessment draws heavily on standardized, norm-referenced methods of assessment—that is, standardized intelligence tests. In contrast, experimental research frequently uses methods unique to the researcher and the researcher's questions.

However, these different approaches are also complementary. That is, researchers' findings often inform clinicians of issues to consider. For example, research helps address the questions of "What are the nature and functions of intellectual processes?" and "How are these processes likely to be affected by deafness?" Also, advances in research methods can inform clinicians with respect to appropriate practices and can be adapted for use in clinical practice. Conversely, clinical assessment practices and tools provide researchers with standardized research protocols and provide data that can be directly compared across research specialties and against large, representative (norm) samples. Generally, research informs practice; appropriate practices for assessment are tried first in controlled, experimental settings. However, there are occasions where practice spurs and informs research. For example, legal mandates to accommodate deaf people in assessments has spurred research in this field, but the practice precedes the research base. Ultimately, research and practice should converge on common methods and conclusions, so that clinicians and researchers share a common understanding of—and methods for assessing—the nature and function of cognitive abilities in deaf people.

REFERENCES

Allinder, R. M., and M. A. Eccarius. 1999. Exploring the technical adequacy of curriculum-based measurement in reading for children who use manually coded English. *Exceptional Children* 65(2):271–83.

American Association of Mental Retardation. 1992. *Mental retardation: Definition, classification, and systems of supports*, 9th ed. Washington, D.C.: American Association of Mental Retardation.

American Psychiatric Association. 1994. *Diagnostic and statistical manual of mental disorders: DSM-IV*. Washington, D.C.: American Psychiatric Association.

Anderson, R. J., and F. H. Sisco. 1977. *Standardization of the WISC-R Performance Scale for deaf children*. Office of Demographic Studies Publication Series T, no. 1. Washington, D.C.: Gallaudet University.

Binet, A., and T. Simon. 1910. Oral and manual methods of teaching the deaf. *American Annals of the Deaf* 55:4–33.

———. 1914. *Mentally defective children*. London: E. Arnold.

Bolton, B. 1978. Differential ability structure in deaf and hearing children. *Applied Psychological Measurement* 2:147–49.

Botterbusch, K. F., and N. L. Michael. 1985. *Testing and test modification in vocational evaluation*. Menomonie, Wis.: Wisconsin University–Stout, Stout Vocational Rehabilitation Institute. [ERIC document no. 267269]

Bracken, B. A., and R. S. McCallum. 1998. *Universal Nonverbal Intelligence Test.* Itasca, Ill.: Riverside.

Brackley, M. H. 1997. Mental health assessment/mental status examination. *Nurse Practitioner Forum* 8(3):105–13.

Braden, J. P. 1985a. LPAD applications to deaf populations. In *Cognition, education, and deafness*, ed. D. S. Martin, 148–50. Washington, D.C.: Gallaudet University Press.

———— 1985b. The structure of nonverbal intelligence in deaf and hearing subjects. *American Annals of the Deaf* 131:496–501.

————. 1985c. WISC-R deaf norms reconsidered. *Journal of School Psychology* 23:375–82.

————. 1994. *Deafness, deprivation, and IQ.* New York: Plenum.

————. 1999. Accommodations in testing: Methods to ensure validity. *Assessment Focus* 8(1):1–3. San Antonio: The Psychological Corp. [Available: http://www.psychcorp.com/pdf/assesspr99.pdf.]

Braden, J. P., and J. M. Hannah. 1998. Assessment of hearing impaired and deaf children with the WISC-III. In *Use of the WISC-III in clinical practice*, ed. D. Saklofske and A. Prifitera, 175–201. New York: Houghton-Mifflin.

Braden, J. P., and C. E. Kostrubala. 1995. *Administration of the WAIS–III in American Sign Language* (videotape). San Antonio: The Psychological Corporation.

Braden, J. P., C. Kostrubala, and J. Reed. 1994. Why do deaf children score differentially on performance v. motor-reduced nonverbal intelligence tests? *Journal of Psychoeducational Assessment* 12:357–63.

Braden, J. P., J. A. Wollack, and T. E. Allen. 1995. Reply to Kishor: Choosing the right metric. *Journal of Psychoeducational Assessment* 13:250–65.

Braden, J. P., and A. Zwiebel. 1992. The intellectual structure of hearing-impaired children as a function of age: A cross-cultural study. Typescript.

Bradley-Johnson, S., and L. D. Evans. 1991. *Psychoeducational assessment of hearing-impaired students: Infancy through high school.* Austin, Tex.: Pro-Ed.

Brody, N. 1997. Malleability and change in intelligence. In *The scientific study of human nature: Tribute to Hans J. Eysenck at eighty*, ed. H. Nyborg, 311–30. Oxford: Pergamon/Elsevier Science.

Chatterji, S., M. Mukerjee, and R. Gupta. 1987. Assessment of intelligence level of hearing impaired children. *Journal of the Indian Academy of Applied Psychology* 13:29–37.

Courtney, A. S., F. B. Hayes, K. W. Couch, and M. Frick. 1984. Administration of the WISC-R Performance Scale to hearing-impaired children using pantomimed instructions. *Journal of Psychoeducational Assessment* 2:1–7.

Falberg, R. M. 1983. Psychological assessment of the verbal functioning of postsecondary educational program applicants: Improving predictive validity. In *Vocational evaluation of hearing-impaired persons: Research and practice*, ed. D. Watson, G. Anderson, P. Marut, S. Ovellette, and N. Ford. Warm Springs, Ark.: University of Arkansas.

Frisby, C. L., and J. P. Braden. 1992. Feuerstein's dynamic assessment approach: A semantic, logical, and empirical critique. *Journal of Special Education* 26:281–301.

Fry, R. R., ed. 1986. *National Forum on Issues in Vocational Assessment: The issues papers.* Menomonie, Wis.: Wisconsin University–Stout, Stout Vocational Rehabilitation Institute. [ERIC document no. 273800]

Gamble, H. W. 1985. A national survey of programs for intellectually and academically gifted hearing impaired students. *American Annals of the Deaf* 131:508–18.

Garrison, W. M., and D. C. Coggiola. 1980. *Practical procedures for test length reduction and item selection.* Rochester, N.Y.: National Technical Institute for the Deaf. [ERIC document no. 209906]

Geers, A. E., H. S. Lane, and the Central Institute for the Deaf. 1984. *Preschool Performance Scale.* Wood Dale, Ill.: Stoelting Co.

Gould, S. J. 1996. *The mismeasure of man,* rev. ed. New York: Norton.

Grigorenko, E. L., and R. J. Sternberg. 1998. Dynamic testing. *Psychological Bulletin* 124(1):75–111.

Heller, B. W., and R. I. Harris. 1987. Special considerations in the psychological assessment of hearing impaired persons. In *Psychosocial interventions with sensorially disabled persons. Mind and medicine series,* ed. B. W. Heller and L. M. Flohr, 53–77. Orlando, Fla.: Grune and Stratton.

Heller, P. J. 1990. Psycho-educational assessment of hearing-impaired children. In *Hearing-impaired children in the mainstream,* ed. M. Ross, 61–79. Parkton, Md.: York Press.

Hiskey, M. S. 1966. *Hiskey Nebraska Test of Learning Aptitude.* Lincoln, Neb.: Author.

Howarth, D. F., J. M. Heath, and F. C. Snope. 1999. Beyond the Folstein: Dementia in primary care. *Primary Care: Clinics in Office Practice* 26(2):299–314.

Jenkinson, J. 1989. Use of the WISC-R Performance Scale with hearing-impaired children: A review. *Psychological Test Bulletin* 2(1):33–38.

Jensen, A. R. 1980. *Bias in mental testing.* New York: Free Press.

———. 1998. *The g factor: The science of mental ability.* Westport, Conn.: Praeger.

Kamphaus, R. W. 1985. Nonverbal Test of Cognitive Skills: Test review. *Journal of Psychoeducational Assessment* 3(1):97–99.

Keane, K. J. 1987. Assessing deaf children. In *Dynamic assessment: An interactional approach to evaluating learning potential,* ed. C. S. Lidz, 360–76. New York: Guilford Press.

Kelly, M. D. 1995. Neuropsychological assessment of children with hearing impairment on Trail Making, Tactual Performance, and Category tests. *Assessment* 2(4):305–12.

Kelly, M., and J. P. Braden. 1990. Criterion-related validity of the WISC-R Performance Scale with the Stanford Achievement Test-Hearing Impaired Edition. *Journal of School Psychology* 28:147–51.

Kishor, N. 1995a. Evaluating predictive validity: A rejoinder to Braden et al. *Journal of Psychoeducational Assessment* 13:241–49.

———. 1995b. Evaluating predictive validity by using different scales of the Stanford Achievement Test for the hearing impaired. *Journal of Psychoeducational Assessment* 13, 241–49.

Lambert, N., K. Nihira, and H. Leeland. 1993. *Adaptive Behavior Scale: Residential and Community,* 2d ed. Austin, Tex.: Pro-Ed.

Leigh, I. W., C. A. Corbett, V. Gutman, and D. Morere. 1996. Providing psychological services to deaf individuals: A response to new perceptions of diversity. *Professional Psychology: Research and Practice* 27(4):364–71.

Lowry, M. 1999. The Glasgow Coma Scale in clinical practice: A critique. *Nursing Times* 95(22):40–42.

Maller, S. J. 1996. WISC-III verbal item invariance across samples of deaf and hearing children of similar measured ability. *Journal of Psychoeducational Assessment* 12(2):152–65.

Maller, S., and J. P. Braden. 1993. The construct and criterion validity of the WISC-III with deaf adolescents. In *Journal of Psychoeducational Assessment: Advances in Psychoeducational Assessment: Wechsler Intelligence Scale for Children*, 3d ed., ed. B. Bracken et al., 105–13. Brandon, Vt.: Clinical Psychology Publishing.

Marschark, M. 1993. *Psychological development of deaf children*. Oxford: Oxford University Press.

Mayberry, R. I. 1992. The cognitive development of deaf children: Recent insights. In *Handbook of neuropsychology*, vol. 7, ed. S. J. Segalowitz and I. Rapin, 51–68. Amsterdam: Elsevier Science.

Messick, S. 1995. Validity of psychological assessment. *American Psychologist* 50(9):741–49.

Mullen, Y. 1999. Assessment of the preschool child with a hearing loss. In *Assessing and screening preschoolers: Psychological and educational dimensions*, 2d ed., ed. E. Vazquez Nuttall and I. Romero, 340–59. Boston: Allyn and Bacon.

Naglieri, J. A. 1985. *Matrix Analogies Test: Expanded form*. San Antonio: The Psychological Corporation.

———. 1988. *Draw a Person: A quantitative scoring system*. San Antonio: The Psychological Corporation.

Neisser, U., G. Boodoo, T. J. Bouchard, A. W. Boykin, N. Brody, S. J. Ceci, D. F. Halpern, J. C. Loehlin, R. Perloff, R. J. Sternberg, and S. Urbina. 1996. Intelligence: Knowns and unknowns. *American Psychologist* 51(2):77–101.

Neuhaus, M. 1967. Modifications in the administration of the WISC Performance subtests for children with profound hearing losses. *Exceptional Children* 33:573–74.

Osberger, M. J., ed. 1986. *Language and learning skills of hearing-impaired students*, ASHA monographs number 23. Rockville, Md.: American Speech-Language-Hearing Association. [ERIC document no. 280232]

Paist S. S., and J. R. Martin. 1996. Brain failure in older patients: Uncovering treatable causes of a diminished ability to think. *Postgraduate Medicine* 99(5):125–28, 130–34, 136.

Pintner, R. 1928. A mental survey of the deaf. *Journal of Educational Psychology* 19:145–51.

Prasse, D. P., and J. A. Schrag. Forthcoming. Providing noncategorical, functional, classroom-based supports for students with disabilities: Legal parameters. In *Functional and noncategorical identification and intervention in special education*, ed. D. Reschly, D. Tilly, and J. Grimes. Austin, Tex.: Pro-Ed.

Raifman, L. J., and M. Vernon. 1996. Important implications for psychologists of the Americans with Disabilities Act: Case in point, the patient who is deaf. *Professional Psychology: Research and Practice* 27(4):372–77.

Ravens, J. C. 1960. *Progressive Matrices–Standard*. San Antonio: The Psychological Corporation.

———. 1965. *Progressive Matrices–Coloured*. San Antonio: The Psychological Corporation.

Raviv, S., S. Sharan, and S. Strauss. 1973. Intellectual development of deaf children in different educational environments. *Journal of Communication Disorders* 6:29–36.

Ray, S. 1979. An adaptation of the Wechsler Intelligence Scales for Children-Revised for the deaf. Natchitoches, La.: Author.

———. 1982. Adapting the WISC-R for deaf children. *Diagnostique* 7:147–57.

Roth, V. 1991. Students with learning disabilities and hearing impairment: Issues for the secondary and postsecondary teacher. *Journal of Learning Disabilities* 24(7):391–97.

Samar, V. J., I. Parasnis, and G. P. Berent, 1998. Learning disabilities, attention deficit disorders, and deafness. In *Psychological perspectives on deafness*, vol. 2, ed. M. Marschark and M. D. Clark, 199–242. Mahwah, N.J.: Lawrence Erlbaum.

Sattler, J. M. 1992. *Assessment of children*, 3d ed. San Diego: Jerome Sattler.

Schalock, R. L., ed. 1999. *Adaptive behavior and its measurements: Implications for the field of mental retardation*. Washington, D.C.: American Association of Mental Retardation.

Schildroth, A. N. and M. A. Karchmer. 1986. *Deaf children in America*. San Diego: College-Hill Press.

Sikora, D. M., and D. S. Plapinger. 1997. The role of informal parent and teacher assessment in diagnosing learning disabilities. *Volta Review* 99(1):19–29.

Sparrow, S. S., D. A. Balla, and D. V. Cicchetti. 1984. *Vineland Adaptive Behavior Scales*. Circle Pines, Minn.: American Guidance Services.

Steinberg, A. G., V. J. Sullivan, and R. C. Loew. 1998. Cultural and linguistic barriers to mental health service access: The deaf consumer's perspective. *American Journal of Psychiatry* 155(7):982–84.

Sullivan, P. M. 1982. Administration modifications on the WISC-R Performance Scale with different categories of deaf children. *American Annals of the Deaf* 127:780–88.

Sullivan, P. M., and L. A. Montoya. 1997. Factor analysis of the WISC-III with deaf and hard-of-hearing children. *Psychological Assessment* 9(3):317–21.

Sullivan, P. M., and L. E. Schulte. 1992. Factor analysis of WISC-R with deaf and hard of hearing children. *Psychological Assessment* 4(4):537–40.

Teasdale, G. M., L. E. Pettigrew, J. T. Wilson, G. Murray, and B. Jennett. 1998. Analyzing outcome of treatment of severe head injury: A review and update on advancing the use of the Glasgow Outcome Scale. *Journal of Neurotrauma* 15(8):587–97.

Tellegen, P. J., and J. A. Laros. 1993. The Snijders-Oomen Nonverbal Intelligence Tests: General intelligence tests or tests for learning potential? In *Learning potential assessment: Theoretical, methodological and practical issues*, ed. J. H. M. Hamers and K. Sijtsma, 267–83. Amsterdam: Swets and Zeitlinger.

Thurlow, M. L., J. E. Ysseldyke, and B. Silverstein. 1995. Testing accommodations for students with disabilities. *Remedial and Special Education* 16(5):260–70.

Tidyman, E. 1974. *Dummy*. Boston: Little, Brown.

Tindal, G. 1998, March. *Models for understanding task comparability in accommodated testing*. Council of Chief State School Officers State Collaborative on Assessment and Student Standards, Assessing Special Education Students. Study Group III. Minneapolis: National Center for Educational Outcomes. [Available: http://www.coled.umn.edu/NCEO/Accommodations/Task_Comparability.htm.]

Tomlinson-Keasey, C., and R. R. Kelly. 1978. The deaf child's symbolic world. *American Annals of the Deaf* 123:452–58.

Tzuriel, D., and N. Caspi. 1992. Cognitive modifiability and cognitive performance of deaf and hearing preschool children. *Journal of Special Education* 26(3):235–52.

Vernon, M., and J. F. Andrews. 1990. *The psychology of deafness: Understanding deaf and hard-of-hearing people.* New York: Longman.

Vonderhaar, W. F., and J. F. Chambers. 1975. An examination of deaf students' Wechsler Performance subtest scores. *American Annals of the Deaf* 120:540–43.

Wechsler, D. 1974. *Wechsler Intelligence Scale for Children-Revised.* San Antonio: The Psychological Corporation.

———. 1989. *Wechsler Preschool and Primary Intelligence Scale for Children-Revised.* San Antonio: The Psychological Corporation.

———. 1991. *Wechsler Intelligence Scale for Children-Third Edition.* San Antonio: The Psychological Corporation.

———. 1997. *Wechsler Adult Intelligence Scale-Third Edition.* San Antonio: The Psychological Corporation.

Yewchuk, C. R., and M. A. Bibby. 1989. Identification of giftedness in severely and profoundly hearing impaired students. *Roeper Review* 12(1):42–48.

Zwiebel, A. 1987. More on the effects of early manual communication on the cognitive development of deaf children. *American Annals of the Deaf* 134:16–20.

Zwiebel, A., and D. M. Mertens. 1985. A comparison of intellectual structure in deaf and hearing children. *American Annals of the Deaf* 130:27–31.

4

THE IMPACT OF SIGN LANGUAGE EXPERTISE ON VISUAL PERCEPTION

Margaret Wilson

A widespread belief among nonpsychologists is that the loss of one sense produces an enhancement of the remaining senses. The blind person is thought to have especially acute hearing, the deaf person to have enhanced visual awareness and high sensitivity to vibration, and so on. This popular and appealing idea is easy to dismiss as an urban myth of psychology, along with the belief that we only use 10 percent of our brains and that Eskimos perceive the world differently from other cultures because they have fifty words for snow.

Nevertheless, investigators have recently begun to take this proposal seriously. In the case of blindness, studies have explored spatial localization abilities and the use of echo information (Ashmead et al. 1998; Lessard et al. 1998; Morgan 1999; Millar 1999; Roeder et al. 1999). In the case of deafness, visual abilities such as allocation of attention (Parasnis and Samar 1985; Stivalet et al. 1998), and movement detection in the periphery (Neville and Lawson 1987) have been explored. Although altered sensory experience may not produce changes in actual sensory acuity, it may cause sensory information to be processed in a different manner, a hypothesis that increasingly appears to be viable. This point is critical not merely for our understanding of perceptual and cognitive processes in special populations, but also for our basic understanding of the development and functioning of the human sensory systems.

In the case of deafness, results from such investigations have produced an unexpected twist on the relationship between deafness and visual perception. Some differences in visual processing between the deaf and hearing populations appear to be mediated not by deafness per se, but rather by the use of a signed language (see Emmorey 1998 for a review). For example, sign language experience appears to enhance the ability to reconstruct movement patterns from dynamic point-light displays (Klima et al. forthcoming). Findings such as this raise profound questions about the current state of our knowledge about sensory processes. Virtually all our knowledge of auditory and visual processing, and the radical differences between the two, derives from the study of hearing indi-

This work was supported by National Institutes of Health grant DC–00128–01 awarded to Margaret Wilson. I would like to thank Kevin Clark for his assistance in stimulus development, and Brenda Falgier, Kevin Clark, Stephen McCullough, Karen Emmorey, and Tracy Love for their valuable suggestions and feedback.

viduals. For this population, the auditory modality is intimately entwined with language expertise, whereas the visual modality has no comparable form of expertise to influence it. If we wish to understand the full scope of human perceptual processing, we must ask how a similarly intimate relationship to language might affect the visual modality.

The extent to which the use of a visual language might affect visual processing is only beginning to be explored. A number of findings indicate that particular visual judgments or discriminations become faster or easier due to practice with a signed language (see Emmorey 1998 for a review). However, a deeper question is whether signed language expertise can actually alter *what* is perceived. One hallmark of human perception is its active, constructive nature. In general, we do not perceive exactly and only the information present in the stimulus. Instead, our perceptions reflect a great deal of "intelligent guessing" on the part of the perceptual system. Examples include illusory contours, the phenomenal absence of the blind spot, and apparent motion, in the visual domain; and phonemic restoration and the influence of familiarity on judgments of background noise, in the auditory domain. Under conditions of ambiguity, then, lifelong experience with a structured system of visual movement such as sign language might well lead to a different perception than would occur without that expertise.

In support of this possibility, it has been found that signers versus nonsigners produce different patterns of similarity ratings for point-light motion displays of signs (Poizner 1981). This finding indicates a shift in categorization boundaries due to sign language expertise. It is, of course, possible that this finding reflects conscious, cognitive judgments, rather than a true perceptual effect. Nevertheless, it strongly suggests that perceptual judgments may be altered by sign language fluency.

VISUAL COMPLETION EFFECTS

To explore this issue more systematically, it is necessary to create conditions of visual ambiguity, in which a stimulus could in principle be seen in two or more ways. Under such conditions, one can look for systematic differences in the perceptual reports of signers versus nonsigners. Such conditions can be created by using known principles of visual "completion" effects. In these effects, the visual system appears to "fill in" information that is ambiguous or absent in the stimulus. As mentioned earlier, these include illusory contours, the phenomenal absence of the blind spot, apparent motion, as well as figure/ground segregation, neon color spreading, and the Gestalt principles of grouping.

One feature that all these completion phenomena have in common is the low-level, mechanistic nature of the principles that govern the filled-in information. In illusory contours, for example, the form taken by the subjectively supplied contours is determined by the geometry of the inducing stimulus. This stands in striking contrast to completion effects in the auditory domain, where the perception of ambiguous speech frequently involves the filling in of complex or "arbitrary" information. For example, in the phonemic restoration effect, an arbitrarily chosen phoneme can be deleted from a word and replaced by noise, and participants will often report hearing the complete word; in fact, they will often have difficulty determining which phoneme was deleted (Samuel 1996; Warren 1970). This is presumably due to the influential role of early language exposure in the development of the perceptual system. Can similar effects occur in the visual domain, provided there is expertise in a visual language?

One way to test this question is to exploit the phenomenon of apparent motion, in which participants perceive a single, moving object when in fact there is only a static stimulus at one location rapidly followed by a static stimulus at another location. Apparent motion is insensitive under most conditions to knowledge about how objects move in the real world. Attributes of the object's identity do not in general influence the perceived path of motion; instead, the object usually appears to take the shortest path between locations, regardless of whether that path of motion is plausible in the real world (e.g., Shepard 1984).

These facts fit well with what is known about the structure of the visual system. The existence of two distinct pathways of visual processing, one devoted largely to processing object identity (the ventral, or "what" pathway) and one devoted largely to processing location and movement (the dorsal, or "where" pathway), suggests that indeed object identity ought not to influence motion perception. In fact, the orientation of an object's longest axis can influence whether the object appears to rotate as it moves (Foster 1975). Nevertheless, it is generally the case that object *identity* does not influence perceived motion (Burt and Sperling 1981). Instead, when the visual system must construct a path of motion based on insufficient information, as in the case of apparent motion stimuli, it does so by inferring "the simplest rigid twisting motion prescribed by kinematic geometry" (Shepard 1984). In most cases, this reduces to a "shortest-path constraint." The visual system chooses among the infinite number of possible paths by assuming the shortest, most direct path.

However, there appear to be certain specific exceptions to this principle, cases in which higher-order knowledge about object identity does influence motion perception. This suggests that apparent motion may be susceptible to the nature of the visual experience that accrues over a lifetime, such as sign language experience. If so, then the contents of visual perception may be partly determined by linguistic experience in that modality.

APPARENT MOTION FOR HUMAN MOVEMENT

In one particular case, it has been found that object identity does influence motion perception (Chatterjee, Freyd, and Shiffrar 1996; Shiffrar 1994; Shiffrar and Freyd 1990, 1993). This special case is biological motion, which growing evidence suggests is treated differently by the visual system from other types of motion (e.g., Johansson 1973; Perrett et al. 1990; Chitty 1990; Shiffrar, Lichtey, and Chatterjee 1997). Shiffrar and Freyd (1990) demonstrated that apparent motion for human figure stimuli sometimes appear to take a longer, indirect path when the shortest path would violate the human body's physical abilities. For example, if a hand is shown first in front of a torso and then behind the torso, the "shortest path constraint" would cause it to appear to pass through the body, and indeed this is what participants report seeing at fast presentation rates. But as the timing parameters of the stimulus presentation are slowed down (across the range of 150–650 ms between presentations), participants become increasingly likely to report seeing the longer but physically possible path in which the hand moves *around* the body. In addition to this "solidity constraint," Shiffrar and Freyd also observed a "joint constraint," in which a long path that was possible given the range of motion of human joints was preferred over a shorter, impossible path.

Further, Chatterjee, Freyd, and Shiffrar (1996) show that the use of the solidity constraint by the visual system depends on the involvement of biological stimuli (or stimuli that have the global structure of a biological form, e.g., a wooden mannequin). When *either* the moving limb or the part of the body it must traverse is replaced by an inanimate object (a board or a chair, respectively), the longer path is perceived more often at slower presentation times. But when *both* are replaced, so that the stimulus is entirely nonbiological, the probability of seeing the longer path remains low across the range of presentation times (figure 1.).

It appears that among the assumptions or "constraints" that the visual system uses to narrow down the problem of interpreting the visual scene, there is a special set of constraints that is specific to the perception of biological stimuli. Motion perception can be influenced by knowledge of possible movements for biological forms. The question posed here, then, is whether additional constraints on apparent motion can be found that are more specific still, relating only to the perception of sign language stimuli and only in participants who are signers.

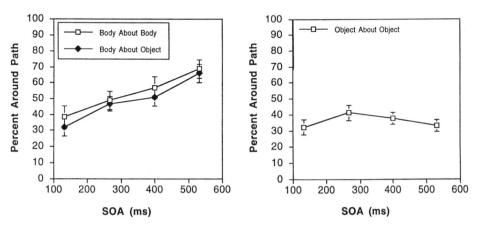

Figure 1. The graph on the left shows probability of reporting one object moving around another rather than through it, when both objects are body parts, and when only one object is a body part. The graph on the right shows performance when neither object is a body part. Adapted from Chatterjee, Freyd, and Shiffrar (1996).

APPARENT MOTION FOR AMERICAN SIGN LANGUAGE STIMULI

Signed languages, like all languages, possess grammatical structure at several levels. In particular, for our purposes, they possess phonological structure.[1] Signs are not holistic gestures but are constructed from a set of meaningless components (handshape, palm orientation, location, and movement) that are combined in rule-governed ways (Battison 1978; Stokoe 1960). In order to test whether American Sign Language (ASL) expertise can influence the perceived path of apparent motion, two types of ASL signs can be compared. The first set consists of signs whose movement is phonologically specified as two contacts (see figure 2 for an example). That is, the dominant hand (the right hand, in right-handers) makes contact with some other body part, such as the torso, arm, or "base" hand, and then makes contact again at a nearby location. The movement between these two points of contact necessarily involves the dominant hand breaking contact, moving in an arced path to the second location, and reestablishing contact. Depending upon emphasis and style, the degree of displacement from a straight path can be very large or more moderate. The critical point, however, is that these signs are never performed with continuous contact between the dominant hand and another body part. In contrast, the second set of signs does involve exactly such continuous contact (see figure 2). These signs are phonologically specified as a single contact with local movement.

These two groups of signs are of interest because each sign involves two endpoints at which the dominant hand is in contact with another body part. Thus, if only the two endpoints are shown in apparent motion display, either type of movement (two contacts or single contact with local movement) could in principle be seen. By using these endpoints as stimuli in an apparent motion paradigm, one can ask whether perceived motion will conform to the path of motion specified in the sign from which the stimuli are taken. In the absence of other constraints, the

Figure 2. The first two photographs show the endpoints of the ASL sign BRIDGE. The two fingers of the dominant hand touch the forearm, break contact, and touch the forearm again closer to the elbow. The last two photographs show the endpoints of the ASL sign CREDIT CARD. The dominant hand slides back and forth along the palm.

---

1. The sublexical structure of ASL exhibits abstract phonological properties such as hierarchically organized feature classes, autosegmental representations, deletion and segmentation rules, a sonority hierarchy, and syllabic structure. For these reasons, the term "phonology" is used by linguists to characterize the sublexical structure of signed languages as well as spoken languages (Brentari 1995; Corina and Sandler 1993; Coulter 1993; Sandler 1995).

shortest-path constraint should bias all participants toward seeing the single-contact movement, which involves a virtually straight path, rather than the two-contact movement, which involves an indirect, arced path. But if expertise with a visual language can influence perceived motion, then one would expect deaf participants who are fluent in ASL to perceive the indirect path for stimuli taken from signs that have such a path more often than would hearing participants who do not know ASL. In other words, signers should perceive the stimulus in such a way as to yield a real sign in ASL, rather than a nonsign movement.

In addition, if deaf signers do reveal a bias toward perceiving movements that result in stimuli that conform to ASL signs, we can be sure that this effect is a purely language-based effect and not one based on cognitive reorganization due to deafness. If there were some overall bias introduced by deafness (say, for the sake of argument, less of a tendency to always see straight paths), then this should apply equally to all stimuli, regardless of whether they come from a two-contact or single-contact sign. Thus, any observed bias toward seeing movements that are compatible with signs in the deaf signing population can be attributed to the effects of sign language expertise.

A TEST OF APPARENT MOTION IN NATIVE SIGNERS

In order to test the predictions just described, a study was performed that followed the methods of Shiffrar and Freyd (1990) in all essential respects with the exception of the nature of the stimulus photographs and the participant population. Five deaf native signers of ASL and ten hearing nonsigners were tested. The deaf participants, all deaf from birth, had hearing loss greater than 80 dB. All had two deaf parents, were exposed to ASL from infancy, and considered ASL to be their primary language. None of the hearing participants knew ASL or any communication system using ASL signs (e.g., Signed English).

To generate the stimuli, a deaf native signer was filmed performing sixteen ASL signs. Eight of these signs consist of two points of contact between the dominant hand and another part of the body, with an arced path of motion between the two contacts (BRIDGE, FOUNDATION, IMPROVE, LAW, MILLION, PARAGRAPH, POLICY, TRASH). The other eight signs consist of movement along a nearly straight path (BUSY, CREDIT CARD, FEVER, SOCKS, TRAFFIC, TRAIN, WOOD, XEROX).[2] For each sign, substituting the other kind of movement (replacing two-contact movement with straight movement or vice versa) but retaining all other characteristics of the original sign (handshape, palm orientation, location) would result in a "pseudo-sign." These pseudo-signs are phonologically legal but are not lexical items in ASL. Thus, when movement information is removed, perceived apparent motion will yield either a real sign or a phonologically legal pseudo-sign, depending on the path of the perceived motion.

---

2. Testing was performed in California. Because of regional differences, the signs listed may not all be two-contact or single-contact signs in other parts of the United States. In addition, some of the signs listed as "single-contact" are sometimes performed without any contact at all (SOCKS, TRAFFIC). Nevertheless, these signs still use a straight movement path, which provides the crucial contrast to two-contact signs.

From the filmed signs, two still frames were chosen, one from each endpoint of the movement (figure 2). When stimuli of this type are presented in alternation with appropriate spatial and temporal parameters, the result is a subjective impression of motion, in which the body part that changes location appears to move back and forth.

Stimuli were presented as digitized pictures on a computer. On each trial, two stimuli were presented alternately at the same location, with a fixed stimulus onset asynchrony (SOA) for that trial, until the participant pressed a key to terminate presentation. Over the course of the experiment, each pair of stimuli was presented at five different SOAs. The shortest SOA was 133 ms, consisting of 100-ms stimulus duration (SD) and 33-ms interstimulus interval (ISI). Sixty-seven ms was added to both SD and ISI to form the next SOA level of 267 ms, and so on for each SOA up to the longest SOA of 667 ms. The order of the eighty trials (sixteen stimulus pairs at five SOAs) was randomized for each participant.

For each trial, participants were asked to report the path of motion that they saw. Of particular interest was whether they perceived the shortest, direct path (called "sliding" in the instructions) or an arced, indirect path (called "hopping"). The "hopping" and "sliding" paths were illustrated for the participant by arrows drawn on photographs. Additional response options included "can see both," "some other movement," and "no movement." After responding, participants initiated the next trial with a key press. For the deaf participants, instructions emphasized that responses should not be made based on how a real sign would look but instead should be based on what they actually saw. Responses were scored for the number of reports of hopping (figure 3).

As would be expected for the single-contact signs, the number of hop responses was low for both groups. This reflects the fact that, for these stimuli, the movement that yields a true sign percept (i.e., sliding) is compatible with the shortest-path constraint. In contrast, for the two-contact signs, deaf participants were almost twice as likely as hearing participants to give hop responses. Further, the two-contact signs for the deaf participants showed a steep increase in the number of hop responses as a function of presentation speed (SOA), in contrast to the other three conditions (figure 4). Shiffrar and Freyd (1990) argue that slower SOAs allow sufficient time for the longer path to be constructed by the visual system. The SOA data reported here suggest that this type of construction process can be induced not only by biomechanical considerations, as shown by Shiffrar and Freyd, but also by experience with an acquired linguistic movement system.

An unexpected finding is that hearing participants showed a small but reliable difference between two-contact signs and single-contact signs. How were the hearing participants, who knew no ASL, able to differentiate the two types of signs? The answer may have to do with movement information implicit in the visual display. Subtle cues from the angle, orientation, or muscle tension of the limbs may have telegraphed to the participants what motion had just taken place or was about to take place. That is, there may be a phenomenon similar to co-articulation of phonemes in speech that would allow information about prior or upcoming movement to be detected. Such an effect would presumably influence the deaf participants as well, but the effect is small and cannot account for the large difference between two-contact and single-contact signs shown by the deaf participants.

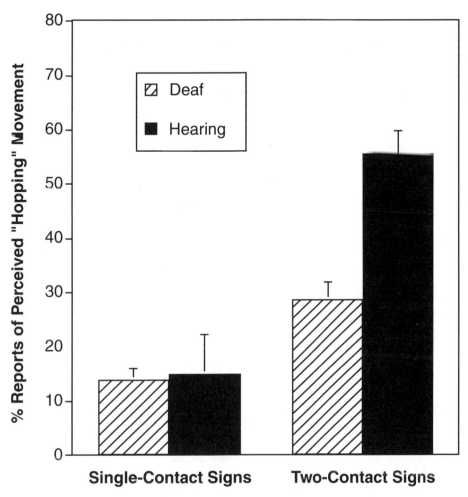

Figure 3. Participants' reports of perceived path of apparent motion, collapsed across SOA. Error bars represent standard error.

Another issue that must be addressed is whether the deaf participants responded based on how they knew the signs should look rather than on what they actually perceived. Several considerations argue against this interpretation. First, the deaf participants were not unwilling to label the two-contact signs as sliding, thus rendering them pseudo-signs. This claim is supported by the fact that deaf participants gave "slide" responses for the two-contact signs on fully 40 percent of trials. Clearly, participants understood that it was acceptable to give responses that corresponded to pseudo-signs rather than real signs. Further, the rather high rate of answers corresponding to pseudo-signs cannot be accounted for in terms of random intermixing of genuinely perceptual shortest-path responses with nonperceptual "how it should look" responses. If participants were mixing strategies in this fashion, the effect size should be constant across SOA. Instead, the tendency to report

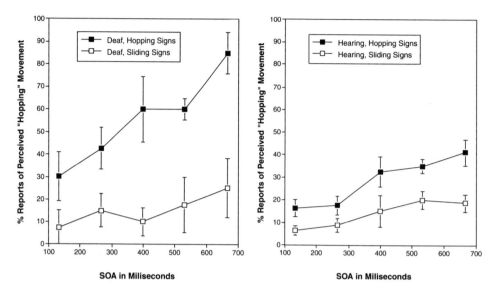

Figure 4.   Reports from deaf participants (left) and hearing participants (right) of perceived path of apparent motion, as a function of SOA. Error bars represent standard error.

hopping is strongly affected by SOA (figure 4). This sensitivity to perceptual qualities of the display suggests that the effect is driven perceptually, not cognitively.

Also relevant to this point is the response of one deaf participant who reported seeing the two-contact signs as alternately hopping and sliding. Further questioning revealed that the participant perceived hopping in the first half of each cycle and perceived sliding as the hand returned to its starting position. For the two-contact signs used to generate these stimuli, the return path is not part of the sign itself but rather is transitional movement. Nevertheless, this transitional movement does break and reestablish contact. Thus, if a participant responds based on how the sign should look, hopping should be reported for the whole display; the transition portion would not be singled out and reported as sliding. Instead, this somewhat peculiar spontaneous response appears to reflect the participant's actual perception. The fact that the report of hopping was restricted to the lexical portion of the display suggests the operation of a linguistically driven perceptual constraint.

Taken together, the results of this study demonstrate that the preference for a direct path (the "shortest path constraint") can be overridden in deaf signers by a preference for a path that renders the movement as a real sign. This "lexicality constraint" is an *object-specific* constraint on motion perception. Featural information about body part and handshape distinguish the cases where an indirect path is preferred from the cases where it is not. In this respect, the lexicality constraint is similar to biomechanical constraints, which are likewise object specific.

As noted earlier, processing of object identity and motion are largely segregated within the visual system, which raises the question of where in the stream of visual processing such object-specific constraints on motion perception occur.

Shiffrar (1994) argues that "what meets where" in areas such as the superior temporal sulcus, which have been implicated in the visual processing of body parts and body movement, and therefore may be involved in the biological motion processing responsible for biomechanical constraints. Given the involvement of such areas in perception of meaningful, goal-directed body movements and other socially relevant stimuli, it is not implausible that areas in this region could be recruited for sign language processing and could therefore be involved in the lexicality constraint as well.

The finding reported here of an effect of sign language expertise on visual perception may also be compared to auditory completion effects, such as the phonemic restoration effect described earlier. It appears that for both speech processing and sign processing, the perceptual system is biased toward interpreting ambiguous information in such a way as to yield a lexical percept. The present findings show that this is not a peculiarity of the auditory modality but is a general characteristic of language perception.

More generally, the study of deaf signers provides an important complement to the study of hearing speakers in understanding the nature of human perception and cognition. Sign language expertise may prove to have an important influence on the organization of visual perception and visual cognition. Understanding these influences can inform our understanding not only of the perceptual and cognitive profile of deaf signers but also of language processing, perceptual processing, and the malleability of the human cognitive system in response to diverse forms of developmental experience.

REFERENCES

Ashmead, D. H., R. S. Wall, S. B. Easton, and K. A. Ebinger. 1998. Echolocation reconsidered: Using spatial variations in the ambient sound field to guide locomotion. *Journal of Visual Impairment and Blindness* 92:615–32.

Battison, R. 1978. *Lexical borrowing in American Sign Language*. Silver Spring, Md.: Linstok Press.

Brentari, D. 1995. Sign language phonology: ASL. In *Handbook of phonological theory*, ed. J. Goldsmith, 615–39. Oxford: Basil Blackwell Ltd.

Burt P., and G. Sperling. 1981. Time, distance, and feature trade-offs in visual apparent motion. *Psychological Review* 88:171–95.

Chatterjee, S. H., J. J. Freyd, and M. Shiffrar. 1996. Configural processing in the perception of apparent biological motion. *Journal of Experimental Psychology: Human Perception and Performance* 22:916–29.

Corina, D., and W. Sandler. 1993. On the nature of phonological structure in sign language. *Phonology* 10:165–207.

Coulter, G. R., ed. 1993. *Phonetics and phonology: Current issues in ASL phonology*. San Diego: Academic Press.

Emmorey, K. 1998. The impact of sign language use on visuospatial cognition. In *Psychological perspectives on deafness*, vol 2, ed. M. Marschark and M. D. Clark. Hillsdale, N.J.: Lawrence Erlbaum.

Foster, D. H. 1975. Visual apparent motion and some preferred paths in the rotation group SO(3). *Biological Cybernetics* 18:81–89.

Johansson, G. 1973. Visual perception of biological motion and a model for its analysis. *Perception and Psychophysics* 14:201–11.

Klima, E., O. Tzeng, A. Fok, U. Bellugi, D. Corina, and J. G. Bettger. forthcoming. From sign to script: Effects of linguistic experience on perceptual categorization. *Journal of Chinese Linguistics*.

Lessard, N., M. Pare, F. Lepore, and M. Lassonde. 1998. Early-blind human subjects localize sound sources better than sighted subjects. *Nature* 395:278–80.

Millar, S. 1999. Veering re-visited: Noise and posture cues in walking without sight. *Perception* 28:765–80.

Morgan, M. 1999. Sensory perception: Supernormal hearing in the blind? *Current Biology* 9:R53–54.

Neville, H. J., and D. Lawson. 1987. Attention to central and peripheral visual space in a movement detection task: An event-related potential and behavioral study: II. Congenitally deaf adults. *Brain Research* 405:268–83.

Parasnis, I., and V. J. Samar. 1985. Parafoveal attention in congenitally deaf and hearing young adults. *Brain and Cognition* 4:313–27.

Perrett, D., M. Harries, A. Mistlin, and A. Chitty. 1990. Three stages in the classification of body movements by visual neurons. In *Images and understanding*, ed. H. Barlow, C. Blakemore, and M. Weston-Smith, 383–405. Cambridge, U.K.: Cambridge University Press.

Poizner, H. 1981. Visual and "phonetic" coding of movement: Evidence from American Sign Language. *Science* 212:691–93.

Roeder, B., W. Teder-Saelejaervi, A. Sterr, and F. Roesler. 1999. Improved auditory spatial tuning in blind humans. *Nature* 400:162–66.

Samuel, A. G. 1996. Does lexical information influence the perceptual restoration of phonemes? *Journal of Experimental Psychology: General* 125:28–51.

Sandler, W. 1995. One phonology or two? Sign language and phonological theory. *Glot International* 1:3–8.

Shepard, R. N. 1984. Ecological constraints on internal representation: Resonant kinematics of perceiving, imagining, thinking and dreaming. *Psychological Review* 91:417–47.

Shiffrar, M. 1994. When what meets where. *Current Directions in Psychological Science* 3:96–100.

Shiffrar, M., and J. J. Freyd. 1990. Apparent motion of the human body. *Psychological Science* 1:257–64.

———. 1993. Timing and apparent motion path choice with human body photographs. *Psychological Science* 4:379–84.

Shiffrar, M., L. Lichtey, and S. H. Chatterjee. 1997. The perception of biological motion across apertures. *Perception and Psychophysics* 59:51–59.

Stivalet, P., Y. Moreno, J. Richard, and P. Barraud. 1998. Differences in visual search tasks between congenitally deaf and normally hearing adults. *Cognitive Brain Research* 6:227–32.

Stokoe, W. C. 1960. *Sign language structure*. Buffalo: Department of Anthropology and Linguistics, University of Buffalo.

Warren, R. M. 1970. Perceptual restoration of missing speech sounds. *Science* 167:392–93.

5

COGNITION AND LANGUAGE IN ITALIAN DEAF PRESCHOOLERS OF DEAF AND HEARING FAMILIES

Elena Pizzuto, Barbara Ardito,

Maria Cristina Caselli, and Virginia Volterra

This chapter describes and discusses some of the major results of a study conducted on a sample of profoundly deaf Italian preschoolers, including children with deaf parents and children with hearing parents. The study explored several aspects of deaf children's cognitive, communicative, and linguistic development. We tried to determine whether and how the patterns we observed could be explained by, or at least related to, some of the major factors that notoriously interact in complex ways in determining a deaf child's developmental outcome. The study focused primarily on the child's family environment (deaf versus hearing parents), language used at home (sign versus speech, or combinations of both), spoken language intervention, and, more generally, educational background.

One of the study's major objectives was to evaluate the children's receptive and expressive language skills, trying as much as possible to use comparable assessment procedures for examining signed as compared to spoken language. It also aimed at defining an evaluation methodology that would allow us to compare the deaf children's developmental achievements with those of their hearing peers. This chapter focuses on the major results obtained by exploring the children's cognition and their receptive language abilities in sign and speech.

The study described here was developed within a broader research project conducted in collaboration with the Vatican Pediatric Hospital "Bambino Gesù" in Rome (Ossella et al. 1994). A key element of the project was the involvement of native LIS signers, deaf colleagues, and LIS interpreters at almost all stages in the planning and execution of the research. We are particularly grateful to Serena Corazza, Maria Luisa Franchi, Paolo Rossini, Benedetto Santarelli, and Vannina Vitale for their help in data collection and analysis; to Barbara Pennacchi for her help with computer graphics; and to Allegra Cattani for first suggesting to us the idea of administering the LIS tasks to hearing children with no knowledge of sign language. Partial financial support from the National Research Council targeted projects "FATMA" (1991–1996), "Safeguard of Cultural Heritage" (1996–2000), and the European Commission Project "Intersign" (1993–1995) (Network, Contract #ERBCHRXCT920023) is also acknowledged. Part of the data and observations reported in this chapter have appeared in a different form in Ossella et al. (1994), Ardito et al. (1998), and Pizzuto et al. (1998). Minor discrepancies between the results reported here and those described in previous reports or publications are due to new analyses of the data conducted for the present chapter.

A few general observations are in order. First, prior to this study, there was little information on Italian deaf preschoolers, their families, language background, or their language abilities in signing as compared to speech. Information on deaf children's family and language background and comparable information on their signed and spoken language skills is vital because these factors have been shown to influence development (Marschark 1993). However, most of the Italian studies that take into account the relevance of this information have been limited to the exploration of early sign language development and the evaluation of spoken language abilities (lexical and grammatical) in older deaf children and adolescents (Caselli et al. 1994). Other studies have explored deaf children's lexical and grammatical abilities in spoken Italian but have ignored the potential influence of sign knowledge on these abilities (Emiliani et al. 1994).

A small number of deaf children (a proportion estimated to be 5–10 percent in western countries, including Italy) have deaf parents who communicate with their child primarily in sign language. Italian Sign Language (LIS) is the primary language of Italian deaf children of deaf parents. Like all the other signed languages investigated to date, LIS is a full-fledged human language, with its own lexical, morphological, and morphosyntactic structures (Volterra 1987; Pizzuto and Corazza 1996; Pizzuto and Volterra forthcoming). A deaf child exposed to LIS as his or her native language acquires it naturally, following developmental steps comparable to those observed in hearing children acquiring spoken language. These patterns of parent–child communication are comparable to those noted among hearing parents and hearing children (Caselli et al. 1994; Capirci, Montanari, and Volterra 1998). Research findings also suggest that native knowledge of LIS may favor the development of deaf children's spoken language abilities, especially if they are exposed to language education programs that include the use of signs (Caselli et al. 1994). In Italy at least, when communicating with their children, many deaf parents often use not only LIS but also forms of Sign Supported Italian (SSI) (i.e., mouthed and/or voiced Italian words accompanied by LIS signs of corresponding meaning). These parents thus provide their children a form of "bimodal" input that may play a role in children's acquisition of spoken Italian, especially with respect to lexical development.

The largest majority of deaf children (the remaining 90–95 percent), however, have hearing parents who communicate with their child primarily in spoken language. In these families, due to the difficulties the child encounters in naturally acquiring spoken language, communication may often be severely restricted, and both the child and the parents may go through a difficult and complex process of psychological adjustment to each other's communicative needs (Gregory 1995; Marschark 1993). Because language plays a key role as the main vehicle for conveying information about the world, it is important to consider whether deaf children of hearing parents show different patterns of cognitive development (Lane, Hoffmeister, and Bahan 1996; Caselli et al. 1994). However, it must also be taken into account that during the last 20 years, in Italy as in other countries, hearing parents' communication abilities and educational choices have changed. This is at least in part due to the dissemination of the results of the LIS research and its use for educational purposes (e.g., Volterra et al. 1995). A growing (albeit still small) number of hearing parents have begun to learn LIS to communicate with their children and/or have chosen sign-based language intervention programs. These include, for the most part, bimodal education, which relies on spoken Italian, SSI, and Exact Signed Italian (ESI) (Massoni and Maragna 1997). Examining the effects these communication and language intervention choices may have on deaf children's communicative and linguistic abilities, in both sign and speech, is necessary and had not been conducted previously to the study reported here.

THE SAMPLE OF CHILDREN AND THEIR FAMILIES

The study examined a total of eleven deaf children—nine males and two females—ranging in age from 3 years, 11 months to 5 years, 11 months. Table 1 summarizes the most relevant information on the children, their families, and school environments. All of the children lived in or near Rome. Five children had deaf parents (indicated by an asterisk), six children had hearing parents, and none of the children had deaf grandparents.

Deaf families had a larger number of language/communication options. All five of the children with deaf parents were in fact exposed primarily to LIS, but four of them also received language input in both SSI and spoken Italian. For these children, the SSI came primarily from their parents, whereas the spoken Italian input came from their hearing grandparents, who in some cases also lived with the child and the child's parents. Only one deaf child of deaf parents (C*) had LIS as single-language input. In contrast, all six children with hearing parents received primarily spoken Italian input at home, but one was also exposed to SSI because his mother had started to learn LIS and used SSI. The children's spoken language experience varied. Among the five children who had deaf parents, three had not received any spoken-language education, two had withdrawn from an oral-language-intervention program at, respectively, 2 and 3 years of age, and one had never received any structured education in spoken Italian. The remaining two children with deaf parents were in bimodal programs with early oral education. All six children with hearing parents were in either oral or bimodal programs.

All the children were attending kindergarten, but again their school environments were rather different. The three children of deaf parents who never received or withdrew from oral language education programs were enrolled in a private school for the deaf that provided no structured language education program at all (either in speech or in sign). The other two children of deaf parents attended public school, one with hearing children and the other in an integrated class with deaf and hearing children in a public school for the deaf that offered a bilingual education program (in LIS and spoken Italian). Of the six children with hearing parents, one was enrolled in the same integrated class with deaf and hearing children, while the remaining five were in hearing-only classes. (One child attended the integrated class with hearing and deaf children on a part-time basis.)

As table 1 shows, all but one of the children were diagnosed as profoundly deaf (i.e., with a hearing loss greater than 90 dB), between the ages of 6 months and 3 years. Only one child had an initially severe deafness (71–90 dB) that subsequently evolved into profound deafness. In terms of deafness typology,

Table 1. A Summary Description of the Eleven Children Examined

Child	Gender	Age	Language at home	Spoken language education (age started, duration, and type)	Type of school attended	Deafness Degree/ Type	Age at diag-nosis	Age at beginning use of hearing aids
M*	F	3;11	LIS, SSI, Ital.	0;10 >Bimodal	H	Profound/1	0;6	0;8
A*	M	4;1	LIS, Ital.	———	D	Profound/3	0;6	1;0
P	M	4;1	Ital., SSI	2;1 >Bimodal	H	Profound/1	1;11	2;0
V	M	4;10	Ital.	3;0 >Bimodal	D&H	Profound/1	3;0	3;6
D	M	4;10	Ital.	1;6 >Bimodal	H	Profound/1	1;1	1;3
J	M	4;10	Ital.	2;2 >Oral +GC	H	Sev/Prof/1	1;11	2;0
F	M	5;1	Ital.	2;2 >Oral	H	Profound/1	2;0	2;2
L*	M	5;5	LIS, SSI, Ital.	1;6 >2;6 >Oral >Bimodal	D&H	Profound/1	0;6	0;8
F*	M	5;7	LIS, Ital.	2;0 - 3;0 ǀ Oral	D	Profound/1	0;8	0;10
C*	F	5;10	LIS	1;0 - 2;0 ǀ Oral	D	Profound/2	0;10	1;0
G	M	5;11	Ital.	1;0 >Oral + GC	H+D&H	Profound/3	0;11	1;0

Guide to symbols:
* = children with deaf parents
F, M = Female, Male
For ages: year and month of age are separated with a semicolon ("5;10" refers to 5 years, 10 months
    old)
LIS = Italian Sign Language
SSI = Sign Supported Italian
Ital. = spoken Italian
> = continued to the time child was observed
ǀ = interrupted
Bimodal = Bimodal education, relying on spoken Italian, SSI, and Exact Signed Italian
GC = gestural communication
H = class with hearing children
D = class for deaf children only
D & H = integrated class with deaf and hearing children
Profound = hearing loss greater than 90 dB
Type 1 = same loss across all frequencies
Type 2 = no residual hearing beyond 2,000 Hz
Type 3 = no residual hearing beyond 1,000 Hz
Sev/Prof/1 = initially severe (hearing loss: 71–90 dB), subsequently evolved into profound, Type 1
    deafness

there were eight children with a Type 1 (same loss across all frequencies), one with a Type 2 (no residual hearing beyond 2000 Hz), and two with a Type 3 (no residual hearing beyond 1000 Hz) deafness. With a single exception, the children with deaf parents were generally diagnosed and started using their hearing aids earlier than their peers with hearing parents (between 2 months to 2 years earlier).

Observation and Evaluation Setting and Materials

The children and their parents were observed and examined in our laboratory by a team of hearing and deaf investigators/examiners during three, fully video-taped observation sessions scheduled over a three-week period. Each child's communicative and linguistic abilities were evaluated during these sessions. Both informal and semistructured child–parent play was elicited. Additionally, cognitive and linguistic tasks in both spoken Italian and LIS were administered to the child by a hearing and/or a deaf examiner. Clinical interviews of the children's parents were also conducted by two hearing clinical psychologists, assisted by LIS interpreters for communicating with deaf parents. These interviews explored emotional–relational patterns within each family, including the following:

- parents' acceptance of, and adjustment to, the child's deafness
- relationship with family of origin (autonomy versus dependence)
- attitudes with respect to the hearing and the deaf world and to signed and spoken language
- degree of participation into the child's educational process.

A detailed description of the cognitive and linguistic tasks used and of the data obtained is given in Ossella et al. (1994). Some of the results have been described elsewhere (Ardito et al. 1998; Pizzuto et al. 1998; Pizzuto et al. 1999). This chapter concentrates on the data obtained from two cognitive and two receptive language tasks.

As mentioned earlier, one of the objectives of this study was to define an evaluation methodology that would allow us to compare the deaf children's developmental achievements with those of their hearing peers. For this reason, assessment tools were adapted from those that had been employed with normally developing Italian hearing preschoolers and for which we had or could obtain data comparable to those collected for the deaf children. Therefore, the Developmental Test of Visual Motor Integration (VMI; Beery 1989) and the Leiter International Performance Scale (LIPS; Leiter 1980) served as the main tools for assessing the children's cognitive abilities. Both measures have been validated with deaf samples (Parasnis et al. [1996] for the VMI; Grimaldi, Lisi, and Zoccolotti [1985] and Porfiri et al. [1985] for the LIPS). The VMI measures the integration of visual perception and motor behavior. A sequence of progressively more difficult geometrical forms are presented to the child, who is requested to copy them. The LIPS provides a culture-free, nonverbal means of assessing general intelligence, based on primarily abstract concepts. Both these scales are nonverbal and therefore do not overlap with the language measures this study focused upon.

The Peabody Picture Vocabulary Test–Form B (PPVT-B; Dunn 1965) was used for exploring children's receptive lexicon, and a standardized Italian Test for

Grammatical Comprehension in Children (TCGB; Chilosi and Cipriani 1995) was used for evaluating sentence comprehension. Because the study also intended to explore the deaf children's abilities in both speech and sign, each test was presented to the deaf children in two versions: one in spoken Italian and the other in LIS. A group of deaf native LIS signers, who are also teachers of LIS, prepared the LIS versions of the tests in collaboration with deaf and hearing researchers who have investigated the lexicon and grammar of LIS. Because both the PPVT-B and the TCGB tests were originally created for hearing children, it is useful to first describe their standard, spoken Italian format.

The PPVT-B is designed for use with children beginning at age 3. It is comprised of 150 pictures of target items, including verbs, nouns, and adjectives, that are ordered by increasing lexical difficulty. Each item is presented orally to the child along with a card with four pictures. The child's task is to point to the appropriate picture on the card.

The TCGB test is designed for use with children from 3 years and 6 months to 8 years of age and includes seventy-six target items. Each item is presented orally to the child along with a series of four illustrations, and the child's task is to point to the appropriate one. The study used a reduced version of the test comprised of thirty target items that are known to be mastered by the majority of normally developing Italian hearing children by age 6. The relative developmental difficulty of each test item can be evaluated on the basis of normative data provided by Chilosi and Cipriani (1995). The target items included the following:

- simple declarative, affirmative, and negative sentences with one or two arguments (e.g., "mommy washes," " the child doesn't sleep," and "the cat chases the dog")
- locative sentences (e.g., "the ball is under the table")
- relative sentences (e.g., "the girl chases the boy who is riding a bike")
- simple nouns and verbs marked for morphological, inflectional contrasts between singular and plural forms. (Italian morphology regularly marks plural inflections not only on nouns, as in "sedia/sedie" = "chair/chairs," but also in verbs, as in "cammina/camminano = he walks/they walk.)

A hearing examiner who is a language therapist fluent in LIS presented the VMI, LIPS, and the spoken versions of both the PPVT-B and the TCGB tests to the children in Italian. A deaf examiner who is a native LIS signer as well as a teacher in a bilingual education program for deaf children presented the LIS version of the PPVT-B and the TCGB tests to the children. Both examiners were highly experienced in interacting with deaf preschoolers. A free interaction time, during which each child became acquainted with both the hearing and the deaf examiners, always preceded the presentation of each test.

The PPVT-B and the TCGB were presented to the deaf children first in their spoken version and then, a week later, in their signed version. Thus, the LIS version of the tests were administered not only to the children of deaf parents but also to those of hearing parents, despite the fact that the latter had only a limited or, in two cases, no exposure at all to LIS. We felt that information on how the children from hearing families responded to single signs and sign sentences, as compared to Italian words and sentences, could be useful for exploring the potential abilities they may have had in their unimpaired, visual–gestural modality. We also wanted to know how this could be related to the amount of exposure they had to signs. We hypothesized that comparing these children's performance (in both LIS and spoken Italian) with that of the deaf signing children could produce a clearer understanding of both modality-dependent and language-dependent factors that intervene in language development.

Methodological Problems Posed by the Language Tests

Both the spoken and the signed versions of the language tests used presented some methodological problems. The spoken version of the PPVT-B was originally created for and standardized on American-English–speaking preschoolers. The choice and ordering of the test items reflect their increasing degree of difficulty in the English language, based on frequency of usage for different age ranges, from 2 to 18 years of age. The Italian spoken version of the test has not yet been standardized, but it has been widely used with Italian children. However, there have been no comprehensive, independent studies of the spoken (receptive or expressive) lexicon of Italian preschoolers (ages 3 to 6).

The signed version of the PPVT-B posed two major methodological problems. First, no appropriate information on the development of the LIS expressive and receptive lexicon is currently available. Thus, we do not have the data we would need for evaluating the adequacy of the choice and ordering of the test items. The second problem concerns the role that iconicity may play in facilitating sign comprehension. In LIS, as in other sign languages, several signs exhibit iconic features. The forms of the signs visually resemble more or less closely their referents. Thus, unlike their corresponding spoken words, the LIS signs may provide visual cues that may facilitate the comprehension process, especially in tasks that are supported by graphic representations of the target items, such as the PPVT. For example, one test item, RING, is shown in LIS with hand configurations and movements closely resembling the action of slipping a ring on one's finger. Other LIS signs do not present this problem, and the relation sign–referent appears to be rather opaque. For example, the sign for the word 'dog' of the PPVT-B is made with a straight hand, palm oriented downward, which repeatedly contacts the signer's neck.

A study conducted by Silberman Miller (1987) directly addressed the issue of whether iconicity could significantly influence children's performance in a signed presentation of the PPVT test. Both a spoken and a signed presentation of the PPVT-R form was administered to twelve nonsigning English-speaking 3-year-olds. Results suggested that, at least in this age range, iconicity did not enable hearing children to understand the meaning of most of the presented signs. A signed administration of this test could thus be viewed as "one measure of receptive single-sign vocabulary development and not merely as a visual–perceptual identification/matching skill" (Silberman Miller 1987, 363).

The TCGB Test also posed problems of cross-linguistic generalizability. Here, the spoken version of the test was adapted from a test of grammatical comprehension originally devised for English-speaking children by Fraser, Bellugi, and Brown (1963). As developed, test items convey a given set of meaningful relations via morphological and morphosyntactic regularities that are specific to spoken Italian. But in the LIS version of the test, the same meaningful relations rely on morphological and morphosyntactic devices that are very different from those employed in spoken Italian. Most important, the grammatical devices used in LIS may impose upon the signing child developmental demands that are not comparable to those imposed by the same sentence in spoken Italian. An illustrative example may be useful. One of the TCGB items is an apparently simple declarative sentence: "il gatto insegue il cane" ("the cat chases the dog"). In Italian (as in English) this sentence requires understanding of the subject-verb-object (SVO) syntactic pattern and overcoming the semantic–pragmatic difficulties created by the unlikely relationship the sentence describes: Cats do not usually chase dogs in real life. But the LIS translation of the same item, in addition to this semantic–pragmatic difficulty, presents a lexical and morphosyntactic structure that appears considerably more complex than its Italian or English counterpart.

The LIS sentence consists of four distinct signs: Three are full lexical signs meaning, respectively, DOG, CAT, and CHASE. The fourth sign belongs to a particular class of morphemes usually described as "classifiers" (hereafter CL), which occur as either independent morphemes or as bound, constituent morphemes of LIS lexical items (Pizzuto and Corazza 1996). The CL used in this sentence can refer to a variety of animate beings and occurs twice: once after the sign DOG, articulated at a marked point "a" in the signing space, and once after the sign CAT, articulated at "b," a different point in space. The same CL morpheme enters into the formation of the two-handed verb sign CHASE. Finally, the verb CHASE is articulated at marked points in space, and these points signal morphological agreement in the signing space with the two CL signs. In fact, CHASE moves in space from point "b" to point "a," and this movement between the two points previously marked by the two CL signs signals that "the cat chases the dog" and not vice versa. While the two CL signs and the predicate sign CHASE move in space, the two noun signs for DOG and CAT have fixed points of articulation on the signer's body. Finally, the order in which the signs are produced can be roughly described as: DOG, CL-a CAT CL-b b-CHASE-a, but the item CL-a is also simultaneously coarticulated with the items CAT and CL-b. In fact, the signer holds the CL-a sign with the left hand, while at the same time producing the two signs CAT and CL-b with the right hand.

Thus, there are several major lexical and morphosyntactic features that differentiate the LIS sentence from its corresponding (English or Italian) form:

- classifier signs (with no analogous morphemes in Italian) and classifier-based lexical items
- the marking of morphological agreement via positions and/or movements of the signs in space
- the ordering of the sentence's main arguments: OVS in LIS versus SVO in Italian
- the simultaneous coarticulation of some signs, which can take place in a visual–gestural language such as LIS, but not in Italian or in any spoken language.

In addition, the signs occurring in the sentences and/or the way in which they are combined may exhibit iconic features, which may in turn provide visual cues and ease comprehension.

There is currently no information on the development of sentence structure (in comprehension or production) in Italian signing children. Taking into account the structural differences between the LIS and the spoken Italian sentences, our study attempted to provide at least some preliminary evidence on this topic. This evidence would reveal whether relevant differences between LIS and spoken Italian may influence the developmental process in one modality or the other.

Collection of Comparison Data between Deaf and Hearing Children

In order to compare the deaf children's performance with that of their hearing peers, normative data were used whenever available (e.g., for the VMI, LIPS, and the spoken version of the TCGB test). When no appropriate comparable information was available, new data were collected. New data were collected for the spoken version of the PPVT-B, which was administered to a control group of thirty normally developing hearing children, divided into three age subgroups (4-, 5-, and 6-year-olds), with ten subjects for each subgroup.

New data were also collected for the LIS versions of both the PPVT-B and the TCGB tests. Both tasks were administered to a second control group of thirty normally developing hearing children with no previous exposure to LIS, divided into three age subgroups (4-, 5-, and 6-year-olds), with ten subjects for each subgroup. These data were collected by the same hearing investigator who had previously tested the deaf children and who was fluent in LIS. The children were told that they would "play a game" in which the experimenter would show them a number of individual "gestural signs," or sequences of signs, along with pictures. The children were encouraged to give their best guess about which picture corresponded to each LIS sign, or sign sentence, and then point to it. First, the children took the PPVT-B test, and then, approximately two weeks later, they took the TCGB test. The data on hearing children's performance in the LIS tasks were particularly necessary in light of the methodological problems pointed out earlier.

Cognitive Abilities

Chronological age (CA) and mental age (MA) as assessed by the VMI and LIPS scales for each deaf child are shown in table 2. IQ scores resulting from the LIPS are reported in brackets. Note that the LIPS scale could not be administered to one of the children.

The deaf children's performance in the VMI test evidenced considerable individual variability that, however, remained within the limits that have been reported for hearing children (Beery 1989). Four children (two from deaf families and two from hearing families) attained an MA that was 6–12 months above their CA, while two children achieved an MA that was 6–7 months below their CA. In

Table 2. The Deaf Children's Chronological Age (CA) and Mental Age (MA) Assessed by the Visual Motor Integration Scale (VMI) and the Leiter International Performance Scale (LIPS) with IQ Values Reported in Brackets

Child	CA	MA: VMI	MA: LIPS (IQ)
M*	3;11	3;11	4;3 (111)
A*	4;1	5;1	——
P	4;1	4;4	4;4 (111)
V	4;10	4;4	5;7 (119)
D	4;10	5;4	4;9 (103)
J	4;10	5;7	6;4 (134)
F	5;1	5;1	6;7 (133)
L*	5;5	5;7	6;7 (116)
Fr*	5;7	5;4	5;5 (99)
C*	5;10	6;5	6;3 (103)
G	5;11	5;4	6;5 (111)

Note: * denotes children with deaf parents. Data not available for A*. "3;11" denotes age 3 years and 11 months.

the remaining five children, the MA was either the same as or closely comparable to the CA (i.e., with differences in a three-month interval). Comparing the children with deaf parents to those with hearing parents, it seems evident that the children's performance did not appear to be significantly influenced by their different family and language backgrounds. Based on a study of visual–spatial abilities in older deaf children of hearing parents, some authors have hypothesized that early exposure to a sign language may be a critical factor for an enhancement of visual–spatial cognition in deaf as compared to hearing subjects (Parasnis et al. 1996). Our data do not support this hypothesis, at least with respect to the age range examined and the assessment tool used.

The children's performance on the LIPS scale also evidenced remarkable individual variability. The IQ scores ranged from 99 to 134, within the normal range reported for Italian hearing children (Grimaldi et al. 1985; Porfiri et al. 1985). The MA assessed by the LIPS scale appeared higher than the CA for most participants (eight out of ten). Similar to what we noted for the VMI test, the children's performance in the LIPS scale did not appear to be related to family or language differences. Three of the eight children with higher MA had deaf parents, and the remaining five had hearing parents. On the whole, the MAs assessed by means of the LIPS scale were higher than those assessed by means of the VMI test. In addition, some children who attained lower MA values at the VMI scale achieved higher MA values at the LIPS scale. These differences indicate that the two non-verbal scales used for this study evaluate different components of visual–spatial and cognitive abilities. They also suggest that generalizations of the results obtained using a single cognitive task need to be assessed with great caution.

LEXICAL COMPREHENSION IN SPOKEN ITALIAN AND LIS

Figure 1 shows the raw scores obtained by all the children on the PPVT-B test administered in spoken Italian. In this as in the remaining figures of this chapter, the children are ordered from left to right by chronological age, distinguishing three small age subgroups. The continuous lines above the columns in figure 1 show the mean raw scores obtained in the same task by age-matched hearing controls.

Focusing first on the deaf children's performance, the data in figure 1 show that on the PPVT-B individual differences among the children appeared to be stronger than either age- or family/language-related differences. Some children from deaf families attained a higher score than some children from hearing families, but others attained a very similar or lower score than their peers from hearing families.

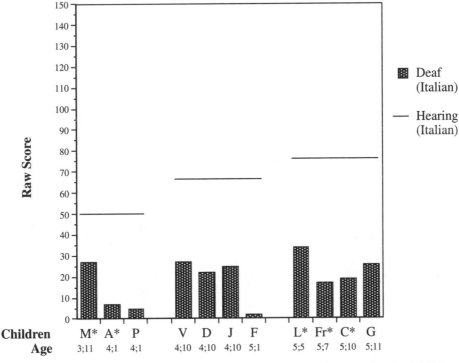

Figure 1. PPVT-B Test in Spoken Italian. Raw scores obtained by the deaf children compared to mean raw scores obtained in the same task by age-matched hearing children. *Note:* * denotes children with deaf parents. "3;11" denotes age 3 years and 11 months.

Looking at the mean raw scores obtained by the hearing controls, one can see that the deaf children's performance was markedly lower than that of the hearing controls. None of the deaf children, not even the oldest ones, reached or even approached in this task the mean raw score of 50 obtained by the youngest group of hearing controls.

Figure 2 shows the deaf children's performance in the LIS version of the PPVT-B task. The continuous lines placed above or across the children's columns indicate the mean raw scores attained by the hearing controls in the spoken version of the test (i.e., the same values described in figure 1). The dotted lines indicate the mean raw scores obtained by the three age-matched subgroups of hearing controls who were administered the LIS version of the PPVT-B task.

Figure 2 shows that the deaf children's performance differed markedly from that observed in the spoken version of the test. In the LIS version of the PPVT-B, all the children obtained considerably higher scores. The majority of them (eight out of eleven) either reached, were close to, or were above the mean raw scores obtained by the hearing controls in the spoken version of the task. Of course, this better performance in the five children of deaf parents was expected. However, it was particularly interesting to find that performance also improved in the children with hearing parents. This was true not only for those children who

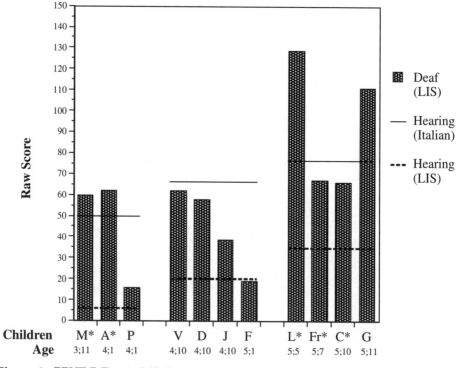

Figure 2. PPVT-B Test in LIS. Raw scores obtained by the deaf children compared to mean raw scores obtained in the same task by age-matched hearing children in the Italian and LIS versions of the test. *Note:* * denotes children with deaf parents. Data not available for A*. "3;11" denotes age 3 years and 11 months.

had been exposed to LIS but also for two children who had not been exposed to LIS.

These results, especially those concerning the deaf children of hearing parents, raise the questions of whether the children's understanding of the LIS signs was facilitated by iconic features that, at least from an adult observer's point of view, characterized many of the LIS signs included in our test. One could hypothesize that these iconic features provided substantial cues for understanding the signs' meaning, especially in a picture choice task such as the PPVT-B. The deaf children's performance could thus have been partially or entirely based on somewhat more general cognitive-representational abilities that allowed the children to exploit these cues rather than on the knowledge of LIS the study intended to explore.

This hypothesis can be evaluated by considering the performance on the same LIS task of our hearing controls with no previous exposure to LIS. The mean raw scores obtained within each age subgroup (see the dotted lines in figure 2) were 6, 20, and 35 respectively for the 4-, 5- and 6-year-old subgroups. In all cases but one, these scores were markedly lower than those obtained by the deaf children. Only one deaf child of hearing parents had a score of 19, which was slightly below the mean raw score of 20 obtained by the hearing peers control subgroup.

The standard procedure for computing the PPVT-B raw scores does not provide sufficient information for assessing whether, in the LIS presentation of the task, the performance of the deaf children or that of their hearing controls was above or below chance level. In order to determine this, we computed for each deaf and hearing child the proportion of correct answers the child provided over the total number of items presented to the child. For a task in which each item provided four choices, as in the PPVT-B, a chance level of performance is equivalent to getting 25 percent of the answers correct.

The performance of all the deaf children (regardless of parental hearing status) was well above chance level. The proportion of correct answers ranged from 73 to 87 percent in deaf children of deaf parents and from 62 to 80 percent in deaf children with hearing parents. However, the mean proportion of correct answers provided by the hearing controls was also above chance level: 32 percent, 44 percent, and 50 percent for the 4-, 5-, and 6-year olds respectively. These data suggest that, in their attempts to guess the meaning of the LIS signs, the hearing controls did make some systematic use of the iconic cues LIS signs provided. The proportion of correct answers also increased with age, which indirectly suggests that 6-year-old hearing children were more capable of detecting iconic/visual cues than hearing 4-year-olds. These data indicate that iconicity did play a role in facilitating the sign comprehension of children, either deaf or hearing, with no or limited exposure to LIS. This conclusion differs somewhat from that of Silberman Miller (1987). Iconic cues may also have contributed to the high levels of performance of some deaf children (including one child who had hearing parents). In addition, the possibility that the signed version of the task required a lower level of lexical knowledge also needs to be more thoroughly explored in future investigations.

At the same time, it is important to emphasize that the performance of the hearing controls in the signed task remained at markedly lower levels compared to that of the deaf children. Even though LIS signs may provide iconically based cues that facilitated their understanding by those with little or no sign exposure, deaf and hearing children did not use the cues in the same manner. Had this been the case, hearing controls would have displayed much higher levels of performance. One plausible explanation for the deaf children's higher performance may be found in visual representational processes specific to deaf children or the particular manner in which they utilize the visual modality for processing information.

Focusing on children who were native signers, one might have expected to find more consistent age-related developmental similarities and/or differences in the LIS task. But this was not the case. In the LIS task, as in its corresponding spoken version, individual variability appeared to be stronger than age-related variability. Thus, no clear developmental progression in relation to age could be noted in these children.

How can we explain these similarities and differences in the group of deaf children of deaf parents? There is no single or simple explanation. Observations regarding individuals' linguistic and communicative skills in spontaneous and semistructured contexts suggested that some aspects of their language environment might have influenced their performance in the PPVT-B task. Children with higher scores tended to be in bilingual programs including both deaf and hearing students where language games, in both sign and oral format, were part of the curriculum. Those children with the lower scores tended to be in the program with no specific language curriculum.

These data indicate two possibilities. On one hand, if we focus our attention only on the children's performance in the LIS task, the data suggest that different educational backgrounds may influence children's functioning even in their native language and may perhaps play a greater role at older ages than they do at younger ages. On the other hand, if we compare the children's performance in the LIS and the spoken Italian tasks, the data suggest that a native knowledge of LIS does not by itself confer an advantage in a spoken language task, where appropriate spoken language education seems to play a role.

GRAMMATICAL COMPREHENSION IN SPOKEN ITALIAN AND LIS

Let us now consider the deaf children's performance in the TCGB grammatical comprehension task administered in spoken Italian. Figure 3 shows the proportion of correct answers each child provided on this test. As in figure 1, the continuous lines show the mean percentage of correct answers that hearing children of comparable age subgroups provided for the same test items. These percentages were drawn from the normative data reported by Chilosi and Cipriani (1995) and reflect the performance of a total of ninety-eight hearing children distributed in three age subgroups: 4-, 5-, and 6-year-olds.

Looking across the children's data, figure 3 show that, as with the findings in the lexical comprehension task, individual differences were more noticeable in the group as a whole than age- or family/language-related differences. Some deaf children of deaf parents performed at considerably higher levels than their peers who had hearing parents, but others did not. How comparable was the deaf children's performance in this task with that of hearing children in the same age ranges? The mean percentages of correct answers provided by the hearing children in this task were 79 percent, 86 percent, and 92 percent respectively for the

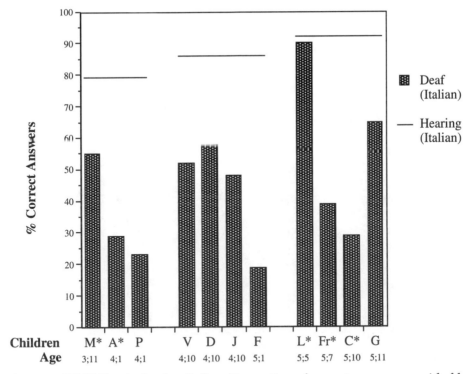

Figure 3. TCGB Test in Spoken Italian. Proportion of correct answers provided by the deaf children compared to mean proportion of correct answers provided in the same task by age-matched hearing children. *Note:* * denotes children with deaf parents. Data not available for A*. "3;11" denotes age 3 years and 11 months.

4-, 5-, and 6-year-olds. All but one of our deaf children remained below these values.

Figure 4 illustrates the deaf children's performance in the LIS version of the test. Comparing the data in figure 4 with those in figure 3, one can see that, in most cases, the performance of deaf children of deaf parents in the LIS presentation of the TCGB differed from that of deaf children of hearing parents. Deaf children of deaf parents provided a greater proportion of correct answers than their peers with hearing parents. In some cases they approached the mean proportion of correct answers provided by their hearing peers in the spoken version of the test. Two of the six deaf children of hearing parents also improved their performance, one to a greater and one to a lesser extent. Because many children of hearing parents performed quite well on the LIS version of the lexical comprehension task, one might have expected them to perform equally well on the LIS grammatical task, but this was not always the case. These results point out that exposure to sign may facilitate the development of lexical receptive skills (as in the case of all the children with hearing parents); this lexical knowledge was not simply and directly employed in the LIS grammatical comprehension task. Exposure to a full, proper sign

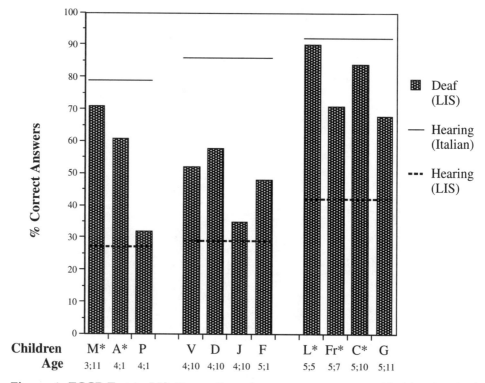

Figure 4. TCGB Test in LIS. Proportion of correct answers provided by the deaf children compared to mean proportion of correct answers provided by age-matched hearing children in the Italian and LIS versions of the test. *Note:* * denotes children with deaf parents. Data not available for A*. "3;11" denotes age 3 years and 11 months.

language system such as LIS appears to be a necessary condition for the development of good receptive skills in both the lexical and the grammatical domain. One child of deaf parents was skilled on both the LIS and the spoken Italian versions of the grammatical task. Albeit limited to one subject, these data indicate that receptive lexical and sentence comprehension skills in one's own native sign language may well favor the development of comparable grammatical comprehension skills in spoken language.

Figure 4 indicates that, although the children of hearing parents produced a markedly lower proportion of correct answers compared to their peers of deaf parents, their performance was always above chance level (25 percent correct answers in a multiple-choice task with four possible items such as the TCGB). Thus, similar to what was found with respect to the PPVT-B task, these children with limited or no exposure to signs appeared to make some systematic use of whatever facilitating cues the LIS signs provided in this grammatical task.

It is interesting to compare the deaf children's performance with that of their age-matched hearing controls with no knowledge of LIS. The dotted lines in figure 4 show that the mean percentages of correct answers provided by the hearing controls in this task were 27 percent, 29 percent, and 42 percent respectively for the 4-, 5-, and 6-year-old groups. These values were always above chance level and showed increasing accuracy with increasing age. These data clearly suggest that some hearing children, especially the older ones, may grasp the meaning of some LIS grammatical constructions despite the fact that they do no not know the language. At the same time, the overall performance of the hearing controls was poorer compared not only to that of the deaf children of deaf parents, which was to be expected, but also to that of the deaf children of hearing parents. These patterns are similar to those found in the LIS presentation of the PPVT-B task. The observations made previously with respect to the signed lexical task can easily be extended to the signed grammatical task.

We have undertaken, but not yet completed, a more in-depth qualitative analysis of the children's responses to the individual items included in both the spoken and the signed presentations of the lexical and grammatical tasks. Preliminary results help clarify some of the factors that may have influenced the deaf versus the hearing children's responses in the LIS version of the TCGB task. For example, the structural properties of the LIS sentences that were briefly described earlier in this chapter clearly appeared to play a role. Sentences that included classifier signs, the use of spatial morphology, and simultaneous coarticulation of signs (e.g., the sentence meaning "the cat chases the dog") were understood by all or, in some cases, only the oldest deaf children of deaf parents. They were significantly more difficult for both deaf children of hearing parents and hearing controls. These sentences thus appeared to require specific linguistic knowledge of LIS grammar, which was not available to deaf or hearing children with limited or no exposure to signs. There were other sentences with coarticulated classifier signs which were also difficult to understand for the hearing controls but which were easily understood by all the deaf children (both of deaf and hearing parents). These sentences somehow provided visual cues for the comprehension of the grammatical relation symbolized (e.g., in a sentence meaning "the ball is under the table," the hand configurations and positions provided visual cues for the locative relation between the two objects). But these cues appeared to be exploited by the deaf children of hearing parents to a degree that was not observed in the hearing controls. These observations suggest that there were qualitative as well as quantitative differences, both within the group of deaf children and between deaf children and their hearing controls, which influenced the way in which they exploited the visual properties of the signs that appeared to ease the comprehension process.

SUMMARY AND CONCLUDING REMARKS

The results of the present study corroborate and extend our knowledge of cognitive and linguistic abilities in deaf preschoolers and provide some indications of how these abilities may be related to different family, language, and educational environments. Our findings concerning the children's cognitive abilities are consistent with those reported in several other studies that have employed nonverbal tasks to assess deaf children's cognition (e.g., see reviews in Mindel and Vernon 1971; Moores 1987; Marschark and Clark 1993; Lane et al. 1996). These findings show that deafness per se neither implies nor causes cognitive impairment. Our children of deaf parents, as those of hearing parents, were all within and often above the norms provided for their hearing peers. The individual variability observed was to be expected in such a relatively small sample of children.

The children's performance in the language tasks also revealed that, on the whole, individual differences were stronger than developmental or family/language-related differences. Once more, individual variability was not surprising given the size of our group and the children's different family and educational backgrounds. But it was interesting to find that, beyond such individual variability, the children from deaf families and those from hearing families exhibited quite comparable performance patterns not only in the two tasks presented in spoken Italian but also in the LIS version of the lexical comprehension task.

In the spoken versions of our lexical and grammatical tasks, with a single exception, the deaf children remained considerably below the level attained by their hearing peers. Regardless of the children's family and school environment and the amount and type of spoken language intervention received, these data demonstrate the difficulties the children had when processing linguistic information in their impaired auditory modality. With respect to the possible role that different spoken language intervention programs may have played, along with the family and school environment, in children's responses to these tasks, it is of interest to recall some information given earlier in this chapter (see table 1) and to note that six of the eleven children in our sample (two of deaf and four of hearing parents) showed higher levels of performance in the spoken language tasks, compared to their peers in the same age subgroup. Four of these were following a bimodal language-intervention program, and the remaining two were in an oral program that included gestural communication. All but one of these children were exposed to LIS and/or SSI in addition to Italian, within the context of the family and/or integrated school classes of hearing and deaf children or bimodal education. In contrast, among the five children who exhibited comparatively lower performances, only one was in a bimodal education program, one attended an oral program, and three children (all from deaf families) had either withdrawn from oral programs or had never received any structured spoken-language education. These observations support our previous comments on the more accurate performance of some, but not all, of the children of deaf parents. Neither native knowledge of LIS nor a school environment with only deaf children appeared to facilitate the children's performance. On the other hand, spoken-language education (in most cases a bimodal program) and an integrated school environment with hearing and deaf children seemed to play a positive role.

In the LIS version of the lexical task, all the deaf children improved their performance, and many of them, including three children of hearing parents exposed to signs in bimodal education or in school, came close to or surpassed the performance level that hearing controls attained in the corresponding spoken task. Although more research is certainly needed to evaluate the comparability of the LIS versus the spoken lexical comprehension task, these data provide a more accurate description of the language skills deaf children can manifest when processing language in sign and more generally through their intact visual–gestural modality.

Clear differences between the deaf children of deaf parents and those with hearing parents emerged, however, in the grammatical task presented in LIS, where most children of deaf parents showed a better comprehension than their peers with hearing parents. As noted, these data indicate that a full exposure to LIS (such as the one that was available to the deaf children of deaf parents) seems to be necessary for developing good receptive skills not only in the lexicon but also in the grammar of the language. These data thus clarify the crucial role that a different input may have in different language domains. A bimodal language input and/or a partial exposure to LIS may enhance single-sign receptive skills but does not appear to be sufficient for the development of grammatical compre hension, for which a complete LIS input is needed.

Finally, we would like to comment on another dimension that appeared to play a positive role in the children's performance on our language tasks. As reported elsewhere (Ossella et al. 1994; Ardito et al. 1998; Pizzuto et al. 1998), most children with high performance levels had parents who, regardless of their hearing or deaf status, were well adjusted to their child's deafness. These parents actively participated in the child's education, promoting the child's autonomy and awareness of the deaf and hearing cultures and their related languages (sign or speech).

Taken together, all of our data and observations provide a relevant methodological indication. The linguistic knowledge that both the deaf children of deaf parents and those with hearing parents possessed would have been largely underestimated if the study had limited its assessment to the spoken modality alone. It is significant, in our view, that the abilities deaf children manifested in the LIS presentations of our language tasks were not displayed in the same manner or to the same degree by the hearing children used as controls for the same LIS tasks. Thus, these abilities appeared to be largely unique to deaf children. Yet our hearing controls, who had never seen LIS signs, performed at above-chance level in both the lexical and the grammatical LIS tasks. We would like to conclude this chapter with some observations on how this finding can be interpreted and evaluated.

The presence of iconicity and consequently of iconic cues facilitating the understanding of single signs and signed sentences is clearly an inherent property of LIS, as of all signed languages investigated to date. The debate over this feature's relevance for our understanding of the use and processing of signed languages is far from settled. But there is clear evidence that the iconic properties of LIS signs may facilitate their comprehension by hearing children (as documented in the present work). Also, hearing and deaf adults with no previous knowledge of LIS may benefit from the iconic properties of LIS signs, as documented in a study conducted on Italian hearing adults (Grosso 1993, 1997) and in a more recent crosslinguistic study on the comprehensibility of LIS signs by hearing and deaf adults of six different European countries (Pizzuto and Volterra 2000; Boyes Braem 1998). It is often implicitly or explicitly assumed that iconicity and the relative transparency of signs or signed sentences somehow "detracts" linguistic properties from any given signed language, rendering the process of comprehending signs less symbolic or abstract. In our view, this assumption is unwarranted because it can be argued that an appropriate understanding of the differences between signed and spoken languages along the dimension of iconicity may ultimately uncover hidden, iconic components in speech that are akin to those found in sign and are grounded in our perceptual–motor experience (Pizzuto and Volterra 2000).

From this perspective, the fact that hearing children (or adults) can grasp the meaning of single signs or sentences should be given the most direct interpretation. It indicates that some aspects of the sign code can be understood based on iconic cues and/or presumably universal (i.e., language-independent) abilities to detect and interpret these cues. Nevertheless, there is no principled reason to infer from this that the knowledge deaf children (or adults) employ when understanding signs requires minor, somewhat nonlinguistic symbolic skills compared to the knowledge that hearing children and adults employ in understanding spoken words. Different (rather than minor) symbolic skills may well be implicated, and it is possible that such skills are inextricably entrenched within linguistic skills. In our view, the investigation of deaf children's linguistic abilities (in both sign and speech) must simply take into account the relevant differences between signed and spoken languages along the dimension of iconicity. Research and language-assessment tools must thus be refined as needed in order to allow an accurate evaluation of both presumably universal processes that hearing and deaf children may employ in interpreting signs and more language-specific processes.

References

Ardito, B., M. C. Caselli, T. Ossella, and E. Pizzuto. 1998. Valutazione del bambino sordo in età prescolare e indicazioni per l'intervento. In *Diagnosi precoce e prevenzione dei disturbi del linguaggio e della comunicazione: Procedure e metodi di trattamento nei disordini della comunicazione*, ed. S. Frasson and L. Lena, 107–30. Pisa: Edizioni del Cerro.

Beery, K. E. 1989. *Administration, scoring and teaching manual for the developmental test of visual-motor integration.* Cleveland: Modern Curriculum Press.

Boyes Braem, P. 1998. Kulturell bestimmte oder freie Gesten? Die Wahrnehmung von Gesten durch Mitglieder unterschiedlicher (hörender und gehörloser). In *Improvisation III*, ed. W. Fähndrich, 192–219. Winterthur, Switzerland: Amadeus.

Capirci, O., S. Montanari, and V. Volterra. 1998. Gestures, signs, and words in early language development. In *The nature and functions of gesture in children's communication*, ed. J. Iverson and S. Goldin-Meadow, 45–60. San Francisco: Jossey-Bass.

Caselli, M. C., S. Maragna, L. Pagliari Rampelli, and V. Volterra. 1994. *Linguaggio e sordità.* Firenze: La Nuova Italia.

Chilosi, A., and P. Cipriani. 1995. *TCGB: Test di comprensione grammaticale per bambini.* Pisa: Edizioni del Cerro.

Dunn, L. M. 1965. *Peabody Picture Vocabulary Test.* Wilmington, Del.: Guidances Associates.

Emiliani, M., D. Baldo, A. Tragni, and R. McKee. 1994. Comprensione di aspetti lessicali e morfosintattici dell'italiano parlato nei bambini ipoacusici. *Età Evolutiva* 48:51–61.

Fraser C., U. Bellugi, and R. Brown. 1963. Control of grammar in imitation, comprehension and production. *Journal of Verbal Learning and Verbal Behaviour* 2:121–35.

Gregory, S. 1995. *Deaf children and their families.* London: George Allen and Unwin, 1976. Reprint, Cambridge, U.K.: Cambridge University Press.

Grimaldi, A., F. Lisi, and P. Zoccolotti. 1985. Analisi delle caratteristiche psicometriche della scala Leiter: Proposta di una ristrutturazione della scala. *Archivio di Psicologia, Neurologia e Psichiatria* 46:114–29.

Grosso, B. 1993. Iconicità e arbitrarietà nella lingua dei segni italiana: Uno studio sperimentale. Ph.D. diss., Department of Psychology, University of Padua. Typescript.

———. 1997. Gli udenti capiscono i segni dei sordi? In *LIS: Studi, esperienze e ricerche sulla Lingua dei Segni in Italia,* ed. M. C. Caselli and S. Corazza, 79–86. Pisa: Edizioni Del Cerro.

Lane, H. L., R. Hoffmeister, and B. J. Bahan. 1996. *A journey into the deaf world.* San Diego: Dawn Sign Press.

Leiter, R. G. 1980. *Leiter International Performance Scale.* Chicago: Stoelting.

Marschark, M. 1993. *Psychological development of deaf children.* New York: Oxford University Press.

Marschark, M., and M. D. Clark. 1993. *Psychological perspectives on deafness.* Hillsdale, N.J.: Lawrence Erlbaum.

Massoni, P., and S. Maragna. 1997. *Manuale di logopedia per bambini sordi.* Milano: Franco Angeli.

Mindel, E. D., and M. C. Vernon. 1971. *They grow in silence; The deaf child and his family.* Silver Spring, Md.: National Association of the Deaf.

Moores, D. 1987. *Educating the deaf: Psychology, practice and principle,* 3d ed. Boston: Houghton Mifflin.

Ossella, T., B. Ardito, P. M. Bianchi, S. Gentile, S. Luchenti, L. Tieri, M. C. Caselli, E. Pizzuto, R. Bosi, and R. Cafasso. 1994. *Lo sviluppo dei processi di simbolizzazione nei bambini sordi, strategie di comunicazione verbale e non verbale e ripercussioni sulle modalità in ambito familiare e sociale.* Research Report 92/02/P/283, Rome: Institute of Psychology, National Research Council, and Ospedale Bambino Gesù.

Parasnis, I., V. J. Samar, J. G. Bettger, and K. Sathe. 1996. Does deafness lead to enhancement of visual–spatial cognition in children? Negative evidence from deaf non-signers. *Journal of Deaf Studies and Deaf Education* 2:145–52.

Pizzuto, E., B. Ardito, M. C. Caselli, and S. Corazza. 1999. The development of Italian Sign Language (LIS) in deaf preschoolers: Data from lexical and sentence elicitation tasks. Paper presented at the Seventh International Congress of the International Association for the Study of Child Language, July 12–16, 1999, San Sebastian, Spain.

Pizzuto, E., M. C. Caselli, B. Ardito, T. Ossella, A. Albertoni, B. Santarelli, and R. Cafasso. 1998. Assessing cognitive, relational, and language abilities in preschool Italian deaf children. In *Issues unresolved: New perspectives on language and deaf education,* ed. A. Wiesel, 41–52. Washington, D.C.: Gallaudet University Press.

Pizzuto, E., and S. Corazza. 1996. Noun morphology in Italian Sign Language (LIS). *Lingua* 98:169–96.

Pizzuto, E., and V. Volterra. Forthcoming. La Lingua dei Segni Italiana (LIS). In *La linguistica italiana alle soglie del 2000*, ed. C. Lavinio and S. Sgroi. Rome: Bulzoni.

———. 2000. Iconicity and transparency in sign languages: A cross-linguistic, cross-cultural view. In *The signs of language revisited: An anthology to honor Ursula Bellugi and Edward Klima*, ed. K. Emmorey and H. Lane, 261–86. Mahwah, N.J.: Lawrence Erlbaum.

Porfiri, E., M. G. Quieti, A. Grimaldi, and P. Zoccolotti. 1985. Analisi delle caratteristiche della scala LEITER: Estensione delle norme a fasce di eta' prescolastiche. *Rassegna di Psicologia* 1/2:101–6.

Silberman Miller, M. 1987. Sign iconicity: Single sign receptive vocabulary skills of nonsigning hearing preschoolers. *Journal of Communication Disorders* 20:359–65.

Volterra, V., ed. 1987. *La lingua italiana dei segni: La comunicazione visivo–gestuale dei sordi*. Bologna: Il Mulino.

Volterra, V., C. Pace, B. Pennacchi, and S. Corazza. 1995. Advanced learning technology for a bilingual education of deaf children. *American Annals of the Deaf* 14:402–9.

6

UNDERSTANDING LANGUAGE AND LEARNING IN DEAF CHILDREN

Marc Marschark and Jennifer Lukomski

Among those concerned with the education of deaf children, there are two broad perspectives on the interaction of language and learning. Many teachers and other professionals, such as Seal, suggest that "deaf and hard of hearing students are just like hearing students" (1998, 128). Assumptions of this sort are consistent with our notions of equity and the flexibility of young learners, and they lie at the heart of arguments in favor of mainstream education for deaf and hard of hearing children (Gearhart, Mullen, and Gearhart 1993). However egalitarian such pronouncements might be, they might also be wrong, and following them blindly may be an even greater disservice to deaf children than treating them as though they are different from hearing children.

This chapter examines the cognitive functioning of deaf learners and the extent to which any reliable differences between them and their hearing peers might explain other observed differences in academic achievement. In that context, we consider ways in which cognitive and academic skills of deaf students are assessed and interpreted. We do not consider language development explicitly in any length, but we explore possible interactions among language fluencies, cognitive abilities, assessment methods, and the academic skills that deaf children bring to the learning context (see also Braden, this volume). We suggest ways in which educational methods might need to change in order to optimize academic success of the individuals, and we emphasize the need for educational programs with sufficient flexibility to match diverse student needs.

Looking ahead, our review of research concerning the cognitive underpinnings and the assessment of learning by deaf students suggests that some differences may occur in their learning, knowledge organization, and approaches to problem solving relative to hearing students. The origins of the observed differences are not entirely clear, nor is the extent to which they may have long-term, significant implications for educational achievement. At a minimum, deaf learners appear more heterogeneous than their hearing age-mates. To the extent that there are also real differences in the cognitive domain, the impact of those differences on classroom learning may be magnified or modified by the variability of the learners.

FOUNDATIONS OF LEARNING

Over the past forty years, investigations of deaf children's cognitive functioning frequently have reported performance that is below the levels of hearing peers (see Marschark 1993 for a review). In some cases, these differences were found to be developmental lags that disappeared over time (e.g., Kusché and Greenberg 1983). In others, the differences remained or appeared to grow larger as the children became older (e.g., Furth 1966). Many earlier studies, however, are now recognized as having confounded cognitive abilities and English language ability, using tasks that required reading, writing, or spoken language skills. For many years, education for deaf children also focused on the written and/or spoken language of the larger hearing community. This focus was with regard to both the primary mode of communication in the classroom and the fact that many areas of study were ignored or received minimal attention because the teaching of language consumed such a large portion of the school day (Bowe 1998; Meadow-Orlans, this volume). Those latter efforts notwithstanding, spoken language development in children with congenital or early-onset hearing losses is typically found to be slow relative to hearing age-mates and marked by significant delays, even when hearing losses are in the mild-to-moderate range (Carney and Moeller 1988; Gregory and Hindley 1996).

With the widespread use of sign language and a greater array of alternative educational placements, deaf children now have significantly improved access to information in the classroom. Still, as a group, they continue to struggle in several academic domains. In particular, reading and writing skills of deaf children continue to lag behind those of hearing peers, a situation that has improved only slightly during the past twenty years (Traxler 2000). Some other academic challenges are likely related to literacy skills, insofar as a large portion of the knowledge expected of children during the middle-school and high-school years is acquired through reading. It thus seems unwise to ignore the influence of language in understanding the cognitive functioning and academic abilities of deaf students, even while remaining vigilant to ensure that relevant evaluations are not confounded by the demands of a particular language. Sign language can serve as an effective mode of communication for young deaf children, providing all of the stages typical of spoken language acquisition when acquired naturally as a first language (Meier and Newport 1990). Early exposure to sign language also appears to be a significant predictor of later academic success (Calderon and Greenberg 1997). At the same time, English-based literacy skills are essential to academic and employment success. Children who do not start early in the acquisition of literacy skills are likely to find themselves increasingly lagging behind their hearing peers.

In the assessment domain, educators and researchers are faced with a related dilemma in evaluating deaf students' abilities. In view of the apparently unfair demands of the verbal portions of intelligence tests, the recommended practice for assessing a deaf or hard of hearing student's intelligence is to use nonverbal scales of intelligence. The utility of such testing, however, is questionable. Nonverbal intelligence scales do serve a function in determining whether a child has mental retardation or other significant learning disabilities. In contrast, they have limited validity for predicting a child's achievement levels or literacy potential or for guiding classroom instruction (e.g., Maller 1997). Simply eliminating the verbal portion of intelligence tests also removes a key component of what those tests are intended to measure: "[I]f performance tests provide fair and accurate assessments of intelligence independent of language skills, . . . why do we persist in using verbal tests for hearing individuals?" (Marschark 1993, 130). Verbal intelligence tests generally are good predictors of academic achievement for hearing children. But using them with children who have severe-to-profound hearing losses and come from predominantly hearing families indicates a lack of sensitivity to the language-related challenges associated with their situations.

In retrospect, many early studies of cognitive functioning in deaf children were motivated by scientific interest in cognitive development in the absence of audition or language (e.g., Myklebust 1960; Furth 1966, respectively). Underlying that research (or at least on the near-periphery) were also a variety of educationally relevant goals consistent with the current zeitgeist concerning the needs of children with disabilities. Today, however, there is much greater recognition that performance differences on cognitive tasks between deaf and hearing children do not imply that deaf children are intellectually disadvantaged. More frequently, our methods of evaluation have been skewed, or the theoretical assumptions and interpretations of research have been flawed (Braden, this volume; Clark and Hoemann 1991; Maller 1997; Marschark 1993). A much more valuable enterprise, therefore, is consideration of deaf children's performance in particular cognitive domains and examination of ways in which the presumed underlying skills converge to influence performance in other domains.

MEANS AND MODES OF EVALUATING DEAF CHILDREN'S COGNITIVE ABILITIES

Beyond methodological issues related to language-based testing, several investigators have argued that deaf children might have early experiences that are different in kind from those of hearing children (Liben 1978; Marschark 2000). If so, then even language-free tests might be limited in their applicability to many deaf children. Studies of intelligence and academic abilities of minority and underprivileged children during the 1960s and 1970s referred to this issue as the lack of *culture fairness*. It had long been recognized that the nature of children's early environments could influence social (Mead 1935) and intellectual (Piaget 1952) development, but the issue was rarely addressed with regard to deaf children (but see Furth 1973; Myklebust 1960; Zweibel 1987). Partially as a result, deaf children were often described as concrete, literal thinkers who were unlikely to be able to grasp the abstract concepts necessary for academic success (e.g., Blackwell et al. 1978; cf. Stokoe, this volume).

It is now clear that although differences are observed between deaf and hearing children in the cognitive domain, many of them are more (falsely) apparent than real. When lags in cognitive development are observed, they can usually be linked to communication barriers at home or in early educational environments rather than to hearing loss per se. The notion of deaf children as unable to understand abstract or multidimensional concepts has now been replaced by a better understanding of the interactions of language and cognitive development in children who often do not have effective access to communication and other environmental information available to parents and hearing peers. The relationship is a complicated one, however, and not to be glossed over.

In order to better understand the relations among language and learning in deaf children, it is important to consider the extent to which deaf and hearing children might develop different patterns of cognitive organization or cognitive functioning as a result of differences in early experience. We can then consider the ways in which such differences might influence learning (broadly defined) and literacy, in particular. Such differences would not be surprising in the context of significant hearing loss because lack of hearing influences the neurological and cognitive development of other systems as well (Marschark 1993, chapter 12; Zweibel 1987). Nevertheless, understanding the nature of those differences opens the possibility of structuring teaching–learning situations and developing instructional materials that might be more effective in educating deaf students. Far from being a reflection of prejudice or discrimination (Lane 1992), work of this sort should be the responsibility and the priority of investigators and educators interested in optimizing academic opportunities for deaf children.

A variety of educators and investigators, for example, have emphasized the obvious importance of the visual modality for deaf children in teaching–learning contexts. Although one may accept this assumption, no strong evidence exists for the corollary that often seems to accompany it: that deaf people are *better* than hearing people in the visual domain. Depending on the specific kind of task used, deaf individuals have been found to be better than, worse than, or the same as normally hearing individuals. Parasnis and Samar (1985), for example, found that deaf college students were more flexible than hearing students in their ability to redirect attention from one spatial location to another. Quittner et al. (1994), in contrast, found that deaf children generally show poorer visual attention than hearing children, particularly in situations in which they are liable to be distracted.

When language is added to the theoretical mix, findings indicate that users of American Sign Language (ASL) tend to exhibit superior performance in some visual-spatial domains, such as the ability to identify emotional facial expressions and on mental imagery tasks involving mental rotation, image generation, and image transformation (see Wilson, this volume). Sign language users and individuals who do not use sign language perform comparably in other domains, including face recognition and other face-processing abilities (e.g., Parasnis et al. 1996; see Emmorey 1998 for a review). Those findings support the suggestion that enhanced visual-spatial skills do not represent some kind of *sensory compensation* in deaf individuals. Rather, exposure to a language that is both visual and spatial appears to result in an organization of function that has some broader cognitive and social advantages.

Beyond the fact that sign language is primarily a visual language (although it is also a kinesthetic one, an essential addition for individuals who are deaf and blind), it seems likely that differences in language exposure among deaf children would have a marked impact on their academic success. In particular, the observed disparity in access to language between deaf children with deaf parents and deaf children with hearing parents is not unrelated to parallel differences observed in several academic domains. Unlike hearing children of hearing parents or deaf children of deaf parents, deaf children of hearing parents frequently do not have effective communication with their parents during their early years. Their social and educational interactions may therefore be less rich when compared with children who share a common language with their parents, regardless of whether that language is signed or spoken (Marschark 1993, 2000; Gray et al., this volume). Let us therefore consider several of the basic components of learning to-gether with ways in which we evaluate both the abilities and potential of deaf children.

Memory Codes and Memory Modes

Deaf children's memory abilities have been of interest to investigators for over a century. Generally, numerous studies concerning short-term memory (or *working memory*) have shown that deaf and hearing individuals may encode information in qualitatively different ways. With lists of simple stimuli such as words, pic-tures, or numbers, hearing people tend to rely on verbal-sequential coding, as-sumed to be phonological, articulatory, or acoustic in nature (Baddeley 1997). Deaf people, in contrast, have been said to rely more heavily on visual-spatial short-term memory codes (Marschark 1993, chapter 8; Wilson, this volume).

The most frequently cited support for the notion that deaf individuals tend to use visual short-term memory codes comes from a series of studies conducted in the 1970s by O'Connor and Hermelin (e.g., O'Connor and Hermelin 1972; Her-melin and O'Connor 1973). They showed deaf and hearing children a series of digits, faces, or other stimuli that varied in the location or order of presentation. O'Connor and Hermelin found that deaf children tended to remember the se-quences using a spatial/location memory code, whereas hearing children's prefer-ences for spatial or temporal/sequential coding varied across different tasks. Most importantly, the results of several studies indicated that temporal and spatial cod-ing of short sequences can lead to equivalent short-term memory performance.

O'Connor and Hermelin's findings provided strong support for hypotheses concerning the primacy of visual-spatial coding in deaf children's short-term memories and for the comparability of those codes to the verbal-sequential short-term memory codes typically employed by hearing children. Belmont, Karchmer, and Bourg (1983) later extended those findings, demonstrating that strategy pref-erences among deaf children for visual-spatial versus verbal coding were difficult to change, whereas hearing children tended to be somewhat more flexible. Their results also emphasized the importance of considering individual differences in coding strategies among deaf children, not only in memory tasks, but also as they might affect performance in other cognitive domains that contain explicit or im-plicit memory components. Individual differences are commonly acknowledged by educators in tasks such as reading, writing, and problem solving, but it is un-clear whether they are also recognized as influencing the knowledge, retrieval strategies, and language fluencies underlying such tasks.

At first blush, there appears to be no a priori reason to expect that one lan-guage modality or another should have any advantage with regard to memory. Nevertheless, research over the past twenty years has indicated that speech-based codes are somewhat more efficient than other codes for remembering sequential information. Early studies by Conrad (1979) and others, for example, indicate that memory for letters and words by "oral" deaf children was closely linked to their spoken language skills and inversely related to their degree of hearing loss. Han-son and Lichtenstein (1990) and Lichtenstein (1998) report that among deaf stu-dents who used both sign language and spoken language, those with better speech skills tended to rely primarily on speech recoding in memory. Further, Campbell and Wright (1990) report that deaf students with low-to-moderate speech-coding abilities tended to use both speech and sign strategies and that students with better speech skills also tended to remember more.

As one alternative to speech-based coding, some deaf individuals do make use of sign language in memory coding. Thus, signs made with similar hand-shapes tend to disrupt memory performance among deaf individuals, just as words that sound the same disrupt memory performance among hearing individuals (e.g., Hanson 1982; Poizner, Bellugi, and Tweney 1981). Such findings suggest that just as variation in English fluency may affect the frequency of phonologically based coding in deaf individuals, variation in sign language fluency should affect the frequency of sign-based coding. Herein lies one possible determinant of short-term memory in deaf students. Consistent with that prediction, Marschark and Mayer (1998) reported a study in which deaf students' spoken language fluency was directly related to their memory spans, whereas their sign language fluency was found to be inversely related to their memory spans (see also Wilson, this volume). At the very least, it must be concluded that the language fluencies of deaf students can influence what they remember and how. As it turns out, the "how" is one of the most interesting parts of the memory story—and one that has much broader implications for learning.

It is now well established that working memory includes a central executive that controls subsystems akin to a visual-spatial sketch pad and an articulatory loop (Baddeley 1997). For the present purposes, the key parameter of working memory is that the *articulatory loop* functionally limits memory span to the amount that can be articulated in roughly two seconds. So, for example, fewer long words than short words can be remembered, and spoken languages in which information takes longer to pronounce yield shorter memory spans than languages in which the same information take less time to pronounce (Ellis and Hennelly 1980). Given that it takes longer to produce a sign in ASL than a word in spoken English (even if the overall rate of information transfer is the same for the two languages), it should not be surprising that deaf people using sign language-based processes in working memory remember less than deaf people or hearing people using speech-based processes in working memory. Deaf and hearing individuals have the same working memory *capacity* (roughly the amount that can be articulated by hand or mouth in two seconds), but fewer ASL signs than English words can be fit into the articulatory loop in that amount of time (Marschark and Mayer 1998; Wilson and Emmorey 1997).

Could alternative memory strategies reduce some of the differences in memory seen between deaf and hearing learners? One possibility is that deaf children might employ visual memory strategies that should be just as efficient as linguistic strategies. We know from investigations by Conlin and Paivio (1975) and Bonvillian (1983), however, that deaf individuals are no more likely than hearing individuals to use a visual imagery code in place of verbal coding for memory.

Perhaps the simplest and earliest-acquired memory strategy is rote repetition, or *rehearsal* (we leave out, for the present purposes, nursery rhymes, which are a related and important early learning tool but not a self-generated strategy). Bebko and McKinnon (1990) demonstrated a strong relationship between language development and the use of memory rehearsal in deaf children. That strategy was seen to emerge at about 7–8 years for hearing students, 10–11 years for deaf students exposed primarily to spoken language, and 12–13 years for students in environments in which both sign language and spoken language were used. Because hearing children appeared more skilled in the application of such strategies, particularly in serial recall, Bebko and McKinnon suggested that memory strategies rather than the modality of memory might have the greatest influence on deaf children's recall performance, a prediction strongly supported by their empirical results. Such findings suggest that deaf children who are taught appropriate memory strategies and who know when to apply them could do as well as hearing children on these tasks (but see Liben 1979).

Rote memorization is seldom seen as an ideal approach to learning, although it is used explicitly in a variety of school settings, and students frequently adopt it as an approach to studying (Richardson et al. 2000). In order to optimize the teaching–learning process, interactions among language, to-be-acquired information, and existing knowledge have to be understood. For that, we have to consider how the learner organizes knowledge.

Organization of Knowledge

The processes by which we acquire new information and retrieve old information from long-term memory are intimately related to the broader organization of our knowledge. Information that we have learned through external sources or discovered for ourselves not only has to be retained, but it also has to be retrieved in order to be utilized. Although we do have occasional retrieval failures, such as when we are unable to put a name to a familiar face, access to information in long-term memory normally happens automatically—"as needed"—in the context of ongoing behavior. Remembering our home telephone number, how to ride a bicycle, or the meaning of "duck" are not things for which we typically have to pay much attention. Of course, "duck" may have different meanings in different contexts, but other cues will tell us which meaning is relevant, and only rarely do such decisions reach consciousness. Because of the need for automatic, rapid access to long-term memory information, the organization of our long-term *semantic memories* is important both for recall and for tasks such as reading, writing, and problem solving.

Research with hearing individuals has provided insight into the ways in which organization and retrieval processes interact under a variety of task conditions. In the present context, it is important to recognize that individuals vary in how much they know about different things and how that information is organized and that both aspects can affect the accessibility and availability of knowledge. Globally, one might expect that organization of general knowledge is roughly the same for most individuals, regardless of whether they are deaf or hearing and independent of how much knowledge each might have about a specific thing. But this does not appear to be the case. People who are experts in an area, for example, may have different ways of organizing relevant information in that area, thus improving its accessibility and availability. Similarly, children may have different, sometimes idiosyncratic, ways of organizing information that reveal its incompleteness and the fact that it is not yet well-interconnected with other knowledge (e.g., a worm may not be considered an animal because it does not have eyes). The organization of knowledge is affected by both explicit teaching and by active and passive self-directed learning, and there is surely a continuum between the extremes we have noted.

Acknowledging differences with regard to early experience, access to language, and the nature of educational contexts raises the possibility that knowledge may be organized, as well as acquired, somewhat differently by deaf learners and their hearing peers (Marschark 2000). Several studies have investigated the relationship between memory performance and conceptual knowledge of deaf individuals, although none has yet examined the way in which differences might specifically affect literacy or performance on standardized assessments. Research conducted during the 1970s, for example, found only small differences in the organization of knowledge in deaf and hearing students when highly familiar concepts were used (Tweney, Hoemann, and Andrews 1975). Investigations involving broader, lower-frequency material appear not to have been conducted. Even with familiar concepts, however, deaf students tended not to use as much meaning-based clustering in recall and typically recalled less than hearing peers even when they did use semantically based retrieval (Liben 1979).

Such findings led to the conclusions that although deaf students recognize and attempt to use associations among words and pictures to improve memory, they might lack flexibility in fully comprehending an item's meaning or automatically recognizing the place of a concept in a hierarchical taxonomic structure (e.g., a duck is an animal, a bird, a farm animal; see Marschark 1993, chapter 9, for a review). Deaf students may know these things, but they still may not automatically activate less-familiar information in memory. For example, the sentence "A shot of sunlight burst from the cage, and the canary was gone" will be understood differently, if at all, by a reader who does not know or does not automatically retrieve the fact that canaries are yellow. Alternatively, a reader's prior experience with canaries, metaphors, or other contexts (e.g., "beaming up" on Star Trek) may overshadow the intended interpretation of the sentence. In any case, the problem is not only that a metaphorical comparison may be missed. The reader may be left confused or misdirected in the comprehension process.

One attempt to determine the extent of lexically based knowledge differences between deaf and hearing students was provided by McEvoy, Marschark, and Nelson (1999). That study examined deaf and hearing college students' knowledge organization using a controlled, single-word association task in which students wrote down the first word that came to mind in response to each in a series of printed words. This controlled-association procedure produces a measure of the associative structure for each word within the mental lexicon, and these associative structures can be used as lexical "fingerprints" to define the word in semantic memory.

McEvoy et al. found that the associative responses given by the two groups were remarkably similar overall ($r = .77$). Nevertheless, they also found that there were significant differences on several dimensions that reflected the coherence or consistency in memory organization, indicating that deaf students' verbal concepts were less homogeneous than those of hearing students. For example, there was significantly less consistency in primary associates across words for deaf than hearing subjects, and hearing subjects had significantly smaller (i.e., less idiosyncratic) and better-defined sets of linkages to other concepts. The observed differences suggested that during complex cognitive tasks, deaf students' activation of meaning in long-term memory may not be as directed, consistent, or inclusive as that of hearing students. Lower frequency, alternative meanings of words might be particularly less likely to be retrieved. In the context of reading, this kind of difference could significantly affect lexical, syntactic, and discourse levels of processing. Thus, the issue here is not simply one of recognizing words per se but the broader involvement of associative memory in higher-level tasks such as reading and other areas of academic performance (Paivio 1971).

Related findings also emerged from a study by Marschark and Everhart (1999). They employed a version of the "Twenty Questions" game in which deaf and hearing children had to discover which of forty-two pictures of common objects the experimenter had chosen. Winning at "Twenty Questions" requires that an individual apply knowledge about relationships among concepts and categories and eliminate alternatives as efficiently as possible. Questions such as "Is it an animal?" or "Is it round?" which make use of taxonomic or other kinds of categorical information, not only provide the best route to a solution but also reflect the application of conceptual knowledge. Marschark and Everhart found, however, that deaf children aged 7–14 years rarely used questions based on the objects' taxonomic, perceptual, or functional characteristics. They tended to guess specific objects in the array instead of attempting to reduce the number of possibilities. Consequently, they were also significantly less likely than hearing peers to win the "Twenty Questions" game. Deaf and hearing children who had played the game before were equally likely to use such strategies, but inexperienced hearing children typically discovered response-limiting strategies, whereas their inexperienced deaf peers did not (Belmont et al. 1983). In a second experiment, Marschark and Everhart found that even among college students, hearing individuals were significantly more efficient in solving the "Twenty Questions" problem than deaf individuals because their questions eliminated more alternative answers. Unfortunately, the study did not examine whether deaf students would discover the more effective strategies with additional training, learn them through modeling (as many hearing children probably do in his task), or generalize them to other tasks.

Taken together, these studies suggest that differences may exist in both knowledge organization and the strategies involved in accessing information between deaf and hearing students. There is clearly considerable overlap in knowledge of concepts and categories across the two groups, but that information is sometimes not applied, or is not successfully applied, by deaf children in contexts in which it is by hearing peers. Whether this situation is related to depth or breadth of the knowledge or a failure to apply such knowledge spontaneously is unclear. Nonetheless, to the extent that conceptual or categorical knowledge from memory is needed but is not successfully used in any particular task, the learning and academic performance of deaf (or hearing) students will suffer. Further, we may misjudge just how much a student actually does know.

ASSESSING COGNITIVE COMPETENCIES IN DEAF CHILDREN

One common explanation for deaf children's observed difficulties in some classroom tasks, as well as in traditional cognitive paradigms such as classification and conservation, is that they are easily distracted by irrelevant aspects of a problem or by other things going on the classroom (Ottem 1980; Quittner et al. 1994). Earlier conclusions arguing that deaf children are more impulsive than hearing peers have now been overshadowed by demonstrations that they are not (Marschark and Everhart 1999). Nevertheless, attentional factors may still be involved. Ottem (1980) reviewed dozens of studies involving deaf adults and children and found that performance of deaf and hearing individuals was essentially equivalent when successful performance required attention to a single dimension of the problems (e.g., number). When problem-solving tasks required joint attention to two or more dimensions (e.g., length and number), in contrast, deaf individuals routinely performed more poorly than the hearing individuals. Ottem attributed the observed pattern of results to the deaf individuals' tendency to focus on a single dimension of a problem situation. He argued that the difficulty is not that deaf children are unable to form coherent concepts or categories but that the dimensions on which they are to be formed is not as obvious or salient as they might be for hearing children (McEvoy et al. 1999). This misdirection could result from lack of verbal/linguistic labeling (e.g., similar objects get the same category name) or from a more basic lack of experience with contexts from which such concepts might be acquired (Gershkoff-Stowe et al. 1997; Marschark and Everhart 1999).

Another explanation for deaf children's difficulty with multidimensional problem solving may lie in their planning abilities or their tendencies to apply planning strategically (Das and Ojile 1995; Tzuriel and Caspi 1992). Das and Ojile (1995) tested groups of deaf and hearing students on a nonverbal strategy task similar to the game "Master Mind." Given a limited amount of information, students were asked to determine the correct pattern of a set of colored chips laid out in predetermined sequence. Students were given the additional clues of how many chips were already in the correct positions. Das and Ojile found that deaf students performed more poorly than the hearing students on the task, and most did not take advantage of the available cues. Whether the problem was that the deaf children did not attend to the salient information or whether they had more difficulty planning a strategy to solve the problem is unclear.

Luckner and McNeill (1994) argued that differences in deaf and hearing students' problem-solving skills derive largely from differences in their language abilities. They explored problem solving using the "Tower of Hanoi" puzzle with groups of deaf, hearing, and hard of hearing students aged 5 and older. Deaf students performed significantly worse than their hearing peers, a difference that Luckner and McNeill attributed to the fact that deaf individuals do not have "strong language skills" that could have mediated performance. Luckner and McNeill did not provide any support for their claim that linguistic deficits impede deaf individuals in the planning stages of problem solving, nor did they offer an explanation for why language skills were deemed necessary in the visual-spatial "Tower of Hanoi" task (cf. Mousley and Kelly 1999).

Aside from possible methodological or theoretical confounds, we already have acknowledged the potential for differences among deaf children that might affect problem solving and other academic tasks. At this point, the important question is whether the apparent lack of flexibility in problem solving can be circumvented or modified through exposure to different experiences or implicit problem-solving instruction. Several studies, for example, have investigated whether teaching deaf students problem-solving strategies can improve their performance (e.g., Keane and Kretschmer 1987; Tzuriel and Caspi 1992). Tzuriel and Caspi (1992) conducted one such study with groups of deaf and hearing children aged 4–6 years. After a baseline assessment, the children were taught mediational strategies such as nonverbal focusing, analyzing task dimensions, and transformational rules. The children then were administered two problem-solving tasks in different modalities (i.e., pictorial and figural). On the post-test, the deaf group was found to have made significant gains on the figural task but not on the pictorial task. Tzuriel and Caspi concluded that the performance differences observed in the two tasks might have been due either to the learning acquired on the figural task transferring to the pictorial task (the two were not counterbalanced) or the relative familiarity of pictorial tasks for children in this age range. Either way, it appears that experience and systematic feedback can be a potent variable in the transfer of learning across problem-solving tasks. Such findings clearly have implications for the classroom even if the field has a relatively poor record of implementing such results in applied settings. Insofar as this seems an apt place for a plea for greater collaboration between researchers and teachers, consider it made.

FROM LABORATORY TO LITERACY

The research just described indicates that we may be able to enhance academic success for deaf students by drawing on research findings and teaching methods from other domains. Beyond studies in cognitive psychology and cognitive development, one possibility that appears to hold particular promise is the borrowing of strategies that have been used effectively in educating children with learning disabilities. Consistent with what we know about improving learning from cognitive and developmental investigations, many strategies used with such children involve direct instruction, emphasis on pictorial materials, repetition, and the incorporation of multisensory information sources (Torgesen and Houck 1980). On the basis of existing research described throughout this book, all of these features seem likely to facilitate learning by deaf children. This is not to suggest that deaf children should be considered learning disabled but rather that tools have already been developed in other domains that could be useful to educators working with this population.

Programs or strategies that encourage multiple levels of processing seem especially likely to match the diverse characteristics of young deaf readers and complement their existing strengths. Although few studies have been conducted in this regard, there is some indication that the approach would be particularly fruitful in the area of reading. In one relevant study, Ensor and Koller (1997) adapted the *repeated readings* methodology for a group of prelingually deaf students aged 15–19 years. The repeated readings strategy was originally developed to increase the automaticity of word-recognition skills in poor comprehenders. It involves reading passages over and over, sometimes in coordination with audiotapes (for hearing children; Conte and Humphreys 1989) until students reach a specified performance criterion (Rashotte and Torgesen 1985). Ensor and Koller found that repeated readings significantly improved both reading rate and recognition accuracy of deaf students relative to children in a comparison group. Still to be determined is whether such enhancements would generalize to other texts for deaf readers. Some evidence exists that they do not transfer for learning-disabled hearing readers if texts have few words in common (Rashotte and Torgesen 1985), but recent evidence suggests that deaf readers cannot be equated with hearing readers who are poor comprehenders (e.g., Garrison, Long, and Dowaliby 1997).

The benefits of repeated reading seem likely to accrue at several levels of text processing, from recognition of morphological units to the elicitation of discourse-level inferences. Although many efforts to enhance deaf children's reading skills focus on lower-level characteristics of text, such as vocabulary and grammar, inference making is a particularly important aspect of text comprehension that appears to present particular challenges for deaf children and others with reading difficulties (Marschark et al. 1993). Oakhill and Cain (2000), for example, demonstrated that poor comprehenders are less likely than good comprehenders to make meaning-relevant inferences that support top-down reading-comprehension strategies. They found that providing access to text- and knowledge-relevant inferences improved reading comprehension in groups of (hearing) poor comprehenders. They suggested that such an approach could be especially valuable for deaf readers who are poor comprehenders.

Consistent with Oakhill and Cain's suggestion, Dowaliby and Lang (1999) provided deaf college students with several kinds of adjunct aids intended to improve text comprehension. In conjunction with short texts on the anatomy of the human eye, low-ability and high-ability readers were given multiple-choice questions (with feedback), content movies, and sign movies (i.e., ASL translations). On an immediate-recall test, low-ability readers who were given the adjunct questions performed as well as high-ability readers who read the text alone. Other combinations of conditions did not significantly improve recall for either group. In a related study, Sartawi, Al-Hilawani, and Easterbrooks (1998) examined the effectiveness of three different reading-comprehension strategies for deaf and hard of hearing students in an "oral" education program. The three approaches were the language experience approach, a modified reciprocal teaching approach, and the key-word strategy. Overall, the key-word strategy, the only approach that combined comprehension with memorization, was found to facilitate reading comprehension better than the alternatives (Richardson et al. 2000).

In short, it appears that strategies that encourage attention to text elements as well as associations among those elements are most effective in optimizing text comprehension. Unfortunately, deaf students frequently focus only on the individual words in texts rather than on connections among them, thus contributing to breakdowns in comprehension (Banks, Gray, and Fyfe 1990; Marschark et al. 1993). Teaching–learning techniques that foster relational processing and information integration thus are likely to benefit deaf children in reading and other domains. They work for learning-disabled students and generally are recognized as beneficial for learning and memory at all ages (Marschark 1993, chapter 9; Paivio 1971). Perhaps it is time to give them some greater attention to such approaches in deaf education, where students have often been allowed or even encouraged to focus on individual concepts, single meanings of words, and isolated facts.

SUMMARY AND CONCLUSIONS

Deaf children are a relatively heterogeneous group of learners, and no single educational technique or approach will remove all academic hurdles. This chapter has argued, however, that it is essential that we understand the constellation of skills and knowledge underlying cognitive and academic performance among deaf children if we are to optimize their learning and educational success. In order to accomplish this, we first have to move away from the notion that recognizing differences between deaf and hearing learners is in some way anathema.

The studies this chapter describes have demonstrated significant performance differences between deaf and hearing children in several domains. These differences appear to derive from variability in language fluencies, experience, knowledge organization, and educational histories. At the same time, there are also remarkable similarities between deaf and hearing children's knowledge and their strategic approaches to various tasks. Some of the observed differences, therefore, are of only minimal or short-term importance, whereas others might have long-lasting implications. In any case, it is essential that we understand both the similarities and the differences as well as the variation among deaf children with different backgrounds if we are to develop teaching and assessment methods that fully and fairly tap deaf children's abilities. Research suggests that some differences in knowledge organization or knowledge utilization, both automatic and strategic, appear to continue into the college years. Attempts to compensate for any such differences that might negatively affect academic achievement must begin much earlier.

In reading, as in other educational endeavors, deaf and hearing students who have broader experience in relevant academic and nonacademic areas tend to have a greater advantage in acquiring new information and new skills. Educational tools are available from work that has been done with children who have specific learning challenges, with second-language learners, and from basic research in cognitive and developmental psychology. We suggest that educators and investigators seeking to enhance deaf children's academic achievement look to these other areas for methods that have proven successful. Drawing on work conducted in other fields will both better utilize existing resources and broaden our understanding of the structures and strategies that underlie effective teaching and learning for deaf students.

REFERENCES

Baddeley, A. 1998. *Human memory: Theory and practice*. Boston: Allyn and Bacon.

Banks, J., C. Gray, and R. Fyfe. 1990. The written recall of printed stories by severely deaf children. *British Journal of Educational Psychology* 60:192–206.

Bebko, J. M., and E. E. McKinnon. 1990. The language experience of deaf children: Its relation to spontaneous rehearsal in a memory task. *Child Development* 61:1744–52.

Belmont, J. M., M. A. Karchmer, and J. W. Bourg. 1983. Structural influences on deaf and hearing children's recall of temporal/spatial incongruent letter strings. *Educational Psychology* 3:259–74.

Blackwell, P., E. Engen, J. Fischgrund, and C. Zarcadoolas. 1978. *Sentences and other systems: A language and learning curriculum for hearing-impaired children.* Washington, D.C.: National Association of the Deaf.

Bonvillian, J. D. 1983. Effects of signability and imagery on word recall of deaf and hearing students. *Perceptual and Motor Skills* 56:775–91.

Bowe, F. 1998. Language development in deaf children. *Journal of Deaf Studies and Deaf Education* 3:73–77.

Calderon, R., and M. Greenberg. 1997. The effectiveness of early intervention for deaf children and children with hearing loss. In *The effectiveness of early intervention,* ed. M. J. Guralnik, 455–82. Baltimore: Paul H. Brookes.

Campbell, R., and H. Wright. 1990. Deafness and immediate memory for pictures: Dissociation between "inner speech" and "inner ear." *Journal of Experimental Child Psychology* 50:259–86.

Carney, A. E., and M. P. Moeller. 1988. Treatment efficacy: Hearing loss in children. *Journal of Speech, Language, and Hearing Research* 41:S61.

Clark, M. D., and H. W. Hoemann. 1991. Methodological issues in deafness research. In *Advances in cognition, education, and deafness,* ed. D. Martin, 423–28. Washington, D.C.: Gallaudet University Press.

Conlin, D., and A. Paivio. 1975. The associative learning of the deaf: The effects of word imagery and signability. *Memory and Cognition* 3:333–40.

Conrad, R. 1979. *The deaf school child: Language and cognition.* London: Harper and Row.

Conte, R., and R. Humphreys. 1989. Repeated readings using audiotaped material enhances oral reading in children with reading difficulties. *Journal of Communication Disorders* 22:65–79.

Das, J. P., and E. Ojile. 1995. Cognitive processing of students with and without hearing loss. *Journal of Special Education* 29:323–36.

Dowaliby, F. J., and H. G. Lang. 1999. Adjunct aids in instructional prose: A multimedia study with deaf college students. *Journal of Deaf Studies and Deaf Education* 4:270–82.

Ellis, N. C., and R. A. Hennelley. 1980. A bilingual word-length effect: Implications for intelligence testing and the relative ease of mental calculation in Welsh and English. *British Journal of Psychology* 50:449–58.

Emmorey, K. 1998. The impact of sign language use on visual-spatial cognition. In *Psychological perspectives on deafness,* vol. 2, ed. M. Marschark and M. D. Clark, 19–52. Mahwah, N.J.: Lawrence Erlbaum.

Ensor, A. D. II, and J. R. Koller. 1997. The effect of the method of repeated readings on the reading rate and word recognition accuracy of deaf adolescents. *Journal of Deaf Studies and Deaf Education* 2:61–70.

Furth, H. G. 1966. *Thinking without language.* New York: Free Press.

———. 1973. *Deafness and learning.* Belmont, Calif.: Wadsworth.

Garrison, W. M., G. Long, and F. Dowaliby. 1997. Working memory capacity and comprehension processes in deaf readers. *Journal of Deaf Studies and Deaf Education* 2:78–94.

Gearhart, B., R. Mullen, and C. Gearhart. 1993. *Exceptional individuals: An introduction.* Pacific Grove, Calif.: Brookes/Cole.

Gershkoff-Stowe, L., D. J. Thal, L. B. Smith, and L. L. Namy. 1997. Categorization and its developmental relation to early language. *Child Development* 68: 843–59.

Gregory, S., and P. Hindley. 1996. Communication strategies for deaf children. *Journal of Child Psychology and Psychiatry* 37:895–905.

Hanson, V. 1982. Short-term recall by deaf signers of American Sign Language: Implications of encoding strategy for order recall. *Journal of Experimental Psychology: Learning, Memory, and Cognition* 8:572–83.

Hanson, V. L., and E. H. Lichtenstein. 1990. Short-term memory coding by deaf signers: The primary language coding hypothesis reconsidered. *Cognitive Psychology* 22:211–24.

Hermelin, B., and N. O'Connor. 1973. Ordering in recognition memory after ambiguous initial or recognition displays. *Canadian Journal of Psychology* 27:191–99.

Keane, K. J., and R. E. Kretschmer. 1987. Effect of mediated learning intervention on cognitive task performance with a deaf population. *Journal of Educational Psychology* 79:49–53.

Kusché, C. A., and M. T. Greenberg. 1983. Evaluative understanding and role-taking ability: A comparison of deaf and hearing children. *Child Development* 54:141–47.

Lane, H. 1992. *The mask of benevolence*. New York: Alfred A. Knopf.

Liben, L. S. 1978. Developmental perspectives on experiential deficiencies of deaf children. In *Deaf children: Developmental perspectives*, ed. L. Liben, 195–215. New York: Academic Press.

———. 1979. Free recall by deaf and hearing children: Semantic clustering and recall in trained and untrained groups. *Journal of Experimental Child Psychology* 27:105–19.

Lichtenstein, E. 1998. Relationships between reading processes and English skills of deaf college students. *Journal of Deaf Studies and Deaf Education* 3:80–134.

Luckner, J. L., and J. H. McNeill. 1994. Performance of a group of deaf and hard of hearing students and a comparison group of hearing students on a series of problem-solving tasks. *American Annals of the Deaf* 139:371–77.

Maller, S. J. 1997. Deafness and WISC-III item difficulty: Invariance and fit. *Journal of School Psychology* 35:299–314.

Marschark, M. 1993. *Psychological development of deaf children*. New York: Oxford University Press.

———. 2000. Education and development of deaf children: Or is it development and education? In *Development in context: The deaf child in the family and at school*, ed. P. Spencer, C. Erting, and M. Marschark, 275–92. Mahwah, N.J.: Lawrence Erlbaum.

Marschark, M., R. De Beni, M. G. Polazzo, and C. Cornoldi. 1993. Deaf and hearing-impaired adolescents' memory for concrete and abstract prose: Effects of relational and distinctive information. *American Annals of the Deaf* 138:31–39.

Marschark, M., and V. S. Everhart. 1999. Problem solving by deaf and hearing children: Twenty questions. *Deafness and Education International* 1:63–79.

Marschark, M., and T. Mayer. 1998. Mental representation and memory in deaf adults and children. In *Psychological perspectives on deafness*, vol. 2, ed. M. Marschark and M. D. Clark, 53–77. Mahwah, N.J.: Lawrence Erlbaum.

McEvoy, C., M. Marschark, and D. L. Nelson. 1999. Comparing the mental lexicons of deaf and hearing individuals. *Journal of Educational Psychology* 91:1–9.

Mead, M. 1935. *Sex and temperament in three primitive societies*. New York: Morrow.

Meier, R. P., and E. L. Newport. 1990. Out of the hands of babes: On a possible sign advantage in language acquisition. *Language* 66:1–23.

Mousley, K., and R. R. Kelly. 1999. Problem-solving strategies for teaching mathematics to deaf students. *American Annals of the Deaf* 143:325–36.

Myklebust, H. E. 1960. *The psychology of deafness*. New York: Grune and Stratton.

Oakhill, J., and K. Cain. 2000. Children's difficulties in text comprehension: Assessing causal issues. *Journal of Deaf Studies and Deaf Education* 5:51–59.

O'Connor, N., and B. Hermelin. 1972. Seeing and hearing and time and space. *Perception and Psychophysics* 11:46–48.

Ottem, E. 1980. An analysis of cognitive studies with deaf subjects. *American Annals of the Deaf* 125:564–75.

Paivio, A. 1971. *Imagery and verbal processes*. New York: Holt, Rinehart, Winston.

Parasnis, I., and V. J. Samar. 1985. Parafoveal attention in congenitally deaf and hearing young adults. *Brain and Cognition* 4:313–27.

Parasnis, I., V. J. Samar, J. G. Bettger, and K. Sathe. 1996. Does deafness lead to enhancement of visual-spatial cognition in children? Negative evidence from deaf nonsigners. *Journal of Deaf Studies and Deaf Education* 1:145–52.

Piaget, J. 1952. *The origins of intelligence in children*. New York: Basic Books.

Poizner, H., U. Bellugi, and R. D. Tweney. 1981. Processing formational, semantic, and iconic information in American Sign Language. *Journal of Experimental Psychology: Human Perception and Performance* 7:1146–59.

Quittner, A. L., L. B. Smith, M. J. Osberger, T. V. Mitchell, and D. B. Katz. 1994. The impact of audition on the development of visual attention. *Psychological Science* 5:347–53.

Rashotte, C. A., and J. K. Torgesen. 1985. Repeated reading and reading fluency and learning disabled children. *Reading Research Quarterly* 20:180–88.

Richardson, J. T. E., J. MacLeod-Gallinger, B. G. McKee, and G. L. Long. 2000. Approaches to studying in deaf and hearing students in higher education. *Journal of Deaf Studies and Deaf Education* 5:156–73.

Sartawi, A., Y. Al-Hilawani, and S. Easterbrooks. 1998. A pilot study of reading comprehension strategies of students who are deaf/hard of hearing in a non-English speaking country. *Journal of Children's Communication Development* 1:27–32.

Seal, B. C. 1998. *Best practices in educational interpreting*. Boston: Allyn and Bacon.

Torgesen, J. K., and D. G. Houck. 1980. Processing deficiencies of learning-disabled children who performed poorly on the digit span test. *Journal of Educational Psychology* 72:141–60.

Traxler, C. B. 1999. The Stanford Achievement Test, ninth edition: National norming and performance standards for deaf and hard of hearing students. *Journal of Deaf Studies and Deaf Education* 5:337–48.

Tweney, R. D., H. W. Hoemann, and C. E. Andrews. 1975. Semantic organization in deaf and hearing subjects. *Journal of Psycholinguistic Research* 4:61–73.

Tzuriel, D., and N. Caspi. 1992. Cognitive modifiability and cognitive performance of deaf and hearing preschool children. *Journal of Special Education* 26:235–52.

Wilson, M., and K. Emmorey. 1997. Working memory for sign language: A window into the architecture of the working memory system. *Journal of Deaf Studies and Deaf Education* 2:121–30.

Zweibel, A. 1987. More on the effects of early manual communication on the cognitive development of deaf children. *American Annals of the Deaf* 132:16–20.

7

VOCABULARY DEVELOPMENT OF DEAF AND HARD OF HEARING CHILDREN

Amy R. Lederberg and Patricia E. Spencer

There has been an explosion of research on early vocabulary development of hearing children (e.g., Golinkoff and Hirsch-Pasek forthcoming; MacWhinney 1999). This exciting new research can be used to stimulate new insights into deaf and hard of hearing children's vocabulary development.[1] Traditionally, the study of vocabulary was limited to descriptions of the content and size of children's lexicons. Recent research has shifted focus to the processes that underlie children's word acquisition (Golinkoff and Hirsch-Pasek forthcoming; Lederberg, Prezbindowski, and Spencer 2001). Cognitive skills such as association, memory, categorization, and social cognition play an essential role in shaping children's vocabulary development. For typically developing hearing children, changes in cognitive skills seem to be, in part, causally connected to changes in the way in which they acquire words (Dromi 1999). Relations between cognition and vocabulary are very different for the vast majority of deaf and hard of hearing children who have hearing parents and thus limited access to linguistic input. For these children, cognitive development typically outpaces their linguistic development (Lederberg and Everhart 2000; Mayberry 1992). Therefore, the cognitive skills that limit and facilitate vocabulary development among hearing children are unlikely to affect language in the same way for deaf children. This opens the possibility that deaf children's vocabulary development may not only be delayed but different from that of hearing children. This chapter reviews and compares studies of vocabulary development of children who are deaf and hard of hearing with that of hearing children in order to discern these differences.

---

1. In this chapter, "deaf" refers to a severe to profound hearing loss while "hard of hearing" refers to a mild to moderate hearing loss.

Our research has been supported by the March of Dimes Foundation and the Office of Special Education. We would like to thank the school administrators, who have given us their support, and the teachers and parents for their participation in our study. With their dedication we are learning more about children's language development. We also want to thank the children for participating and allowing us to learn from them. We are also grateful to Dr. Robert E. Johnson of the Gallaudet University Department of ASL, Linguistics, and Interpretation and Ms. Linda Stamper of the Gallaudet Research Institute for their help in developing the nonce signs used in our research. Finally, we are most grateful to Amy Prezbindowski for her continual support and significant contributions to our research.

Of course, we do not expect vocabulary to develop similarly among all children who are deaf or hard of hearing. A variety of factors are likely to affect acquisition of vocabulary, including type of linguistic environment and cognitive abilities. As we and others have discussed extensively elsewhere (e.g., Spencer and Lederberg 1997), a vast majority of deaf and hard of hearing children are relatively deprived of linguistic input and develop language in a less rich linguistic environment than hearing children or deaf children with deaf parents. We expect factors that affect the frequency, complexity, and diversity of linguistic input to influence vocabulary development. For children who are in a speech-only environment, degree of hearing loss and the type and age of amplification affect how much access the children have to linguistic input. For children acquiring sign, the skill and number of people who sign in the children's environment have a similar impact. Finally, children's cognitive abilities may influence their abilities to learn from their linguistic input and thus affect their pattern of vocabulary development. When data are available, the influence of these variables on deaf and hard of hearing children's vocabulary development are discussed. However, an extensive analysis of these variables is outside the scope of this chapter.

Vocabulary development can be characterized along three dimensions: (1) the quantity and nature of words that a child knows; (2) the rate of vocabulary growth (i.e., the speed at which new words are learned and added to a child's vocabulary); and (3) word-learning processes or strategies that children use to facilitate and guide the learning of new words. These three dimensions are clearly interrelated and should be seen as different "windows" onto the changes to the way children learn new words as their skills develop. Past research on vocabulary development has primarily concentrated on ways to assess the extent of vocabulary knowledge (i.e., number of words children know at a given age). Only a few studies with small numbers of subjects have examined the trajectory of vocabulary growth. Even less is known about deaf children's word-learning processes. However, some initial conclusions emerge from recent research that provide a framework for observations of vocabulary development and possibilities for future research.

In addition to reviewing results from several recent research projects by other investigators, we report results from our own on-going research project. To our knowledge, our on-going study is the first to address all three issues (i.e., vocabulary, rate of growth, and word-learning processes) related to deaf and hard of hearing children. We have completed one study of vocabulary development of nineteen deaf and hard of hearing children between the ages of 3 and 6 years (Lederberg et al. 2001) who were enrolled in a state day school for the deaf where teachers communicated with the children simultaneously in speech and sign. We are in the process of replicating and extending our initial study to a larger range of children from a variety of communication environments: oral only, speech and sign used together, and bilingual-bicultural programs that emphasize American Sign Language (ASL) (Lederberg, Spencer and Prezbindowski 2000). The study includes children who have mild to profound hearing loss and who have mild to moderate cognitive, motor, or behavioral disabilities if they are participating in programs for deaf and hard of hearing children. Participants are from rural, suburban, and urban areas from three widely separated geographic areas of the United States. Cross-sectional data have been collected to date on seventy-nine children. Our data include initial vocabulary size and the use of specific vocabulary learning processes when the children entered the study. Children who have vocabularies of fewer than 250 words at initial testing are being followed longitudinally for a year to describe rate of vocabulary growth and acquisition of word-learning processes at multiple time points. These children will provide information about change in vocabulary over time and the degree to which changes in acquisition rate relate to use of specific learning strategies. Although some information is available now (Lederberg et al. 2000), the study is ongoing and data collection and analysis are not complete. Therefore, although information in this chapter represents current understandings, much remains to be learned.

Characterization and Assessment of Vocabulary Knowledge

Vocabulary Size

Vocabulary development is frequently studied by assessing the number of words that a child understands or can express meaningfully. Because of the variety of language systems used by deaf and hard of hearing children, a word is typically defined as any recognizable conventional, arbitrary (i.e., linguistic) symbol. Speech or sign, ASL or English can be used to express a word. The extent of vocabulary knowledge (size of lexicon) is usually assessed to determine the age-appropriateness of deaf and hard of hearing children's development (vis-à-vis hearing children or other deaf and hard of hearing children). This research also frequently examines the range of knowledge among deaf and hard of hearing children of a given age and the factors that predict that range. Measurement of the level of vocabulary knowledge is the starting point for describing the rate of vocabulary growth and change in word-learning processes (the other two aspects of vocabulary development are described later). Therefore, in addition to reporting results concerning deaf children's vocabulary knowledge, this section discusses the strengths and weaknesses of different assessment methods. Assessment of the number of words a child knows (or uses) usually proceeds by one or more of the following methods: direct testing of child performance; language sampling in an interactive context; and parent and/or teacher report.

Direct Testing

Direct testing of child performance most often occurs through the use of structured or standardized instruments that elicit evidence of comprehension or production of words. Vocabulary is assessed by asking children either to label an object or picture (to test expressive vocabulary) or to select an object or picture labeled by the examiner (to test comprehension or receptive vocabulary). Such tests make no attempt to provide an actual census of words but instead provide a sample from which to generalize, comparing a child's number of correct responses to norms established from earlier use of the test. Although most tests provide a number of different ways to characterize a child's performance, age norms are frequently used in interpreting performance. In this case, a child's number of correct responses is compared to the number typical for a certain age.

Tests Normed for Hearing Children

Some researchers have used tests designed and normed for hearing children, with modifications made in administration to accommodate the language modality used by deaf children. One of the most extensive studies of older deaf children used a variety of standardized test instruments to assess both receptive and expressive vocabulary development. Moeller, Osberger, and Eccarius (1986) used simultaneous communication (English-based sign, plus speech) to assess the receptive vocabulary of 150 children between the ages of 4.5 and 20 using the Peabody Picture Vocabulary Test (PPVT; Dunn 1959) and the picture vocabulary subtest of the Test of Language Development (Newcomer and Hammill 1977). On average, the children and adolescents showed severe delays in receptive vocabulary compared to the hearing age norms. In addition, delays increased with chronological age, with the average age equivalent never exceeding 9.8 years of age. Osberger et al. (1986) report a similar delay for the same sample of deaf children and adolescents on expressive vocabulary tests.

On all tests, there was a large variance in the vocabulary knowledge of the deaf children and adolescents. Part of the variance seemed to be related to the children's nonverbal cognitive skills. Children's scores on expressive and receptive vocabulary correlated with their score on the performance scale of the WISC-R, suggesting that higher cognitive ability is at least associated with and probably facilitates the acquisition of vocabulary.

Davis et al. (1986) find similar delays for children (5 through 18 years old) who had mild to moderate losses. Specifically, on average, the forty children scored well below age norms for the PPVT, with only six children scoring at or above age norms. Similarly, Gilbertson and Kamhi (1995) found children with mild to moderate learning losses (M age = 9;0) performed similarly on the PPVT to a group of hearing children who were 2.5 years younger (M age = 6;5). These two studies suggest that even mild hearing loss negatively affects vocabulary development.

Tests Normed for Deaf and Hard of Hearing Children

There are only a few vocabulary assessment instruments developed specifically for children with hearing loss. The Grammatical Analysis of Elicited Language-Presentence Level (GAEL-P) (Moog, Kozak, and Geers 1983) was devised to test the language skills of young (2 to 5 years old) children with hearing loss. The vocabulary ("single word") section tests the child's ability to imitate, produce, and understand the labels for thirty objects whose labels are learned early in development (e.g., shoe, ball, boat). The GAEL-P was normed with oral children with "educationally significant hearing losses" (Moog et al. 1983). Scores are also reported in the manual for a sample of younger hearing children (2.5 to 3.11 years of age). The deaf and hard of hearing children performed similarly to the younger hearing children, indicating once again the significant lag in vocabulary development experienced by young deaf children compared to hearing children. Although the GAEL-P provides norms that can be used to compare oral deaf and hard of hearing children's vocabulary knowledge with other deaf children, interpretation of the norms may be questionable for children acquiring sign as a first language.

The Carolina Picture Vocabulary Test (Layton and Holmes 1985) is a receptive vocabulary test developed for deaf children in total communication settings. It is modeled after the PPVT and requires children to select from a group of four pictures the one that depicts the word being spoken and signed by the tester (e.g., ball, sit, constitution). The test was normed on 761 deaf children ages 2.5 to 16 years. It is used frequently in assessments of deaf children because it is one of the few vocabulary tests available to test signing deaf children across a wide age range (Bradley-Johnson and Evans 1991). However, we know of no research that has used it to study vocabulary development. We are presently using the test in our ongoing study.

In summary, assessment of deaf and hard of hearing children's vocabulary knowledge using standardized tests clearly shows that they are, in general, delayed in their level of vocabulary knowledge compared to hearing children. The kind of information available from such tests is useful for comparing a child's performance with the accomplishments of others. Thus, significant delays can be identified, and a rough measure of growth over time is provided. However, scores on standardized tests provide minimal if any specific information about the actual size, content, or growth of children's vocabulary knowledge.

Naturalistic Language Sample

For more naturalistic and extensive assessment of language skills, researchers and practitioners often collect and analyze language samples obtained from young children by audio- or videotaping them interacting with an adult. These samples are sometimes collected during free-play sessions, sometimes in response to pictures or wordless picture books and sometimes by extensive data collection over a number of naturally occurring or elicitation situations (Day 1986; Nelson 1973). The more extensive language samples, especially if drawn over a period of several days in the natural environment, can provide useful information about a child's expressive vocabulary.

However, there are several drawbacks to this method of assessing vocabulary. First, transcribing and analyzing a language sample is highly labor-intensive and requires special training. The more extensive samples, which provide the best information, require too much time for analysis to be a practical means of assessing vocabulary for researchers, clinicians, and teachers. Second, language samples (especially if obtained from relatively short sessions) may fail to provide valid information about the breadth of children's actual vocabulary knowledge. Especially during the early stages of vocabulary development, individual words are infrequent, and their occurrence is unpredictable (Bates and Carnevale 1993). Many occur only in specific contexts that may not appear in the data collection session. Bates, Bretherton, and Snyder (1988) concluded that language samples from hearing toddlers (during the second year of life) did not show sufficient internal reliability and failed to predict later language development.

Using language samples to assess the vocabulary development of deaf and hard of hearing children can be even more problematic. Unlike audiotape recordings, capturing language behavior (especially when signed) on videotape requires elaborate equipment set-ups, usually including more than one camera and sometimes special effects generators so that most of the signing can be seen. Although the collection of language samples from deaf and hard of hearing children has become relatively common in laboratory settings, this can put child and communication partner in a restricted and an atypical context. Special skills are required to understand and transcribe the expressive language of young signing children. Moreover, the spoken language of young deaf and hard of hearing children is usually difficult to understand, and the somewhat degraded signal obtained through a videotape may make transcription unreliable if not impossible. Everhart and Lederberg (1991; Everhart 1993) raise further questions about the validity of laboratory-obtained language samples for deaf children. They found that the language measures obtained from language samples of deaf 3- and 4-year-olds, with mothers during free play and with a researcher during a storybook elicitation task, did not correlate highly with each other or with a standardized vocabulary test (the Total Communication Vocabulary Test, an out-of-print test; Scherer 1981). Only elicited language using a storybook correlated with children's performance on the standardized vocabulary test.

Although a number of researchers have used language samples to study deaf children's overall level of language development (Lederberg and Everhart 1998, 2000; Spencer 1993a, 1993b), very few have focused on vocabulary. Shafer and Lynch (1981) collected 20- to 30-minute language samples of six deaf children between the ages of 15 and 34 months who were exposed to a variety of different communication environments (described as oral, aural, and total communication). They found that the number of words used in these sessions seemed to be delayed compared to published reports of hearing children.

In summary, naturalistic observation studies have tended to use brief samples instead of extensive data collection over several days in a home and school environment. Therefore, it is unlikely that these assessments provide a comprehensive description of the children's lexicon. The laborious nature of data collection required to assess lexical size with confidence has led researchers and practitioners to seek alternative assessment tools.

Parent and Teacher Reports

Diaries

In response to the problems standardized testing and language sampling pose to those assessing young hearing, deaf, and hard of hearing children, instruments based on parent reports of child functioning have gained in popularity. Parental diaries (i.e., parents write down new vocabulary words in a diary) are a traditional way to study early vocabulary development. Rich diary data of hearing children are available because several developmental psychologists and linguists have kept detailed records of their own children's vocabulary growth (Dromi 1999). The attraction of diaries is their potential to be a record of the whole corpus of children's growing vocabulary. There are two published studies in which researchers asked mothers to keep a notebook of the words their deaf children used. From such diaries, Griswold and Commings (1974) were able to compile lists describing the size and type of words nineteen deaf children used. In comparison with published reports of hearing children's vocabularies, these deaf children had much smaller vocabularies (e.g., a mean of 161 words at 4 years of age compared to over 300 words by the average 2.5-year-old hearing child). Griswold and Commings (1974) suggest that the lexicons of the deaf children were similar to those of hearing preschoolers in terms of the proportions of nouns, verbs, types of prepositions, number words, and question words. The deaf children's vocabularies were less likely to contain articles and auxiliary/modal verbs compared to those of hearing preschoolers. Deaf children's vocabulary size correlated with time in intervention and amount of sign used at home but did not correlate with age. The lack of correlation with age suggests that characteristics of the linguistic environment had a greater effect on vocabulary than did cognitive development (as measured by the child's age).

Gardner and Zorfass (1983) used both language samples and a hearing mother's diary to study the vocabulary development of a deaf child who was acquiring both sign and speech. In contrast with other studies, they found this child's vocabulary development similar to that typical of hearing children. The authors attribute the child's success to the fact that his hearing mother "provided consistent total communication input by speaking and signing simultaneously. . . . Her input was not stilted as might be expected from a person just learning to sign" (23).

Parent Report Instruments

Keeping a diary of children's vocabulary is a time-consuming process that is frequently difficult to obtain from parents or teachers, especially as vocabulary grows (see Gregory and Mogford 1981; Griswold and Commings 1974; Shafer and Lynch 1981). In search of a better assessment instrument, both researchers and practitioners have developed parental report instruments that ask parents to recognize (not recall) words that are part of their children's vocabulary.

Two early studies of vocabulary development show the extremes of vocabulary development among children who are deaf and hard of hearing. Howell (1984) asked mothers to record their children's vocabulary by checking any words that the children used from a preschool vocabulary checklist that contained 1,655 words (created at the Maryland School for the Deaf). The four 4-year-old deaf children (two with hearing parents and two with deaf parents) had much larger vocabularies than has been reported by other investigators (range = 750 to 1300 words). Howell notes that the extensiveness of these children's vocabulary was probably due to the fluent sign communication that was present in the homes of all four children. Thus, deafness per se does not necessarily limit the size of children's vocabulary.

Contrasting findings were reported by Gregory and Mogford (1981), who used a checklist of 150 words created for their study to examine early vocabulary development of eight deaf and hard of hearing children in oral communication environments. For six children, attainment of all vocabulary milestones (first word, 10, 50, and 100 words) was delayed an average of 10 months. Two deaf children did not even have 10 words by 4 years of age.

More recently, a parent report assessment instrument has been developed that has important potential in the study of vocabulary development. Based on two decades of research with young hearing children and their families (Bates et al. 1979; Bates, Bretherton, and Snyder 1988), the MacArthur Network developed two parent-report instruments to assess early language development (Fenson et al. 1993, 1994). Parts of both instruments are word checklists that measure children's vocabulary. The MacArthur Communicative Development Inventory: Words and Gestures (CDI-Words and Gestures) was developed for hearing infants between 8 and 16 months of age and includes checklists for both receptive and expressive vocabulary, as well as items related to early gestural, communicative, and syntactic development. To assess vocabulary, parents are asked to check the words that a child understands and/or produces from a list of 396 words arranged into categories (e.g., animals, vehicles, toys, food and drink, clothing, furniture and rooms, action words, descriptive words). The CDI-Words and Sentences was developed for hearing children from 16 to 30 months of age who are at a more advanced language level. It contains a 680-word expressive vocabulary checklist. Because judging receptive vocabulary becomes more difficult at larger vocabulary levels, this version of the CDI does not assess receptive knowledge.

The CDIs seem to measure early language more accurately than other methods discussed in this chapter. The CDI, when used with typically developing hearing children, has high internal reliability, correlates with language samples taken concurrently, and predicts later language development better than measures derived from language samples (Bates et al. 1988; Fenson et al. 1994). Although the instruments were not designed to provide a complete census of a child's lexicon, the large number of words listed provides a nearly complete assessment of words used by children with emerging vocabulary skills. Norms for each word, as well as for overall performance are available based on 671 and 1,142 hearing toddlers for the two inventories (Fenson et al. 1994). The instruments require no specialized training either to administer or to score and are clearly more cost effective than either standardized administered tests or language samples. First developed for spoken English, modified versions are now available in many languages—including a version in preparation for ASL (Povine, Reilly, and Anderson 1993).

Some researchers have begun to use the two versions of the English CDI (which are normed for hearing children only) with deaf and hard of hearing children. Bornstein et al. (1999) used an earlier version of the CDI and modified the items to allow assessment of children whose first language was ASL (although those modifications are not specified in their report). Their study included eighty-nine children in four groups (hearing children with hearing mothers; hearing children with deaf mothers; deaf children with deaf mothers; deaf children with hearing mothers) ranging in age from 17 to 30 months. This measure seemed to reliably measure the children's English vocabulary development: The number of words parents reported correlated highly with expressive and comprehension scores on the Reynell Developmental Language Scales, a standardized test administered to each child. Correlations between the CDI and Reynell scores ranged for the sample as a whole and within each group from .47 to .81. Deaf children with hearing mothers had smaller vocabularies than both groups of hearing and deaf children with Deaf mothers. In addition, hearing children with hearing mothers were reported to know more words than did deaf children with Deaf parents. This difference was not limited to pronouns, preposition, and auxiliaries—a difference that might be expected given the variations in ASL and spoken English. Deaf parents reported that their deaf children knew fewer names of common items, places, and people than typical of hearing children.

Given consistent reports that deaf children with Deaf parents acquire first words at least as early (on average) as hearing children (Meier 1990; Spencer and Lederberg 1997), the difference reported by Bornstein et al. (1999) between these two groups' vocabulary size is puzzling. A possible explanation may lie in the way some word meanings are lexicalized in ASL and English. For example, the CDI includes some words that are represented by a single symbolic unit in English but require either fingerspelling or multiple signs in ASL. One example from the CDI is the word "pony," which we have observed fingerspelled or represented by the signs BABY HORSE by signing Deaf mothers when communicating with young deaf children. Deaf children who are in the single-word stage would not be ex- pected to produce the two words to express the concept *pony;* even if they did, they would not be "credited" with another word. Blumenthal-Kelly (1995) and Erting, Thumann-Prezioso, and Benedict (2000) reported that Deaf mothers fin- gerspell representations during their deaf children's early months and years of life. For example, a Deaf mother labeled a kitten by signing BABY CAT K-I-T-T-E-N to her 2-year-old daughter (Erting et al. 2000). The children themselves did not pro- duce fingerspelled words until well into the second and third years of life. This suggests that, at least when expressive vocabulary is considered, the lexicons of signing deaf children and hearing children may differ during the early years. Given these differences in ASL and English lexicalization, parent report instru- ments such as the CDI should be interpreted cautiously (i.e., not implying deficits) when used with children whose linguistic environment is primarily ASL and not English. Perhaps because of ASL–English differences, the preliminary version of the CDI for ASL (Provine, Reilly, and Anderson 1993) contains fewer words on the vocabulary list than does the English CDI.

Mayne, Yoshinaga-Itano, and Sedey (2000; Mayne et al. 2000) have used cur- rent versions of the English CDI to assess the vocabulary of relatively large num- bers of young deaf and hard of hearing children with hearing parents. The 202 children, ranging in age from 8 to 37 months, were participating in a variety of types of language programming. Both versions (Words and Gestures and Words and Sentences) of the English CDI were used without modification. One goal of this ongoing study is to provide normative statistics for deaf and hard of hearing children. The data they report are especially helpful in that the researchers have considered a number of potentially influential variables when interpreting the vo- cabulary measures.

A subsample of deaf and hard of hearing children (*n* = 118), ranging in age from 8 to 22 months, was used to report developmental trends in receptive vo- cabulary (Mayne et al. 2000) as assessed on the Words and Gestures version of the CDI. No significant associations were found for the deaf and hard of hearing sample between receptive vocabulary size and variables including age of identi- fication of hearing loss, language modality used, and family demographic char- acteristics. However, performance on cognitive tasks was associated with recep- tive vocabulary. When only the noncognitively delayed children are considered, the median vocabulary scores for the deaf and hard of hearing children fell be- tween the tenth and twenty-fifth percentile scores established for hearing chil- dren. Mayne et al. (2000) also report expressive language scores for a group of

202 deaf and hard of hearing children ages 8 to 37 months. The CDI-Words and Gestures form was used for the younger or less linguistically advanced children; the Words and Sentences form was used for older or more linguistically advanced children. As with receptive scores, general cognitive level related to expressive scores. In addition, expressive vocabulary was associated with age of identification of hearing loss, with an advantage for children identified by 6 months of age. A median expressive vocabulary size of 396.5 words was found for those children in the 35- to 37-month group who had age-typical cognitive abilities and who had hearing loss identified before the age of 6 months. This median is higher than reported previously for deaf and hard of hearing children at this age, but it remains below the average expressive vocabulary size of 530 words reported for hearing 30-month olds (Fenson et al. 1993).

We have also collected data on the vocabulary development of deaf and hard of hearing children (some of whom had mild cognitive or attention disabilities) using the CDI (Lederberg et al. 2001; Lederberg et al. 2000). One goal of this ongoing study is to compare assessments of vocabulary size using various procedures in order to determine the usefulness and reliability of the procedures. Lederberg et al. (2001) report a comparison between child vocabulary size as measured on the CDI-Words and Sentences version and on child performance on the vocabulary ("single word") items of the GAEL-P. The participants in the study included nineteen deaf and hard of hearing children who attended a state day school that provided a simultaneous communication language environment. Administration of the CDI in this study differed in two ways from its typical administration. First, teachers instead of parents were asked to provide the report. Second, teachers marked both receptive and expressive knowledge instead of the expressive-only measure that is usually obtained on the Words and Sentences version. To provide a comparison measure from a direct test situation, a researcher administered the vocabulary items of the GAEL-P to the children using the school's simultaneous communication system. Because GAEL-P norms have been established only for oral children, and the norms are based on a score for the entire test (including syntax items that were not relevant), a raw score (total number of object labels that the children provided expressively and receptively) was used to represent performance. The raw scores obtained from the GAEL-P vocabulary items correlated with teacher-reported CDI expressive (r (18) = .59, $p < .01$) and receptive vocabulary (r (16) = .77, $p < .001$). Thus, the teacher-completed CDI produced a measure of the size of deaf and hard of hearing children's vocabulary that was consistent with their performance on a direct elicitation procedure. Both procedures showed that the level of vocabulary development of this group of deaf and hard of hearing children was below that expected for hearing children of the same chronological age.

In summary, research with a variety of assessment instruments consistently shows that vocabulary of the vast majority of deaf and hard of hearing children lags behind that of their hearing peers when assessed with a variety of different techniques. Several variables seem to affect vocabulary knowledge of the deaf and hard of hearing children; these include hearing status of parents (Bornstein et al. 1999; Howell 1984), age of identification and intervention (Mayne, Yoshinaga-Itano, and Sedey 2000; Mayne et al. 2000), and nonverbal intelligence (Gilbertson and Kamhi 1995; Mayne, Yoshinaga-Itano, and Sedey 2000; Mayne et al. 2000; Moeller et al. 1986; Osberger et al. 1986).

Rate of Early Vocabulary Growth

Hearing Children

Even more important than the number of words children know is the rate at which they add new words to their vocabulary. This aspect of vocabulary development has been studied in some depth for young hearing children, with special attention directed to the presence (or absence) of a "spurt" or exponential increase in rate of growth during the toddler period (e.g., Bates et al. 1988; Dromi 1999; Goldfield and Reznick 1990; Mervis and Bertrand 1994; Nelson 1973). Initially, hearing toddlers learn new words very slowly, averaging one new word per week. Then, sometime during the second year of life, most hearing toddlers experience a rapid acceleration in the rate of learning new words, acquiring more than one new word a day. This increased rate of word learning seems to mark a qualitative change of some kind in the learning process (Dromi 1999; Goldfield and Reznick 1990; Mervis and Bertrand 1995b; Nelson 1973).

Vocabulary development in hearing children with developmental disabilities seems to proceed in a slower but similar pattern to that seen for those without disabilities. Children with Down syndrome have a longer initial period of slow, deliberate word learning before beginning an acceleration in the rate at which new words are learned (Mervis and Bertrand 1995a, 1997; Miller 1992a, 1992b). Similar to typically developing children, children with Down syndrome appear to experience an acceleration in word acquisition when they have acquired approximately fifty words (Mervis and Bertrand 1995a). This similarity in pattern of growth between hearing children without disabilities and those with Down syndrome suggests the change in learning is linked to the number of words a hearing child knows. Explanations for the link between vocabulary knowledge and acceleration in word learning are both varied and controversial. Some researchers have proposed that these changes are related to changes in general cognitive skills such as categorization abilities (Mervis and Bertrand 1994), while others suggested that increasing the number of words in a child's lexicon fuels changes in word retrieval and associations (Merriman 1998; Smith 1999) and word-learning strategies (Dromi 1999; Golinkoff and Hirsch-Pasek forthcoming; MacWhinney 1999).

Deaf Children with Deaf Parents

Assessment of vocabulary growth requires frequent assessment of the number of words that individual children know. The few studies that have examined vocabulary growth of deaf children acquiring ASL as a first language have studied changes in the number of words children use in language samples obtained over a year or more. The authors of two studies that examined vocabulary growth of children with signing deaf parents (thus children with ASL as their first language) reached contradictory conclusions. Petitto (1988) reported that a small sample of deaf children with Deaf parents showed the same pattern of growth in sign vocabulary as reported for hearing children with hearing parents, including evidence of a vocabulary spurt. However, Bonvillian, Orlansky, and Folven (1994) found no evidence of a vocabulary spurt in children with Deaf parents despite reporting very early production of signs and an overall fast rate of word acquisition.

Deaf and Hard of Hearing Children with Hearing Parents

Case studies of deaf and hard of hearing children with hearing parents who are skilled signers have tended to show patterns similar to those of hearing children and the deaf children studied by Petitto (Gardner and Zorfass 1983; Hoffmeister and Wilbur 1980; Howell 1984; Shafer and Lynch 1981; Schlesinger and Meadow 1972). For instance, Gardner and Zorfass reported on one child who started to sign at 14 months, knew 100 signs at 22 months, and then showed a rapid rise to 150 signs by 23 months of age. Thus, the pattern of initial slow acquisition followed by acceleration was apparent.

In contrast, studies of deaf and hard of hearing children who are acquiring speech or whose hearing parents are *not* skilled signers suggest that their vocabulary development is much more delayed and may show a different pattern from that of hearing children (Gregory and Mogford 1981; Griswold and Commings 1974; Lederberg et al. 2001). Only one study (Gregory and Mogford 1981) assessed individual deaf and hard of hearing children's vocabulary frequently enough to demonstrate clearly the rate and pattern of word learning. Gregory and Mogford studied eight orally trained deaf and hard of hearing children from the ages of 15 to 18 months to their fourth birthday and concluded that their early vocabulary development differed in pattern and rate from that of hearing children. Two profoundly deaf children had not learned ten words by their fourth birthday. The other six deaf and hard of hearing children appeared to require more direct instruction than hearing children to produce their first words, took more time than hearing children to progress from first words to a vocabulary size of ten words, and showed no dramatic increase or acceleration in subsequent vocabulary growth. The researchers conclude, "We feel confident . . . that the deaf child develops language differently from the hearing child . . . from the early stages" (1981, 231). However, these conclusions seem based on group data. An examination of the data presented for individual children's development reveals wide individual differences. Tucker, Hostler, and Nolan (1984) note that two of the children studied by Gregory and Mogford showed an accelerated period of vocabulary growth, increasing their vocabulary from 50 to 100 words in a 2-month period. Tucker et al. conclude that accelerations (or "spurts") in rate of vocabulary acquisition may occur for some orally trained deaf and hard of hearing children but not for others.

Although few studies have plotted the trajectory of vocabulary growth over time, studies that examine group vocabulary sizes of deaf and hard of hearing children of hearing parents support the conclusion that these children experience a slower growth of their vocabulary. Most deaf and hard of hearing children are delayed in acquisition of their first words, sometimes not producing them until the end of the second year or even later (Lederberg and Everhart 1998; Mayne et al. 2000). Even deaf and hard of hearing infants who produce initial words or signs within age ranges typical for hearing children's first words frequently fall far behind those children on size of vocabulary by 30 months of age (Spencer and Lederberg 1997). This suggests that the deaf and hard of hearing children's vocabulary development continued at a slow pace and that no period of rapid acceleration occurred by that age.

The data reported by Mayne et al. (2000) are also relevant to the issue of rate of vocabulary acquisition; however, we must keep in mind that they report 368 expressive vocabulary scores (from the CDI) for only 202 children. That is, cross-sectional and longitudinal data are combined in their reports of average vocabulary size at various ages. They first considered only those whose hearing loss was identified by 6 months of age and who functioned in the normal range on a cognitive measure. These children's group norms for number of words learned at different ages seemed to show an acceleration in vocabulary growth; the acceleration was reported to occur after 20 to 25 months of age, later than for hearing children. For children who are less advantaged and slower in vocabulary growth, the acceleration appears later or may even be nonexistent.

Thus, existing reports conflict on the presence of a "spurt" or acceleration in vocabulary growth for deaf and hard of hearing children. To date, only limited longitudinal data are available, and longitudinal data are required to provide a more valid description of rate and pattern of growth. We are now collecting longitudinal data using monthly updates on the CDI with the expectation that these data will clarify developmental patterns. The monthly CDI data will allow us to plot individual growth curves over a year. Meanwhile, the preceding reports suggest that individual factors and characteristics influence the rate and pattern of vocabulary growth. Deaf and hard of hearing children who are identified early and have typical cognitive functioning may show acquisition rates and patterns similar (although later) to those of hearing children, even when vocabulary development is delayed (Mayne, Yoshinaga-Itano, and Sedey 2000; Mayne et al. 2000). Those deaf and hard of hearing children experiencing less fortunate circumstances may show development that is different in pattern as well as being delayed (Gregory and Mogford 1981; Mayne, Yoshinaga-Itano, and Sedey 2000; Mayne et al. 2000). These latter children may be much older when (and if) they experience acceleration in vocabulary growth. Therefore, deaf and hard of hearing children who have optimal resources to support development and those who do not have such support may differ in the methods used to learn new words and in their trajectory of vocabulary growth.

Hearing Children's Word Learning Processes

Both the number of words that children know and the rate at which they acquire new words are descriptive measures of vocabulary development. Recently, there has been an increased focus on explaining developmental change in vocabulary growth. Among hearing children, acceleration in vocabulary is accompanied by (and may be caused by) the acquisition of new word-learning skills (Dromi 1999; Mervis and Bertrand 1994).

There seem to be two major types of changes in word-learning processes that occur during early vocabulary development and that are implicated in the acceleration of word learning. First, children become capable of rapid word learning or forming an initial representation of a word after hearing or seeing it only a few times. Diary data of hearing infants suggest that young 1-year-olds need to hear a new word multiple times in order to retain the word-referent connection. In contrast, during the first half of the second year of life, toddlers become capable of learning a new word after hearing it only a few times (Dromi 1999).

Second, children become capable of establishing reference for new words in an increasingly broad variety of contexts. As both philosophers (Goodman 1983; Quine 1960) and psychologists (Clark 1991; Golinkoff, Hirsh-Pasek, and Holich 1999) have stressed, determining the reference of a new word should be a difficult problem. Even when an adult explicitly gives cues that a word refers to an object, how does one know whether it refers to an object, attribute, action, or event? For instance, a mother points to an elephant in a zoo, and says "Oh look, an elephant" to her child. How is the child to know "elephant" means that specific animal instead of animals in general or the characteristics of "gray" or "big"?

Although theoretically establishing reference should be a difficult task for young children, it is not. The facility with which young children figure out reference in seemingly ambiguous situations was initially noted by Carey (1978). She observed that hearing 3-year-olds were able to learn a new color term when it was contrasted with a known term after hearing the term only once. Specifically, she found that children were able to infer which color was "chromium" when told, "Bring me the chromium tray, not the blue one, the chromium one." Although Carey's initial interest was in the speed with which young children learn new words (a process she referred to as "fast-mapping"), subsequent research that has replicated and extended her work has focused more on the different linguistic and cognitive skills children use when inferring the meaning of a word.

Researchers have studied word-learning processes by testing the way children use linguistic and nonlinguistic cues to acquire novel words. Nonce (or nonsense) words that are consistent with the phonological rules of the English language (e.g., *dax, bipi*) are used in order to control for prior exposure to the words. Typically, after the experimenter uses the nonce word in a given context, the child is then asked to select a referent for the word (e.g., "Give me a *dax*"). By varying the cues present when the nonce word is initially presented, researchers have found that children become sensitive to different linguistic and nonlinguistic cues as they develop. Although much about these strategies is still controversial (MacWhinney 1999), we next summarize some general conclusions about the development of different types of word-learning processes that hearing children have available when learning new words.

Types of Word-Learning Processes

1. *Word learning when reference is explicit.* Even when adults make the word-referent connection explicit (by either pointing or holding up the object), the child needs to know how words are used in order to correctly identify the referent. Specifically, mapping a word onto an object requires use of the principles of reference (i.e., that words "stand for" things in the world), extendibility (i.e., that words refer to more than just the exemplars that someone has

labeled), and object scope (i.e., words are most likely to refer to a whole object rather than to just part of it). These strategies lead children to infer that when an adult connects a new word to an object, that new word refers to the whole object and should be used to refer to other objects that are part of the same basic category in other contexts. These strategies allow children to engage in true word learning (i.e., learning that words refer to a category of objects) in contexts when adults make explicit the connection between word and referent. Evidence suggests that these strategies are available to children during early word learning (Golinkoff et al. 1999).

2.   *Word learning based on knowledge of adults' social intentions.* The preceding strategies enable children to learn words when adults show the referent via pointing or holding an object and therefore make the word's referent obvious. However, in many circumstances reference is much more ambiguous. Hearing 18- to 24-month-olds become adept at using a variety of social cues to determine a speaker's intentions. Thus, one reason that children's vocabulary learning accelerates is that they may no longer be dependent on adults explicitly teaching them vocabulary words. For example, toddlers infer that a word refers to an object that the speaker is looking at even if the toddler is initially attending to a different object (Tomasello forthcoming). The children will also use a speaker's facial expression and other social behaviors to help them determine reference. For example, in one study (Tomasello and Barton 1994), the adult said "Let's go find the *toma*" while looking directly at the child and then began pulling out toys from buckets. Children were able to establish reference when the adult pulled several toys in succession out of the box, shook her head, and put them back in the box until she found the target object, then smiled and handed the object to the child. In another word-learning task (Tomasello and Barton 1994), toddlers knew that a novel verb ("I'm going to *plunk* Big Bird") referred to an action that the experimenter performed intentionally (an action followed by the examiner exclaiming "there"), rather than one performed accidentally (an action followed by the examiner exclaiming "Whoops!"), even when the accidental action was done first. Note that the child could not use gaze direction or temporal contiguity to determine reference in these situations. Tomasello (forthcoming) suggests that toddlers become skilled at figuring out adults' intentions by using their knowledge of social conventions while determining reference.

3.   *Word learning based on internal strategies.* Older children seem to have biases or strategies that allow them to make inferences about what the referent of a word is even when the speaker gives no pragmatic cues for reference. One of the most firmly documented "internal" strategies is the novel mapping strategy. Namely, hearing children (after 2 years of age) and adults consistently choose an unfamiliar object for the referent of a novel word even when there are no explicit or pragmatic cues from the speaker (Merriman, Marazita, and Jarvis 1995). For example, if a child is looking at a lion, an elephant, and a gazelle, and an adult says, "Look, a gazelle," the young child who already knows "elephant" and "lion" will assume "gazelle" refers to the novel animal. Even without explicit

feedback from the speaker, this novel mapping bias is sufficient to lead children and adults to fast-map the meaning of the word such that they are willing to generalize the word to other exemplars of the same category (e.g., another gazelle) (Golinkoff et al. 1992). Thus, children using this novel mapping strategy infer that a word refers to a category of objects. This strategy provides children with an internal mechanism to learn new words that makes them less reliant on adults' explicit instruction for adding new words to their vocabulary (see Merriman 1998 for discussions of the ways this type of strategy facilitates word learning). They can therefore learn new words in naturally occurring conversations, such as when an adult is conversing with a child (or with more than one child) and is not necessarily monitoring what words are "new" for the child and need to be explicitly referenced.

Deaf and Hard of Hearing Children's Word-Learning Processes

Two aspects of deaf and hard of hearing children's novel word learning have been studied by researchers. We have examined deaf and hard of hearing children's ability to use different cues to fast-map the meaning of new words (Lederberg et al., 2000, 2001). This research is similar to that conducted with hearing children. Gilbertson and Kamhi (1995) examined the ability of older oral deaf children to accurately *encode and produce* the phonological structure of new words. This skill, done with ease by hearing children, is frequently challenging to deaf and hard of hearing children.

Fast Mapping of Novel Words

Both our completed (Lederberg et al, 2000, 2001) and ongoing studies have examined deaf and hard of hearing children's ability to quickly map meaning onto new words. The objective of the studies has been to determine whether and when these children develop similar word-learning processes as hearing children. The deaf and hard of hearing children's ability to learn new words was tested in two contexts: when reference was explicitly established and when word learning required the use of a novel mapping strategy.

Procedure   For both contexts, we exposed children to nonce words. The nonce words in our study were created to be consistent with the phonological system of both speech and sign. For example, some of the spoken words used were *dax, bipi, nupa,* and *toma.* The nonce signs for the initial study were created with assistance from an ASL linguist and a deaf ASL instructor. Persons from the Gallaudet University Center on ASL Literacy provided additional assistance. One example of a created sign is the one made to accompany the nonce spoken word *dax.* This novel sign, which consisted of Y handshapes on both hands, was produced with elbows bent so that forearms were upright in front of the signer's body with palms facing each other. The Ys were then tapped together twice. The reduplicated movement is a morphological marker in ASL indicating that a sign represents a noun (Supalla and Newport 1978; Valli and Lucas 1995) and was used in production of the novel signs created for this study. The created signs were also reviewed and pronounced acceptable by teachers in participating programs that used a simultaneous communication approach and therefore used a form of signed English. Nonce spoken words were similarly checked with teachers of children in oral programs.[2] The novel words were presented to the children in the language of their school's linguistic environment (i.e., spoken and signed for all sign/speech combination environments, spoken only for oral programs, and signed only for bilingual/bicultural programs).

In both the completed and ongoing studies, children were taught four nonce words in two contexts: the explicit reference and novel mapping contexts. These contexts were identical in their structure. Both contexts tested children's ability to learn new words quickly because they saw or heard the new words only two or three times. In both contexts, learning the new word required the children to extend the word to more than one exemplar of that category of objects. Thus, these word-learning contexts assessed deaf and hard of hearing children's ability to engage in true word learning after minimal exposure to a word. The two contexts differed in the way in which the word-referent link was established, thus assessing the development of different word-learning processes.

The *explicit reference* context tested children's ability to learn a novel word quickly and to generalize that word to a new exemplar of that category of objects when the connection between word and referent was made explicit by the researcher. For example, during an exposure trial, an unusual novel object (e.g., a corkscrew) was shown to the child and labeled three times (KUBAN, KUBAN, LOOK A KUBAN) in both speech and sign. Three familiar objects were also shown and labeled for the child (e.g., apple, shoe, baby). The child was then asked to select the kuban (KUBAN WHERE KUBAN?) from among the four objects (i.e., corkscrew, apple, shoe, baby). (A familiar object was also requested.) On the generalization trial, the child was shown different exemplars of the same categories of objects (e.g., another corkscrew, baby, apple, shoe) and a new novel object (e.g., bottle stopper) without any of the objects labeled. (The second novel object was included in the generalization trial to ensure the child was not just biased toward choosing any novel object.) The child was asked again for a "kuban" and for a familiar object in counterbalanced order. In order to be credited with learning a word, children had to select the correct novel object in both the exposure and generalization trials.

In this context, children had to employ the principles of reference, extendibility, and object scope to learn the new words. They also had to be able to map an initial representation onto the novel word quickly because they were exposed to each novel word only a few times. Performance on this task is indicative of children's ability to quickly learn new words that are explicitly taught.

The *novel mapping* context tested children's ability to infer that a novel word refers to an unfamiliar object even when the adult does not explicitly link word to referent (i.e., a novel mapping strategy). This task was almost identical to the explicit reference task, except that the researcher did not label the objects and provided no pragmatic cues that the novel word referred to the novel object. In the exposure trial, the children played briefly with three familiar objects (e.g., banana,

---

2. A complete description of nonce spoken words and signs can be obtained from the authors. Nonce signs are also available on videotape.

cookie, car) and one novel "target" object (e.g., a cherry pitter) without the researcher labeling any of the objects. Then the researcher (while looking directly at the child so that there would be no pragmatic cues for reference) asked for a referent for a nonce word (lep, lep, where lep?) and later for a familiar object (e.g., banana). The children were not corrected if they chose a familiar object as the referent for the nonce word. For the generalization trial, four new exemplars of the same objects (e.g., cherry pitter, banana, cookie, car) and a new novel object (e.g., egg slicer) were shown, and the child was again asked for the "lep" and for another familiar object.

Hypotheses   In both of these studies, we expected to identify deaf and hard of hearing children at each of three levels of word-learning abilities. Children at initial stages of language development were expected to learn a new word only after repeated exposures in which word and referent were explicitly linked. Therefore, children who were just beginning to acquire vocabulary should not learn words in either explicit reference or novel mapping context because the words were not demonstrated many times in either one. Children at the next level of language development were expected to learn new words after only a few exposures (i.e., to fast-map new words) when the association between object and referent was made explicit by the examiner (the explicit reference context). Finally, children at the highest stage of vocabulary development, who were thought to have developed internal word-learning strategies, were expected to learn words in both explicit reference and novel mapping contexts. Because these strategies are hypothesized to be related to children's knowledge of and experience with word learning, we expected these three levels of word-learning abilities to be related to the number of words in deaf children's vocabulary rather than to their age.

Results and Discussion   The hypotheses were supported in the initial study of nineteen deaf and hard of hearing children from a state day school (Lederberg et al. 2001). Three levels of word learning were observed. Two children with the lowest vocabularies (61 and 71 words respectively), at an age of 4 years, 4 months, did not consistently learn new words in either context (the *slow word learners*). Five children with moderate vocabularies ($M = 153$ words; $SD = 25$; M age = 4;2; $SD = 14$ months) learned new words rapidly in the explicit reference context but not in the novel mapping context (referred to as *rapid word learners*). These children had developed the ability to learn new words after only a brief exposure and to generalize those words to new exemplars. Children with larger vocabularies ($M = 312$ words, $SD = 146$; M age = 5;7 years; $SD = 14$ months) learned words rapidly in both contexts (*novel mappers*). These children had developed internal word-learning mechanisms that allowed them to infer that a novel word referred to a novel object without any explicit reference being demonstrated.

The slow and rapid word learners were followed longitudinally to examine their development of word-learning processes. All of the children eventually acquired the ability to learn new words in both contexts. The two children who were slow learners were able to learn new words in the explicit reference but not the novel mapping task when tested 6 months later. Four months after that, they were able to learn words in both tasks. This pattern suggests that the word-learning processes develop sequentially. Within the rapid word learner group, those children who experienced the fastest vocabulary growth and therefore had a larger lexicon at the second testing acquired the novel mapping strategy before those whose vocabulary grew slowly. The age of children in this group varied widely. Some of the children did not acquire the novel mapping strategy until they were more than 5 years old, more than 3 years after the age that is typical for hearing children (Graham, Poulin-Dubois, and Baker 1998; Golinkoff et al. 1992). Furthermore, these word-learning skills sometimes took over a year to develop. Acquisition of this strategy seemed to occur some time after children had a lexicon of more than 200 words, no matter what the child's age. Although the preschoolers in this study were older and more advanced in most areas of nonverbal cognition than hearing toddlers at the same level of word learning, there was no evidence that the novel mapping strategy occurred at smaller vocabulary sizes for the deaf and hard of hearing children. Therefore, although such general cognitive processes of association, attention, and memory seem to form the basis for these word-learning processes, the ability to use those processes for word learning seem to be specifically tied to linguistic development.

In addition, acquisition of these strategies seemed tied to affective changes in children's approach to learning new words. Although not objectively measured, examiners reported the impression that development of these word-learning processes brought with them a sense of certainty and ease about word learning. For instance, when the slow and rapid word learners were asked for the nonce word in the novel mapping task, they appeared uncertain and searched for pragmatic cues to guide their response. They seemed very aware they had no basis for choosing a referent. In contrast, the novel mappers chose the novel object with almost the same degree of confidence as they chose a referent for a familiar word. These children's certainty that they knew the referent for the nonce word was striking even though they had never heard or seen the word before and there were no pragmatic cues establishing reference. This skill, and the confidence with which it was employed, would seem to support word learning in naturally occurring conversations.

The study just summarized (Lederberg et al. 2001) was restricted to studying word-learning processes of deaf and hard of hearing children in one language environment (simultaneous communication). A goal of the ongoing research is to replicate these findings with a larger and linguistically more diverse sample. Preliminary findings (Lederberg et al. 2000) suggest that these three levels of word learning accurately depict word-learning abilities of children educated in a variety of communicative environments (simultaneous communication, oral, and bilingual/bicultural). To date, seventy-nine children have been assessed. Eleven children with the lowest vocabularies did not consistently learn new words in either context. Twenty-nine children with moderate vocabularies learned new words in only the explicit reference context. Thirty-nine children with the largest vocabularies learned words in both contexts. The forty slow and rapid word learners are now being tested every 4 months to record their acquisition of the strategies and their growth in vocabulary. As in the initial study, the vast majority of these children appear to be acquiring these word-learning strategies as their vocabulary development progresses.

Encoding the Phonological Structure of Novel Words   In addition to assigning meaning, learning new words will depend on deaf and hard of hearing children's ability to represent or encode the phonological structure of words. Gilbertson and Kamhi (1995) found that many oral hard of hearing elementary-school children had difficulty quickly learning new words. In an explicit-reference word-learning task, half of the children could not accurately produce some spoken novel words after ten exposures although they had no problems rapidly acquiring the words' correct meaning. Half the children learned to produce the words quickly. The children who had difficulty acquiring the new words had much smaller vocabularies (as measured by standardized tests) than the rapid word-learning children. Thus, vocabulary development may be very slow for those oral children who have difficulty representing the phonological structure of new words. This skill seemed linked to the hard of hearing children's cognitive processing abilities rather than their hearing abilities.

SUMMARY, CONCLUSIONS, AND IMPLICATIONS FOR PRACTICE

Researchers and practitioners have known for a long time that hearing loss significantly delays vocabulary development (Brannon 1968). However, assessment instruments such as standardized tests and language samples do not lend themselves to developing a more detailed analysis of this delay. The CDI promises to allow practitioners and researchers to explore both group and individual patterns of development. It seems to correlate highly with standardized tests of overall language (Bornstein et al. 1999) and vocabulary development (Lederberg et al. 2001). By completing the CDI at regular intervals, children's acquisition of individual and classes of words, as well as the rate of vocabulary growth, can be tracked over time. Although not available yet, expectations for vocabulary size and rate of growth of young deaf and hard of hearing children will soon be available from the studies we have underway and by Mayne and colleagues (Mayne, Yoshinaga-Itano, and Sedey 2000; Mayne et al. 2000).

For teachers, information gathered from completing the CDI can be helpful in planning curriculum. In our research, teachers reported that they felt it useful to complete the CDI. They were comfortable completing the CDI without directly testing the children's vocabulary, suggesting that the small classes and intensive language focus of the early intervention preschool provides an environment in which teachers are aware of individual children's vocabulary knowledge. Teachers also reported becoming more aware of which words they might need to emphasize in their classrooms. For instance, in one oral classroom, teachers realized recently that none of the children knew the word "purse" even though they were clearly exposed to their mothers' purses on a daily basis. They subsequently added children's purses to the classroom and provided opportunities for the children to be exposed to the word during pretend play. Therefore, the CDI may be both a valid assessment of children's vocabulary knowledge and a tool to guide teachers and parents in their efforts to facilitate children's vocabulary growth.

Vocabulary development consists not only of the acquisition of words but also of developing new learning processes for acquiring those words. Our research suggests that the acquisition of two word-learning processes—fast-mapping based on explicit reference and novel mapping—is linked to deaf and hard of hearing children's level of vocabulary knowledge. These results have some important implications for the construction of interventions for facilitating word learning. Our tasks can be seen as reflecting the learning contexts that are needed at the three levels of vocabulary development. Children with low levels of vocabulary seem to be unable to rapidly learn words even when reference is explicitly established. They therefore will require multiple, explicit exposures to new vocabulary for acquisition to occur. Children with intermediate levels of vocabulary knowledge may acquire new words quickly but only when the object-referent link is made explicit. Children with the highest levels of vocabulary may quickly pick up new words in naturally occurring, less structured, language-learning contexts. However, some oral children who have large vocabularies may not be able to represent the phonological structure of certain words quickly even when they have accurately fast-mapped the meanings of the words (Gilbertson and Kamhi 1995).

Categorization of children into levels of word-learning abilities can provide therapists and teachers with information about the kinds of contexts and teaching strategies that will be most effective with an individual child at a specific time in his or her development. In addition, categorization of a child as belonging to one of these three levels of vocabulary development can give professionals an idea of the child's potential rate of acquisition of new vocabulary (i.e., slow versus accelerated) in the short term and can aid in the setting of short-term goals for programming.

In summary, hearing loss is associated with a delay in children's vocabulary development (at least for those with hearing parents). This impact results in smaller lexicons, slower rates at which new words are acquired, and a narrower range of contexts that result in word learning. Our research suggests that, although delayed, deaf and hard of hearing children eventually acquire strategies that should lead to acceleration in word learning. Future research that uses the methodologies described here should result in a better understanding of deaf and hard of hearing children's vocabulary development that can be used to improve early intervention programs.

References

Bates, E., L. Benigni, I. Bretherton, L. Camaioni, and V. Volterra. 1979. *The emergence of symbols: Cognition and communication in infancy.* New York: Academic Press.

Bates, E., I. Bretherton, and L. Snyder. 1988. *From first words to grammar: Individual differences and dissociable mechanisms.* New York: Cambridge University Press.

Bates, E., and G. F. Carnevale. 1993. New directions in research on language development. *Developmental Review* 13:436–70.

Blumenthal-Kelly, A. 1995. Fingerspelling interaction: A set of deaf parents and their deaf daughter. In *Sociolinguistics in deaf communities,* ed. C. Lucas, 62–73. Washington, D.C.: Gallaudet University Press.

Bonvillian, J., M. Orlansky, and R. Folven. 1994. Early sign language acquisition: Implications for theories of language acquisition. In *From gesture to language in hearing and deaf children*, ed. V. Volterra and C. Erting, 219–32. Washington, D.C.: Gallaudet University Press.

Bornstein, M., A. Selmi, O. Hayes, K. L. Painter, and E. Marx. 1999. Representational abilities and the hearing status of child/mother dyads. *Child Development* 70:833–52.

Bradley-Johnson, S., and L. D. Evans. 1991. *Psychoeducational assessment of hearing-impaired students*. Austin, Tex.: Pro-Ed.

Brannon, J. B. 1968. Linguistic word classes in the spoken language of normal, hard of hearing, and deaf children. *Journal of Speech and Hearing Research* 11:279–87.

Carey, S. 1978. The child as word learner. In *Linguistic theory and psychological reality*, ed. M. Halle, J. Bresnan, and G. Miller, 264–93. Cambridge, Mass.: MIT Press.

Clark, E. V. 1991. Acquisitional principles in lexical development. In *Perspectives on language and thought*, ed. S. A. Gelman and J. P. Byrnes, 31–71. New York: Cambridge University Press.

Davis, J. M., J. Elfenbein, R. Schum, and R. A. Bentler. 1986. Effects of mild and moderate hearing impairments on language, educational, and psychosocial behavior of children. *Journal of Speech and Hearing Disorders* 51:53–62.

Day (Spencer), P. E. 1986. Deaf children's expression of communicative intentions. *Journal of Communication Disorders* 19:367–86.

Dromi, E. 1999. Early lexical development. In *The development of language: Studies in developmental psychology*, ed. M. Barrett, 99–131. Philadelphia: Psychology Press.

Dunn, L. 1959. *Peabody Picture Vocabulary Test*. Circle Pines, Minn.: American Guidance Service.

Erting, C., C. Thumann-Prezioso, and B. Benedict. 2000. Bilingualism in a deaf family: Fingerspelling in early childhood. In *The deaf child in the family and at school*, ed. P. Spencer, C. Erting, and M. Marschark, 41–54. Hillsdale, N.J.: Lawrence Erlbaum.

Everhart, V. 1993. The development of sign language use in deaf preschoolers and their hearing mothers. Ph.D. diss., University of Texas at Dallas.

Everhart, V., and A. R. Lederberg. 1991. The effect of mothers' visual communication use on deaf preschoolers' visual communication. Poster presented at the biennial meeting of the Society for Research in Child Development, April 18–20, Seattle.

Fenson, L., P. S. Dale, J. S. Reznick, E. Bates, D. J. Thal, and S. J. Pethick. 1994. Variability in early communicative development. *Monographs of the Society for Research in Child Development* 59(5), no. 242.

Fenson, L., P. S. Dale, J. S. Reznick, D. Thal, E. Bates, J. P. Hartung, S. Pethick, and J. S. Reilly. 1993. *MacArthur Communication Development Inventories: User's guide and technical manual*. San Diego: Singular Publishing Group.

Gardner, J., and J. Zorfass. 1983. From sign to speech: The language development of a hearing-impaired child. *American Annals of the Deaf* 128:20–24.

Gilbertson, M., and A. Kamhi. 1995. Novel word learning in children with hearing impairment. *Journal of Speech and Hearing Research* 38:630–42.

Goldfield, B., and J. S. Reznick. 1990. Early lexical acquisition: Rate, content, and the vocabulary spurt. *Journal of Child Language* 17:171–83.

Golinkoff, R., and K. Hirsh-Pasek, eds. Forthcoming. *Breaking the word learning barrier: What does it take?* Oxford: Oxford University Press.

Golinkoff, R. M., K. Hirsh-Pasek, L. M. Bailey, and N. R. Wenger. 1992. Young children and adults use lexical principles to learn new nouns. *Developmental Psychology* 28(1):99–108.

Golinkoff, R. M, K. Hirsh-Pasek, and G. Hollich. 1999. Emerging cues for early word learning. In *The emergence of language,* ed. B. MacWhinney, 305–29. Mahwah, N.J.: Lawrence Erlbaum.

Goodman, N. 1983. *Fact, fiction, and forecast.* Cambridge, Mass.: Harvard University Press.

Graham, S. A., D. Poulin-Dubois, and R. K. Baker. 1998. Infants' disambiguation of novel object words. *First Language* 18:149–64.

Gregory, S., and K. Mogford. 1981. Early language development in deaf children. In *Perspectives on British Sign Language and deafness,* ed. B. Woll, J. Kyle and M. Deuchar, 218–37. London: Croom Helm.

Griswold, L. E., and J. Commings. 1974. The expressive vocabulary of preschool deaf children. *American Annals of the Deaf* 119:16–29.

Hoffmeister, R., and R. Wilbur. 1980. The acquisition of sign language. In *Recent perspectives on American Sign Language,* ed. H. Lane and F. Grosjean, 61–78. Hillsdale, N.J.: Lawrence Erlbaum.

Howell, R. F. 1984. Maternal reports of vocabulary development in four-year-old deaf children. *American Annals of the Deaf* 129:459–65.

Layton, T. L., and D. W. Holmes. 1985. *Carolina Picture Vocabulary Test.* Austin, Tex.: Pro-Ed.

Lederberg, A. R., and V. Everhart. 1998. Communication between deaf children and their hearing mothers: The role of language, gesture, and vocalization. *Journal of Speech, Language and Hearing Research* 41:887–99.

———. 2000. Conversations between deaf children and their hearing mothers: Pragmatic and dialogic characteristics. *Journal of Deaf Studies and Deaf Education* 5:303–22.

Lederberg, A. R., A. K. Prezbindowski, and P. E. Spencer. 2001. Word learning skills of deaf preschoolers: The development of novel mapping and rapid word learning strategies. *Child Development,* 71:1571–85.

Lederberg, A. R., P. E. Spencer, and A. K. Prezbindowski. 2000. *Deaf children's expressive vocabulary and its relation to their word learning strategies: A cross-sectional study.* Poster presented at the biennial meetings of the International Society of Infant Studies, July 16–19, Brighton, Great Britain.

MacWhinney, B., ed. 1999. *The emergence of language.* Mahwah, N.J.: Lawrence Erlbaum.

Mayberry, R. I. 1992. The cognitive development of deaf children: Recent insights. In *Handbook of neuropsychology: Child neuropsychology,* vol. 7, S. J. Segalowitz and I. Rapin, 51–68. New York: Elsevier.

Mayne, A., C. Yoshinaga-Itano, and A. L. Sedey. 2000. Receptive vocabulary development of infants and toddlers who are deaf or hard of hearing. *Volta Review* 100:29–52.

Mayne, A., C. Yoshinaga-Itano, A. L. Sedey, and A. Carey. 2000. Expressive vocabulary development of infants and toddlers who are deaf or hard of hearing. *Volta Review* 100:1–29.

Meier, R. 1990. Language acquisition by deaf children. *American Scientist* 79:60–70.

Merriman, W. E. 1998. CALLED: A model of early word learning. *Annals of Child Development* 13:67–112.

Merriman, W. E., and L. L. Bowman. 1989. The mutual exclusivity bias in children's word learning. *Monographs of the Society for Research in Child Development* 54(3–4), no. 220.

Merriman, W. E., J. Marazita, and L. Jarvis. 1995. Children's disposition to map new words onto new referents. In *Beyond names for things: Young children's acquisition of verbs,* ed. M. Tomasello and W. E. Merriman, 149–63. Hillsdale, N.J.: Lawrence Erlbaum.

Mervis, C. B., and J. Bertrand. 1994. Acquisition of the novel name-nameless category (N3C) principle. *Child Development* 65:1646–62.

———. 1995a. Acquisition of the novel name-nameless category (N3C) principle by young children who have Down syndrome. *American Journal on Mental Retardation* 100(3):231–43.

———. 1995b. Early lexical acquisition and the vocabulary spurt: A response to Goldfield and Reznick. *Journal of Child Language* 22:461–68.

———. 1997. Relations between cognition and language: A developmental perspective. In *Research on communication and language disorders: Contributions to theories of language development,* ed. L. B. Adamson and M. A. Romski, 75–106. New York: Brookes.

Miller, J. F. 1992a. Development of speech and language in children with Down syndrome. In *Down syndrome: Advances in medical care,* ed. I. T. Lott and E. E. McCoy, 39–50. New York: Wiley.

———. 1992b. Lexical development in young children with Down syndrome. In *Processes in language acquisition and disorders,* ed. R. S. Chapman, 202–16. St. Louis: Mosby Year Book.

Moeller, M. P., M. J. Osberger, and M. Eccarius. 1986. Receptive language skills. In Language and learning skills in hearing-impaired children, ed. M. Osberger. *Monographs of the American Speech, Language, and Hearing Association* 23:41–53.

Moog, J., V. Kozak, and A. Geers. 1983. Grammatical analysis of elicited language: Pre-sentence level. St. Louis: Central Institute for the Deaf.

Nelson, K. 1973. Structure and strategy in learning to talk. *Monographs of the Society for Research in Child Development* 38(1–2), no. 149.

Newcomer, P., and D. Hammill. 1977. *Test of language development.* Los Angeles: Western Psychological Services.

Notoya, M., S. Suzuki, and M. Furukawa. 1994. Effects of manual instruction on the oral-language development of two deaf children. *American Annals of the Deaf* 139:348–51.

Osberger, M. J., M. P. Moeller, M. Eccarius, A. M. Robins, and D. Johnson. 1986. Expressive language skills. *Monographs of the American Speech-Language-Hearing Association* 23:54–65.

Petitto, L. 1988. "Language" in the prelinguistic child. In *The development of language and language researchers,* ed. F. Kessel, 187–221. Hillsdale, N.J.: Lawrence Erlbaum.

Povine, K., J. Reilly, and D. Anderson. 1993. *Language development of deaf children: The CDI for ASL.* Poster presented at the American Speech-Language-Hearing Association Annual Convention, November 19–21, Anaheim, Calif.

Quine, W. V. O. 1960. *Word and object*. Cambridge, Mass.: MIT Press.

Scherer, P. 1981. *Total communication receptive vocabulary test*. Northbrook, Ill.: Mental Health and Deafness Resources.

Schlesinger, H. S., and K. P. Meadow. 1972. *Sound and sign: Childhood deafness and mental health*. Berkeley: University of California Press.

Shafer, D., and J. Lynch. 1981. Emergent language of six prelingually deaf children. *Journal of the British Association of Teachers of the Deaf* 5(4):94–111.

Smith, L. B. 1999. Children's noun learning: How children's learning processes make specialized learning mechanisms. In *The emergence of language*, ed. B. MacWhinney, 277–303. Mahwah, N.J.: Lawrence Erlbaum.

Spencer, P. E. 1993a. Communication behaviors of infants with hearing loss and their hearing mothers. *Journal of Speech and Hearing Research* 36:311–21.

———. 1993b. The expressive communication of hearing mothers and deaf infants. *American Annals of the Deaf* 138:275–83.

Spencer, P. E., and A. R. Lederberg. 1997. Different modes, different models: Communication and language of young deaf children and their mothers. In *Research on communication and language disorders: Contributions to theories of language development*, ed. L. B. Adamson and M. A. Romski, 203–30. Baltimore: Brookes.

Supalla, T., and E. Newport. 1978. How many seats in a chair? The derivation of nouns and verbs in American Sign Language. In *Understanding language through sign language*, ed. P. Siple, 91–132. New York: Academic Press.

Tomasello, M. Forthcoming. Perceiving intentions and learning words in the second year of life. In *Language acquisition and conceptual development*, ed. M. Bowerman and S. Levinson. Oxford: Oxford University Press.

Tomasello, M., and M. Barton. 1994. Learning words in non-ostensive contexts. *Developmental Psychology* 30:639–50.

Tucker, I., M. Hostler, and M. Nolan. 1984. *The hearing impaired child developing language*. Typescript.

Valli, C., and C. Lucas. 1995. *Linguistics of American Sign Language: An introduction*. 2d ed. Washington, D.C.: Gallaudet University Press.

8

THEORY OF MIND DEVELOPMENT IN DEAF CHILDREN

Ethan Remmel, Jeffrey G. Bettger, and Amy M. Weinberg

Theory of mind development in deaf children is a new and exciting area of research. The first study on the topic was published in 1995, and to date only about a dozen studies have been published or presented. But even in this relatively short period of time, researchers have learned a great deal. Research teams from around the world (Australia, France, the United States, and Great Britain) have produced converging evidence on a number of important issues. This chapter provides a brief overview of theory of mind in general, including some of the major theoretical debates, and then reviews the existing research on theory of mind development in deaf children. The authors summarize the patterns that have emerged thus far and point out where issues remain unresolved and further research is needed.

OVERVIEW OF THEORY OF MIND

What Is Theory of Mind?

Theory of mind is a type of social cognition (i.e., thinking about people). Theory of mind refers to the body of knowledge that individuals use to predict and explain people's behavior. Adults in European–American cultures typically predict and explain people's behavior via the attribution of mental states such as beliefs and desires.[1] That is, adults assume that people have minds and that there are lawful causal relations between people's experiences, their mental states, and their intentional actions. For example, if Max wants a cookie and believes that there are cookies in the cookie jar, then adults will predict, *ceteris paribus*, that Max will go to the cookie jar.

This material is based on work supported by a National Science Foundation graduate fellowship to Ethan Remmel.

---

1. See Lillard (1998) for a review of possible cultural variation in theory of mind. This discussion focuses on what Lillard calls the "European–American Social Science Model" of theory of mind.

Both philosophers of mind (Dretske 1988; Stich 1983) and social psychologists (Heider 1958; Ross 1977) have examined theory of mind in adults, although they usually use the labels "folk psychology" and "intuitive psychology," respectively. These labels are useful in distinguishing theory of mind from academic or scientific psychology. Theory of mind knowledge is neither learned in psychology class-rooms nor revised in research laboratories. "Folk" or "intuitive" conceptions of how the mind works and influences behavior are used by ordinary people from an early age to make sense of their social worlds. This chapter uses the term "theory of mind" because that is the most common label within developmental psychology.

In the past decade or so, research on theory of mind development has become one of the most active and productive areas in developmental psychology (Flavell and Miller 1998). This research program is related to two earlier research traditions with which readers may be more familiar. The first is Piagetian research on egocentrism and perspective-taking. A mature theory of mind requires an under-standing that other people have minds and that other people's mental states (per-ceptions, desires, beliefs, emotions, etc.) may be different from one's own. The sec-ond is research on metacognition (thinking about thinking). But whereas research on metacognition typically concerns children's knowledge of higher-level mental strategies (e.g., the relationship between rehearsal and memory), research on the-ory of mind concerns children's knowledge of more basic mental processes (e.g., the relationship between perception and belief).

Representational Theory of Mind

As mentioned earlier, adults in Western cultures typically predict and explain peo-ple's actions with reference to the actor's beliefs and desires. In many situations, however, reference to desires is sufficient. To return to our earlier example, if asked to explain why Max went to the cookie jar, the statement "because he wanted a cookie" would ordinarily be sufficient. The fact that "He thought there were cookies in the cookie jar" is implied but not typically stated. As long as everyone shares the same beliefs about the state of the world, people's actions can be predicted and explained on the basis of their desires. One leading developmen-tal psychologist, Henry Wellman, proposes that young children understand the social world in this way. According to Wellman (1990), 2-year-olds have a "desire psychology"; that is, they appreciate that other people may have different desires but not that other people may have different beliefs about the state of the world (a sort of Piagetian egocentrism).[2]

When people's beliefs differ, reference to beliefs becomes necessary to accu-rately predict and explain people's behavior. To return to our example, suppose that while Max is out of the room his mother takes the cookies out of the jar and hides them in the cupboard. Now Max holds a false belief about the cookies' location. If asked to predict "Where will Max look for a cookie?" a "desire psychologist" will

---

2. Research in social psychology shows that even adults often fail to appreciate that other people may construe the same "facts" differently (Ross and Ward 1996).

reason "Max wants a cookie, and the cookies are in the cupboard" and thus will answer incorrectly, "the cupboard." Wimmer and Perner (1983) developed the first such "false-belief task," and variants have subsequently been used in many studies to establish that children begin to use a "belief-desire psychology" around age 4 (Wellman 1990).[3] That is, after about age 4, children begin to reason as follows: "Max did not see his mother move the cookies to the cupboard, so Max still thinks the cookies are in the jar, so if Max wants a cookie, he will look in the jar."

Success on a false-belief task, that is, the ability to consider that people may act on the basis of beliefs that differ from one's own, is a marker of a "representational" theory of mind (Perner 1991). By late preschool age, children seem to understand that people's minds contain mental representations of reality (i.e., beliefs) and that these representations may misrepresent reality (i.e., can be false). Of course, children may not be able to verbalize their knowledge in these terms, but they are able to demonstrate it in situations such as the false-belief task. Other important markers of a representational theory of mind include understanding of "representational change" (Gopnik and Astington 1988) and the "appearance–reality distinction" (Flavell, Flavell, and Green 1983). Understanding of representational change concerns the fact that the same person can have conflicting beliefs at two different points in time and is typically tested by asking the child to recall a previous false belief (i.e., to recognize that his or her own mental representation has changed). Understanding of the appearance-reality distinction concerns the fact that the same thing (e.g., a sponge painted to look like a rock) can be represented in different ways at the same time (e.g., as a rock with respect to its appearance, but as a sponge with respect to its real identity) and is typically tested by asking the child to report both the appearance and the reality.

The emergence of a representational theory of mind during the preschool years is a critical transition in theory of mind development. However, success or failure on tests of understanding of mental representation, such as false-belief tasks, do not indicate the presence or absence of a theory of mind altogether. Even a 2-year-old's desire psychology is a sort of theory of mind (albeit a nonrepresentational one); it is just not as good a theory as a belief-desire psychology because it is not as accurate in predicting and explaining people's behavior in situations in which people have different beliefs (mental representations of reality). The incorporation of beliefs gives the child's theory of mind greater predictive and explanatory power and thus enables the child to navigate the social world more successfully (Watson et al. 1999).

Theories versus Modules

Developmentalists disagree about how children's theory of mind knowledge develops. One influential position, the "theory theory" (Gopnik and Wellman 1994), holds that children construct their folk or intuitive theories of mind in the same way that scientists construct scientific theories. Children observe people's behavior, postulate

---

3. This discussion glosses over the intermediate stage of "desire-belief psychology" proposed by Bartsch and Wellman (1995), during which children begin to talk about subjective beliefs but do not yet use them to predict and explain people's behavior.

theoretical entities (e.g., beliefs and desires) and causal relationships, and revise their theories or devise new ones in response to events that cannot be accommodated by their existing theory. According to this view, theory of mind development is shaped by the child's experience within a particular social and cultural context.

An alternative position holds that theory of mind knowledge is contained in a dedicated and encapsulated cognitive "module," in the sense of Fodor (1983). According to this view, theory of mind development is primarily a matter of neurological maturation (Leslie 1994). A certain amount or type of experience may be necessary to "trigger" the process, but the course of development is largely biologically constrained (Scholl and Leslie 1999).[4] The fact that autistic children perform poorly on theory of mind tasks is taken as evidence of neurological impairment to the theory of mind module (Baron-Cohen 1995).

Domain Specific versus Domain General

Both theory theorists and modular theorists hold that theory of mind forms a distinct domain of knowledge. That is, individuals reason about people's behavior using concepts and rules that are specific to the social domain (Wellman and Gelman 1998). According to this "domain-specific" view, children's performance on theory of mind tests such as false-belief tasks depends primarily on conceptual developments specific to theory of mind, such as understanding of mental representations.

An alternative position holds that children's performance on theory of mind tasks depends primarily on their general level of cognitive development, such as their ability to reason about (a) representations in general, including mental representations such as beliefs and physical representations such as photographs (Zaitchik 1990) or (b) logical rules, particularly embedded rules such as "if X then (if Y then Z)" (Frye, Zelazo, and Palfai 1995). According to this "domain-general" view, reasoning about events in the social domain depends on the cognitive complexity of the situation and not on the child's understanding of mental phenomena specifically.

The Role of Language

Language and theory of mind are indubitably related, but the relationship is complex and not completely understood. As evidence of this relationship, verbal ability predicts performance on false-belief tasks better than chronological age or non-

---

4. Some modular accounts of development hold that experience sets various "parameters" of the module (Stich and Nichols 1998). However, a highly parameterized modular account is empirically indistinguishable from the theory theory (Gopnik and Meltzoff 1997) and thus, in the authors' opinion, not very theoretically interesting. This discussion is thus restricted to nonparameterized modular accounts of theory of mind development, such as Scholl and Leslie (1999).

verbal cognitive ability, and a certain threshold level of verbal ability seems to be necessary to pass false-belief tasks (Happe 1995; Jenkins and Astington 1996). There are many different ways in which language and theory of mind may be related (de Villiers and de Villiers 1999). Three possibilities are as follows:

1. language as task demand

2. language as data for theory construction

3. language as representational structure

Theory of mind tests are often administered verbally, and so children's performance may be related to their ability to follow the narrative and understand what is being asked (Lewis 1994; Siegal 1999). Language may also serve to stimulate theory of mind development. According to the theory theory, children construct their theories of mind through social interaction, and so conversations, particularly those that refer to mental states, are a rich source of data. In support of this possibility, the amount of mental state talk within families predicts children's performance on theory of mind measures (Dunn et al. 1991; Brown, Donelan-McCall, and Dunn 1996; Ruffman, Perner, and Parkin 1999). Finally, the structure of language may enable a representational theory of mind. According to Jill and Peter de Villiers (1999), certain syntactic features of language, such as complementation, may provide the means for children to represent embedded propositions, such as false beliefs (e.g., "Max thinks that *the cookies are in the jar*"). These possibilities will be discussed more later, in light of the evidence from deaf children. Because deaf children's language experience varies widely, research on theory of mind development in deaf children has the potential to explicate the role of language in theory of mind development.

THEORY OF MIND IN DEAF CHILDREN

Delayed Development?

In the first published study of theory of mind in deaf children, Peterson and Siegal (1995) found that only 9 of 26 deaf children (35 percent), ages 8 to 13 years (average age of 10 years), passed a false-belief test. The test was a version of the "unexpected location" false-belief task originally developed by Wimmer and Perner (1983), in which the child is asked to predict where a person will look for an object after the object has been, unbeknownst to the person, moved to a second location. Recall that normally developing hearing children typically pass this test (i.e., predict that the person will look for the object in the first location, even though it is not there anymore) by around age 4. Some aspects of the procedure may have hampered the deaf children's performance (e.g., the procedure was administered using a combination of spoken English and Signed English, although some of the children preferred to communicate in Australian Sign Language). Nevertheless, the deaf children's poor performance at a relatively advanced age suggested a significant delay in their theory of mind development. Furthermore, the children were of normal nonverbal intelligence, and neither nonverbal IQ nor chronological age distinguished between the false-belief passers and failers.

Peterson and Siegal noted that the deaf children performed as poorly as autistic children in previous research (i.e., Baron-Cohen, Leslie, and Frith 1985) and took this as evidence against the modular view of theory of mind development and for the role of language as data for theory construction. Recall that modular theorists explain the poor theory of mind performance of autistic children as the result of neurological impairment. Peterson and Siegal argued that the poor performance of both deaf children and autistic children could be more parsimoniously explained as the result of conversational deprivation. Many deaf children (due to the inaccessibility of spoken language) and autistic children (due to their social aloofness) receive attenuated linguistic input, which may delay their theory of mind development.

Representational Theory of Mind

Although the Peterson and Siegal (1995) study suggested delayed theory of mind development in deaf children, it left many questions unanswered. Peterson and Siegal used only one theory of mind measure, the unexpected-location false-belief task. Would deaf children have difficulty with other theory of mind measures? Success on false-belief tasks requires a representational theory of mind. Would deaf children succeed on theory of mind tasks that do not require the concept of mental representation?

Subsequent research has established that deaf children's difficulty is not confined to the unexpected-location false-belief task. Deaf children show similar levels of performance on other types of false-belief tasks (Courtin 2000b; de Villiers, Pyers, and Salkind 1999; Gale, de Villiers, de Villiers, and Pyers 1996; Peterson and Siegal 1999; Remmel et al. 2000), on tests of representational change (de Villiers et al. 1999; Gale et al. 1996; Peterson and Siegal 1999; Remmel et al. 2000), and on tests of the appearance–reality distinction (Courtin 1998; Remmel et al. 2000). Although it is difficult to compare success rates across different tests, samples, and procedures, the difficulty that some deaf children exhibit on theory of mind tasks seems to extend across a wide range of tests of understanding of mental representation.

As discussed earlier, however, failure on tests of understanding of mental representation does not indicate the absence of a theory of mind altogether. Even if the development of a representational theory of mind is delayed, children may understand other nonrepresentational mental phenomena, such as desires and emotions.[5] In a study by Steeds, Rowe, and Dowker (1997), deaf children, ages 5 to 12 years (average age of 9 years), showed better understanding of desires than of beliefs. Specifically, the children had no difficulty predicting a person's emo-

---

5. The research reviewed in this chapter focuses on deaf children's understanding of representational mental phenomena, such as beliefs. For a review of research on deaf children's understanding of emotions, see the chapter by Gray, Hosie, Russell, and Ormel in this volume.

tional reaction on the basis of the person's desires (e.g., that a person will be happy if she gets what she wants) but had some difficulty predicting a person's actions or emotional reaction on the basis of the person's beliefs (e.g., that a person will be happy if she *believes* she is getting what she wants, even if that belief is false). This finding suggests that some deaf children may be operating at the level of a "desire psychology" at a relatively late age, but more research is needed to explore this possibility.

Theories versus Modules

Deaf children are an extremely heterogeneous population. An accurate account of theory of mind development in deaf children must consider some of the ways in which deaf children differ from one another and how these differences are related to their theory of mind development. These relationships may illuminate the processes that underlie theory of mind development in general. At a basic level, deaf children differ in the degree and onset of their hearing loss. The existing research on theory of mind in deaf children has focused on children with severe or profound hearing loss, with onset before language acquisition; therefore, this discussion is limited to such children, except as otherwise noted.

Two other important variables are (a) parental hearing status and (b) method of education. Some deaf children are born into deaf families. These "DD children" (deaf children of deaf parents) typically acquire a sign language as their native language on the same timetable that hearing children acquire spoken language (Emmorey 1994; Hoff-Ginsberg 1997). However, 90 percent of deaf children are born into hearing families. These "DH children" (deaf children of hearing parents) often have delayed language acquisition and difficulty communicating with their hearing families (Marschark 1993; Meadow et al. 1981). DH children are often not exposed to sign language until school age or later, depending on their method of education.

Methods of educating deaf children vary widely, and a full discussion of the differences is beyond the scope of this chapter. One major division is between programs that emphasize spoken language (oral programs) and those that use some signed communication. Methods of signed communication vary also, from natural sign languages such as American Sign Language (ASL) to signed versions of spoken languages (e.g., Signed English) and to combinations of speech and sign.

According to the theory theory, differences in deaf children's home and school environments may have a major impact on their theory of mind development. On this view, theory of mind development is shaped by social and linguistic experience. According to the modular view, however, these differences in social context should have little effect on deaf children's theory of mind development. On this view, theory of mind development is largely determined by chronological age, barring neurological impairment to the theory of mind module or insufficient environmental stimulation to trigger the maturational process.

Parental Hearing Status
The Peterson and Siegal (1995) study provided the first hint that parental hearing status might be an important variable in deaf children's theory of mind development. The two DD children in their sample, both native signers of Australian Sign

Language, passed the false-belief test. Subsequent research has confirmed that DD children outperform DH children across a range of theory of mind tests (Courtin 2000; Courtin and Melot 1998; Peterson and Siegal 1997, 1999; Remmel et al. 2000).

DH children perform worse on theory of mind tests than expected for their chronological age. In general, the performance of DH children in the 5- to 12-year age range on tests of a representational theory of mind is better than that of hearing 3-year-olds but worse than that of hearing 4-year-olds (de Villiers and de Villiers 1999; Gale et al. 1996; Peterson and Siegal 1998). This asynchrony between age and theory of mind performance seems to support the theory theory over the modular view of theory of mind development. Theory theorists can attribute a delay in DH children's theory of mind development to their atypical and often attenuated social and linguistic experience. Modular theorists must attribute a delay in DH children's theory of mind development to neurological impairment or insufficient input to trigger maturation. At first blush, the neurological explanation seems plausible. DH children are much less likely than DD children to have inherited their deafness, and nongenetic causes of deafness are more likely to have associated neurological damage (Marschark 1993). But the modular view holds that neurological damage to the theory of mind module results in autism, and DH children are obviously not autistic. The "insufficient input" explanation is harder to evaluate because modular theorists have not specified what sort of environmental input would be sufficient to trigger theory of mind development. Although the existing evidence is not conclusive, the authors' opinion is that the strong relationship between parental hearing status and deaf children's theory of mind performance fits more naturally and comfortably with the theory theory than with the modular theory.

DD children outperform DH children on theory of mind tests, but their performance relative to the age norms for hearing children is less clear. In Peterson and Siegal (1997, 1999) and Remmel et al. (2000), DD children performed near ceiling on tests of understanding of mental representation. It is difficult to compare these results to the age norms for hearing children, however, because these DD samples were much older (average ages of 9 to 10 years) than the ages at which hearing children reach ceiling on these tasks (around age 5 or 6). Only Courtin (1998, 2000; Courtin and Melot 1998) has conducted age-controlled comparisons of DD children and hearing children. Courtin (2000) found that DD children, ages 5 to 6 years, actually performed *better* than an age-matched sample of hearing children on a set of false-belief tasks. However, the performance of the hearing sample was worse than expected from the theory of mind literature (only eleven of the twenty-four hearing 5- and 6-year-olds passed two out of the three false-belief tasks). This could be due to the fact that the age norms in the theory of mind literature are largely based on research with middle-class children, whereas Courtin's hearing sample was drawn from a more underprivileged class in order to match the socioeconomic status of the deaf children. Holmes, Black, and Miller (1996) examined false-belief understanding in an underprivileged hearing population and found performance more similar to that of Courtin's hearing sample (e.g., the average success rate of 5-year-olds was 57 percent). Furthermore, the inconsistent performance of DD children on conceptual perspective-taking tasks suggests that their good performance on false-belief tasks may actually overestimate their understanding of the representational nature of mind (Courtin forthcoming).

More research with DD children, especially younger DD children, is needed to determine whether DD children's theory of mind development is accelerated, delayed, or equivalent to that of hearing children. The existing research, however, suggests that DD children's theory of mind development is not delayed, relative to that of hearing children. If so, the poor performance of DH children, relative to that of both DD children and hearing children, cannot be attributed to deafness per se (i.e., the absence of auditory input does not necessarily result in delayed theory of mind development).

The experiences of DD and DH children differ in many ways (Marschark 1993), which makes it difficult to determine which of the variables associated with parental hearing status has an effect on theory of mind development. It seems likely, however, that differences in early social and linguistic experience, particularly in effective parent–child communication, are causally related to the gap between the theory of mind performance of DD children and that of DH children. The role of language in particular is considered in more detail later.

Method of Education
Researchers have tested theory of mind performance in DH children from several different educational environments:

1. total communication programs, which use combinations of speech, signed versions of spoken language, fingerspelling, and natural sign language (Peterson and Siegal 1995, 1997, 1998; Russell et al. 1998; Steeds et al. 1996)

2. oral programs, which use only spoken language (de Villiers and de Villiers 1999; de Villiers et al. 1997; de Villiers, Pyers, and Salkind 1999; Gale et al. 1996)

3. one bilingual-bicultural program, which emphasizes a natural sign language (ASL), as well as competence in written, but not spoken, English (Remmel et al. 2000).

DH children have shown age-delayed theory of mind performance in each of these studies, suggesting that their difficulty is not specific to a particular method of education. It is difficult, however, to compare absolute levels of performance across studies, due to differences in samples (e.g., in age) and procedures. There are other confounding factors as well. To take one example, Steeds et al. (1996) did not collect detailed family background information, so there may have been some DD children in their sample, which may have inflated their sample's performance. To take another example, all of the children in the study by Gale et al. either used hearing aids or had received cochlear implants, but Gale et al. (1996) did not collect aided hearing test information. To the degree that these children were able to hear spoken language, their experience would be more similar to that of hearing children, and thus one would expect better theory of mind performance.

The only studies to date that directly compare the theory of mind performance of DH children from different educational environments are those by Courtin (1998, 2000; Courtin and Melot 1998), and Peterson and Siegal (1999). These studies compared the performance of DH children from oral programs (oral DH children) with that of DH children from programs that use some signed communication (signing DH children). Such comparisons are inevitably somewhat confounded by two factors. First, deaf children are not randomly assigned to different educational environments. Preexisting differences between deaf children and their families are likely to be associated with the method of education chosen for the child, and it is difficult to control for all the potentially relevant variables. Second, the administration of verbal tests cannot be held completely constant because instructions must be given in spoken language to the oral deaf children and in signed language to the signing deaf children. This confound could be minimized in future studies by using theory of mind tests with fewer verbal demands. Despite these caveats, the comparisons in these studies offer the best existing evidence on the relationship between method of education and deaf children's theory of mind development.

Courtin (1998; 2000; Courtin and Melot 1998) found better performance by signing DH children than by oral DH children on a set of false-belief tasks and on "identity" appearance–reality tests (in which an object appears to have a different identity, e.g., a sponge appears to be a rock) and equivalent performance on "property" appearance–reality tests (in which an object appears to have a different property, e.g., a white sheet of paper appears red under a colored filter). Peterson and Siegal (1999), on the other hand, found better performance by oral deaf children than by signing deaf children on a set of false-belief tasks. However, degree of hearing loss was confounded with method of education in the Peterson and Siegal study but not in Courtin's studies. In Courtin's studies, both the signing DH children and the oral DH children had profound hearing loss (more than 90 decibels in the better ear). In the Peterson and Siegal study, the signing DH children had severe to profound hearing loss, but the oral DH children had only moderate to severe hearing loss (presumably measured unaided, although Peterson and Siegal do not specify) and had used hearing aids since infancy. In the Peterson and Siegal study, the signing DH children and the oral DH children differed in their early language experience (because the oral DH children had greater access to spoken language) as well as their method of education.

Thus Courtin's results more directly address the relationship between method of education and deaf children's theory of mind development. Among DH children with profound hearing loss, those from educational environments that use some signed communication show better theory of mind performance than those from oral programs. Although subject to the caveats discussed earlier, this relationship presumably reflects the fact that signed language is more accessible to these children than is spoken language. Peterson and Siegal's results, on the other hand, suggest that the accessibility of early language within the family may be more important to theory of mind performance than the accessibility of language in school, at least up until the ages tested (5 to 13 years). Peterson and Siegal's oral DH sample had partial access to the spoken language used in their hearing families and their school programs, whereas their signing DH sample had little access to the spoken language used in their hearing families but full access to the signed language used in their school programs. Although the comparison is confounded with onset and duration of linguistic exposure, the fact that these oral DH children outperformed these signing DH children on the false-belief tasks suggests that the quality of early communication within the family is critical to theory of mind development. In general, the relationship between accessible linguistic experience and theory of mind performance supports the theory theory over the modular view of theory of mind development.

Critical Period Hypothesis

In their original article, Peterson and Siegal (1995) noted that their sample of DH children demonstrated poor false-belief understanding for their age and furthermore that performance did not improve with age within the sample. Peterson and Siegal speculated that the preschool years may represent a critical period for theory of mind development and that if children do not receive adequate accessible linguistic stimulation during this period, then they may never develop a representational theory of mind. According to this critical-period hypothesis, DH children's difficulty with theory of mind tests reflects a permanent deficit rather than a temporary delay.

Chronological age predicts DH children's theory of mind performance in some studies (de Villiers and de Villiers 1999; de Villiers et al. 1997; Peterson and Siegal 1999; Russell et al. 1998) but not in others (Courtin 2000; Courtin and Melot 1998; Peterson and Siegal 1995; Steeds et al. 1996). But in every study in which age predicted theory of mind performance and a measure of the DH children's language was taken, the language measure predicted theory of mind performance better than age. These language measures have included general verbal ability (Peterson and Siegal 1999), receptive vocabulary (de Villiers and de Villiers 1999; de Villiers et al. 1997), and production of complements (de Villiers and de Villiers 1999; de Villiers et al. 1997). Production of complements (e.g., "He thinks that X," "She says that Y") is a particularly good predictor of theory of mind performance in oral DH children, a result that is discussed further in the language section. Contrary to the critical-period hypothesis, it appears that DH children's theory of mind performance does improve after the preschool years, but improvements are directly related to language ability and only indirectly to chronological age (i.e., age predicts theory of mind performance only insofar as it is also correlated with language ability). These relationships provide additional indication that theory of mind development depends on linguistic experience and not simply on neurological maturation.

Additional evidence against the critical-period hypothesis comes from theory of mind research with DH adolescents and DH adults. Russell et al. (1998) found that DH adolescents (ages 13 to 16) outperformed DH children (ages 4 to 12) on two unexpected-location false-belief tasks. The performance of the DH children was unusually poor, however, relative to previous studies (only three of the twenty-two children passed both false-belief tasks). Russell et al. speculated that the acquisition of a representational theory of mind is often delayed in DH individuals until adolescence, due to delayed language acquisition and thus reduced opportunities to learn about mental states. Clark et al. (1996) asked DH adults to rate cognitive verbs (e.g., "thinking," "guessing," "observing") according to their conceptual similarity. Clark et al. found that DH adults and hearing adults organized these verbs along similar dimensions (e.g., certain versus uncertain, conceptual output versus perceptual input), although there was less agreement among DH adults. Clark et al. concluded that DH adults and hearing adults conceptualize mental activities similarly. Although more research on theory of mind in deaf adults is needed, this study suggests that most DH individuals eventually acquire a theory of mind similar to that used by hearing adults (i.e., that the critical-period hypothesis is false).

Domain Specific versus Domain General

According to the domain-specific view of theory of mind development, children's performance on theory of mind tests depends on their understanding of mental phenomena, which may be more or less advanced than their understanding of other types of phenomena (e.g., physical events). According to the domain-general view, children's performance on theory of mind tasks depends on their general level of cognitive development. On this view, as in Piaget's theory of cognitive development, children use a consistent level of reasoning across different domains of knowledge.

The research on theory of mind in deaf children bears on this debate. Although DH children perform poorly for their age on theory of mind tests, their performance does not seem to be due to delayed cognitive development in general. In every theory of mind study in which nonverbal IQ has been assessed, DH children have scored in the normal range (de Villiers et al. 1997; de Villiers, Pyers, and Salkind 1999; Gale et al. 1996; Peterson and Siegal 1995, 1999; Russell et al. 1998). Furthermore, two of these studies compared the average nonverbal IQs of DH children who passed false-belief tests and those who failed and found no significant difference between the false-belief passers and the false-belief failers (de Villiers et al. 1997; Peterson and Siegal 1995). Nonverbal IQ does not predict theory of mind performance in DH children, which suggests that theory of mind development is not simply a function of general level of cognitive development.

Other evidence points more directly to the domain-specificity of DH children's difficulty. Three studies have compared DH children's performance on false-belief tasks and "false photograph" tasks (de Villiers et al. 1999; Peterson and Siegal 1997, 1998). False photograph tasks, originally developed by Zaitchik (1990), are similar to false-belief tasks except that they involve physical representations of reality (photographs) rather than mental representations (beliefs). For example, the child watches as a photograph is taken of an object in one location. Before the child sees the photograph, the object is moved to a second location, and then the child is asked where the object is represented in the photograph. As in the unexpected-location false-belief task, the correct answer is the first location, even though the object is no longer there. When all extraneous task demands are controlled, as in Peterson and Siegal (1998, experiment 2), hearing 3-year-olds fail both false-belief and false-photograph tasks, whereas hearing 4-year-olds pass both types of tasks. This sort of synchrony has led some theorists (e.g., Zaitchik 1990) to argue that children's performance on representational theory of mind tests depends on their understanding of representations in general, rather than their understanding of mental representations specifically. However, this synchrony is not found in DH children. DH children perform much better on false photograph tasks than on false-belief tasks (de Villiers et al.

1999; Peterson and Siegal 1997, 1998). This finding suggests that DH children's difficulty with false-belief tasks reflects a domain-specific delay in understanding of mental representations rather than a domain-general delay in representational reasoning.

Frye, Zelazo, and Palfai (1995) propose that improvements with age in children's performance on theory of mind tests reflect developments in domain-general logical reasoning rather than developments in domain-specific knowledge. Frye et al. argue that success on representational theory of mind tests, such as false belief, representational change, and appearance–reality tasks, depends on the ability to reason using embedded rules (e.g., "if X then (if Y then Z)"), rather than on understanding of mental representation. In support of this hypothesis, Frye et al. found that hearing preschoolers' performance on a set of representational theory of mind tests was significantly positively correlated with performance on the Dimensional Change Card Sort (DCCS) task, which requires embedded rule reasoning but does not involve reasoning about mental states.

Contrary to Frye et al.'s proposal, Remmel et al. (2000) state that domain-specific understanding of mental representation appears to be the limiting factor on DH children's theory of mind performance. Remmel et al. tested DD children and DH children (average age of both groups was 9 years) on both the DCCS task and a set of theory of mind tests. As expected, the DD children performed perfectly on the DCCS task and near ceiling on the theory of mind tasks. Among the DH children, however, DCCS performance did not predict theory of mind performance. In fact, seven of the twelve DH children scored perfectly on the DCCS task, but these DH children scored at chance on the theory of mind tasks. This finding suggests that embedded rule reasoning may be necessary for success on representational theory of mind tests, but it is certainly not sufficient.

The Role of Language

In several previous sections, language has been implicated as playing a role in theory of mind development. Language and theory of mind may be related in multiple ways. Different aspects of language (e.g., narrative understanding, conversational experience, syntactic competence) may play different roles. This section examines how the research on theory of mind development in deaf children bears on some of the proposed relationships between language and theory of mind.

Language as Task Demand
One obvious way in which language and theory of mind are related is that language is used to administer theory of mind tests. Some critics (Lewis 1994; Siegal 1999) have charged that theory of mind tests really measure the child's ability to comprehend the procedure and infer the intent of the experimenter's questions, rather than theory of mind per se. This criticism is especially germane to research with DH children because they often have age-delayed language skills. Theory of mind researchers have countered this criticism by including "control questions" in their procedures, which check the child's comprehension and retention of the facts, as well as ability and willingness to answer simple questions. If a child does not answer the control questions correctly, then that child's data are not used. All

of the theory of mind studies with deaf children have included such control questions and, with one exception (Steeds et al. 1997), discarded the data of the few children who failed such questions. The use of control questions gives some assurance that the deaf children's performance, particularly the DH children's age-delayed performance, is not simply due to insufficient language skills. The fact that DH children perform well on false photograph tasks, which have equivalent linguistic complexity, provides additional indication that their difficulty with theory of mind tasks is conceptual and not simply linguistic.

Studies by Gale et al. (1996) and de Villiers and de Villiers (1999) provide additional evidence that deaf children's performance on theory of mind tests is not simply a function of linguistic task demands. These studies tested oral deaf children using theory of mind tasks with reduced linguistic demands. The "sticker-finding" task, adapted by Gale et al. (1996) from Povinelli and deBlois (1992), tests the child's understanding that a person who saw where an object (the sticker) was hidden can provide a better hint as to its location than a person who did not see (i.e., that seeing leads to knowing). Importantly, neither the hints (pointing gestures) nor the child's response (looking in a location) are linguistically demanding. In the "what face?" task described in de Villiers and de Villiers, the child is shown a series of pictures in which a person either sees that a container holds unexpected contents (e.g., a crayon box contains a key) or does not see this information. The child is then asked to choose which facial expression ("surprised" or "not surprised") the person will display upon opening the container. Pretesting with hearing preschoolers established that these tasks were similar in difficulty to standard false-belief tasks, which have greater verbal demands. Oral deaf children's performance on the sticker-finding and "what face?" tasks was equivalent to, and significantly positively correlated with, their performance on standard false-belief tasks. Although these children's performance on both types of theory of mind tasks (more verbal and less verbal) was poor for their age, linguistic task demands do not seem to be the critical factor. In general, although a certain level of linguistic competence is certainly required to pass verbal theory of mind tests, linguistic task demands do not seem to be the constraining factor on deaf children's theory of mind performance.

Language as Data for Theory Construction

Rather than simply being a constraint on children's performance on theory of mind tasks, language may play a positive causal role in the development of children's social-cognitive competence. According to the theory theory, language is an important means by which children learn about the mind. On this view, children acquire mental state concepts through social interaction, especially through participation in conversations that make reference to mental states (e.g., thoughts, feelings, desires). Research with hearing children has found that the amount of mental state talk between children and their parents and peers predicts the children's performance on false-belief tasks (Brown et al. 1996; Dunn et al. 1991; Ruffman et al. 1999).

Peterson and Siegal (1995, 1997, 1998, 1999) have consistently and cogently argued that the data on theory of mind development in deaf children are consistent with this sort of relationship between language and theory of mind. Specifically, Peterson and Siegal argue that the poor theory of mind performance of DH children is the result of the fact that DH children, unlike DD children and hearing children, do not have full access to the language used in their families. DH children's early communication with their hearing parents and peers is often limited to concrete visible referents, which excludes discussion of mental states (Meadow 1975; Meadow et al. 1981). Although more research on the nature and amount of mental state talk between DH children and their families is needed, DH children may have delayed theory of mind development because they do not receive as much data with which to construct their theories.

Language as Representational Structure

Rather than simply being the vehicle by which information about the mind is carried to the child, language may provide the necessary structure for the child to represent that information. Jill and Peter de Villiers (de Villiers 1995; de Villiers and de Villiers 1999) have argued that in English the syntactic process of complementation provides the means to represent embedded propositions (e.g., "Max thinks *the cookies are in the jar*"), in which the truth of the entire sentence does not depend on the truth of the embedded proposition. On this view, the acquisition of this syntactic feature enables the child to understand that people may hold and act upon false beliefs (e.g., that Max may look in the jar even though the cookies are in the cupboard). Embedding propositions under mental verb complements (e.g., "He thinks that X") allows the child to represent other people's mental representations—that is, to attain a representational theory of mind.

In research with hearing children and oral deaf children, de Villiers and de Villiers have accumulated evidence for this relationship between language and theory of mind. In a longitudinal study of hearing preschoolers, de Villiers and Pyers (1997) found that production of complements had a significant positive correlation with performance on false-belief tasks and was more highly correlated than were more general language measures. Furthermore, memory for complements predicted false-belief performance four months later, but false-belief performance did not predict later memory for complements, suggesting that mastery of complementation is a prerequisite for false-belief understanding. In three studies of theory of mind in oral deaf children, the de Villiers group has found that production of complements is a better predictor of theory of mind performance (on both verbal and nonverbal tasks) than more general language measures, age, nonverbal IQ, or hearing loss (de Villiers et al. 1997; de Villiers and de Villiers 1999; Gale et al. 1996).

These results indicate a tight developmental relationship between the acquisition of complementation and the acquisition of a representational theory of mind in English-speaking children. However, all these data are correlational, so the existence and direction of a causal relationship between language and theory of mind cannot be inferred (although the longitudinal data come closest). The de Villiers group is testing the effect of complementation training on theory of mind performance, but these data are not yet available (P. de Villiers, personal communication, April 16, 1999). Furthermore, it is not clear how this relationship transfers to other languages, particularly sign languages. English-style complementation is not completely natural in ASL (Pyers, personal communication, August 27, 1998). More research is needed to determine whether other syntactic features of sign language (perhaps referential shifting; Poulin 1996) show the same relationship to theory of mind development in signing deaf children as complementation appears to in oral deaf children.

Sign Language and Theory of Mind

The previous proposals regarding the relationship between language and theory of mind were originally developed in the context of hearing children and spoken language. Courtin and Melot (1998; Courtin 2000) have proposed that some of the unique features of sign language may have a beneficial effect on theory of mind development. Certain syntactic features of sign language require the manipulation of multiple perspectives. For example, a signer may use referential shifts to take the perspectives of different characters in a story (Poulin 1996). Courtin and Melot suggest that exposure to and use of sign language may accelerate the development of spatial and visual perspective-taking skills in signing deaf children, particularly DD children. As discussed earlier, the ability to consider other people's perspectives is an important part of theory of mind development. Therefore, Courtin and Melot argue, native signing children may show earlier theory of mind development than hearing speaking children.[6] Courtin's (2000) evidence that signing DD children outperform hearing children on false-belief tasks is consistent with this proposal, although more research using other theory of mind tests is needed.

New Research Directions

Researchers have only scratched the surface of the topic of deaf children's theory of mind development. The existing research has largely focused on deaf children's understanding of false belief. Although important, this focus has left many areas of deaf children's theory of mind knowledge unexplored (see Flavell and Miller 1998 for a review of the research on theory of mind in hearing children). A recent study by Remmel et al. (2000) examined one of these other areas: deaf children's understanding of aspectuality.

Aspectuality refers to the fact that people's experience of the world is composed of various perceptual properties, or "aspects," such as color and weight. Understanding of aspectuality refers to an understanding of how perceptual access in different sensory modalities, such as vision or touch, leads to knowledge of different aspects of the world. For example, looking at an object leads to knowledge of its color, but touching the object does not. Understanding of aspectuality (i.e., of the modality-specific nature of the relationship between perception and knowledge) typically appears around age 4 in hearing children (O'Neill, Astington, and Flavell 1992; Pillow 1993), although slightly earlier competence has been found under some circumstances (Remmel 1999).

Remmel et al. (2000) tested understanding of aspectuality in DD children and DH children (average age of both groups was 9 years). All the children attended a bilingual/bicultural school for the deaf and used ASL as their primary mode of

---

6. Courtin and Melot (1998) also predict that hearing children of signing deaf parents may show earlier theory of mind development than hearing children of hearing parents. This prediction remains untested.

communication. Remmel et al. focused on the children's understanding of vision and touch as sources of knowledge because these seem to be the most important modalities for deaf children's knowledge acquisition. On each test trial, the child was presented with one of two pairs of objects. One pair differed visually (in color) but not tactilely. The other pair differed tactilely (in weight) but not visually. On some trials (the "action choice" trials), the experimenter hid one of the objects in a box and then asked the child to find out which one was in the box by either looking or feeling inside. On these trials, the child demonstrates understanding of aspectuality by choosing to look when the objects differ visually and to feel when the objects differ tactilely. On other trials (the "knowledge assessment" trials), the child hid one of the objects in the box and then watched as another person either looked or felt inside the box. The child was then asked whether the other person now knows which object is in the box. On these trials, the child demonstrates understanding of aspectuality by attributing knowledge to the other person only when the objects differ visually and the person looks inside or when the objects differ tactilely and the person feels inside.

The DD children performed well on these tests, whereas the DH children performed at chance levels. The high level of performance of the DD children was expected, given their age and the unimpaired theory of mind performance of DD children in previous studies (Courtin 2000; Courtin and Melot 1998; Peterson and Siegal 1997, 1999). The poor performance of the DH children, however, indicates that an understanding of how perception in different modalities leads to knowledge of different aspects of the world requires more than just sensory experience in those modalities. Instead, as Perner (1991) argues, understanding of aspectuality also requires an understanding of mental representation, which seems to be delayed in DH children.

CONCLUSIONS

The existing research on theory of mind development in deaf children can be largely summarized in the following sentence: DH children (but not DD children) show a delay (but not a permanent deficit) in understanding of mental representation (but not in understanding of physical representation). This sentence, however, contains a number of important distinctions and implications. The fact that DD children do not show delayed theory of mind development indicates that neither the absence of auditory input nor the use of sign language (versus spoken language) causes delayed theory of mind development. In fact, as Courtin and Melot (1998) argue, the use of sign language may promote theory of mind development. The fact that DH children do not have as much difficulty with tests of equivalent logical and linguistic complexity in other domains (e.g., false photograph tasks) indicates that their difficulty with tests of understanding of mental representation is not simply due to delayed cognitive development in general or to linguistic task demands. Finally, the fact that many DH children seem to lack an understanding of mental representation does not indicate that they lack a theory of mind altogether. It does suggest, however, that many DH individuals may possess a nonrepresentational theory of mind, such as a desire psychology, until adolescence or perhaps even adulthood.

The cause or causes of this delay are not clear, but the fact that DH children, unlike DD children or hearing children, lack full access to the language used in their families seems to be important. It may be important because it reduces the opportunities for the child to discuss and learn about mental states. It may also be important because it delays the child's acquisition of syntactic structures of sufficient complexity to represent other people's mental representations. In general, the fact that deaf children's theory of mind development seems to depend more on their social and linguistic experience than on their chronological age supports the theory theory over the modular view of theory of mind development.

Parental hearing status and method of education both affect the deaf child's social and linguistic experience, and both seem to be related to deaf children's theory of mind development. DD children outperform DH children on theory of mind tests (Courtin 2000; Courtin and Melot 1998; Peterson and Siegal 1997, 1999; Remmel et al. 2000), and signing DH children seem to outperform oral DH children, although there is less evidence on the latter point (Courtin 2000; Courtin and Melot 1998). Future studies need to consider, measure, and report these variables, as well as hearing loss (degree, age of onset, and aided hearing levels if aids are used) and socioeconomic status. In particular, future studies should control for socioeconomic status, given the relationship between socioeconomic status and theory of mind development observed in hearing children (Holmes et al. 1996).

All of the existing research assumes that theory of mind development in deaf children follows the same course as that found in hearing children, although the rate of development may differ. That is, it is assumed that deaf children's theory of mind development may be accelerated or delayed, relative to that of hearing children, but that the goal state is the same. This assumption deserves to be questioned, given (a) the evidence of cultural variation in theory of mind (Lillard 1998; admittedly, this evidence is controversial and based largely on ethnographic report rather than experimental research), and (b) the growing recognition of Deafness as a cultural identity (hence the capital "D") rather than just an audiological condition (Parasnis 1996). The Clark et al. (1996) study is an important first step, but more research on theory of mind in deaf adults, particularly those who identify themselves as culturally Deaf, is sorely needed. If there is a distinct Deaf theory of mind, then Deaf children's theory of mind development may follow a different course from that of hearing children, in which case terms such as "accelerated" and "delayed" become somewhat moot. From a theoretical perspective, any evidence that theory of mind development is shaped by culture and not determined by biology would be strong evidence for the theory theory against the modular view.

The existing research on theory of mind development in deaf children has focused on basic theoretical questions specific to theory of mind. Future research should explore the links between social cognition and actual social behavior in deaf children. In the theory of mind research with hearing children, these links have always been assumed but only recently confirmed. For example, false belief understanding is correlated with social interaction skills in hearing children (Watson et al. 1999). Future research should also explore how parents, educators, and policymakers can promote theory of mind development in deaf children. The existing research highlights the importance of linguistic stimulation in an accessible modality (i.e., signed rather than spoken language) at as early an age as possible. Discussion of mental states (e.g., thoughts, feelings, desires) may be particularly beneficial for theory of mind development. For example, parents' reference to other people's feelings during disciplinary situations predicts false belief understanding in hearing preschoolers (Ruffman et al. 1999).

Research on theory of mind development in deaf children has the potential to inform many other areas of research on deafness and cognition. Developments in theory of mind may underlie the development of many abilities that involve social cognition, including story understanding (Gray and Hosie 1996), symbolic play (Spencer 1996), role-taking ability (Cates and Shontz 1990; Kusché and Greenberg 1983), and referential communication (MacKay-Soroka, Trehub, and Thorpe 1987). Consideration of the common conceptual basis of these abilities will provide a more complete picture of the developing deaf child. The authors hope that inclusion of this chapter in this volume will help to integrate the theory of mind research into the larger context of deafness and cognition.

References

Baron-Cohen, S. 1995. *Mindblindness: An essay on autism and theory of mind.* Cambridge, Mass.: MIT Press.

Baron-Cohen, S., A. M. Leslie, and U. Frith. 1985. Does the autistic child have a theory of mind? *Cognition* 21:37–46.

Bartsch, K., and H. M. Wellman. 1995. *Children talk about the mind.* New York: Pergamon Press.

Brown, J. R., N. Donelan-McCall, and J. Dunn. 1996. Why talk about mental states? The significance of children's conversations with friends, siblings, and mothers. *Child Development* 67:836–49.

Cates, D. S., and F. C. Shontz. 1990. Role-taking ability and social behavior in deaf school children. *American Annals of the Deaf* 135:217–21.

Clark, M. D., P. J. Schwanenflugel, V. S. Everhart, and M. Bartini. 1996. Theory of mind in deaf adults and the organization of verbs of knowing. *Journal of Deaf Studies and Deaf Education* 1:179–89.

Courtin, C. 1998. Surdité, langue des signes et développement cognitif. Ph.D. diss., Paris University, France.

———. 2000. The impact of sign language on the cognitive development of deaf children: The case of theories of mind. *Journal of Deaf Studies and Deaf Education* 5:266–76.

———. Forthcoming. Is false-belief attribution a litmus test for estimating theories of mind? Negative evidence from conceptual perspective-taking abilities in second-generation deaf children. Manuscript submitted for publication.

Courtin, C., and A.-M. Melot. 1998. Development of theories of mind in deaf children. In *Psychological perspectives on deafness,* ed. M. Marschark and M. D. Clark, 79–102. Mahwah, N.J.: Lawrence Erlbaum.

de Villiers, J. 1995. Steps in the mastery of sentence complements. Paper presented at the biennial meeting of the Society for Research in Child Development, March, in Indianapolis, Ind.

de Villiers, J. G., and P. A. de Villiers. 1999. Linguistic determinism and the understanding of false beliefs. In *Children's reasoning and the mind*, ed. H. P. Mitchell and K. Riggs. Hove, U.K.: Psychology Press.

de Villiers, J., and J. Pyers. 1997. Complementing cognition: The relationship between language and theory of mind. In *Proceedings of the Twenty-first Annual Boston University Conference on Language Development*, ed. E. Hughes, M. Hughes, and A. Greehill, 138–47. Somerville, Mass.: Cascadilla Press.

de Villiers, P. A., B. Hosler, K. Miller, M. Whalen, and J. Wong. 1997. Language, theory of mind, and reading other people's emotions: A study of oral deaf children. Poster presented at the biennial meeting of the Society for Research in Child Development, April, in Washington, D.C.

de Villiers, P. A., J. Pyers, and S. Salkind. 1999. Language-delayed deaf children understand "false" photographs but not false beliefs. Poster presented at the biennial meeting of the Society for Research in Child Development, April, in Albuquerque, N.M.

Dretske, F. 1988. *Explaining behavior: Reasons in a world of causes.* Cambridge, Mass.: MIT Press.

Dunn, J., J. Brown, C. Slomkowski, C. Tesla, and L. Youngblade. 1991. Young children's understanding of other people's feelings and beliefs: Individual differences and their antecedents. *Child Development* 62:1352–66.

Emmorey, K. 1994. Sign language. In *Encyclopedia of human behavior* 4:193–204. New York: Academic Press.

Flavell, J. H., E. R. Flavell, and F. L. Green. 1983. Development of the appearance-reality distinction. *Cognitive Psychology* 15:95–120.

Flavell, J. H., and P. H. Miller. 1998. Social cognition. In *Handbook of child psychology: Cognition, perception, and language*, vol. 2, 5th ed., ed. D. Kuhn and R. S. Siegler, 851–98. New York: Wiley.

Fodor, J. A. 1983. *Modularity of mind: An essay on faculty psychology.* Cambridge, Mass.: MIT Press.

Frye, D., P. D. Zelazo, and T. Palfai. 1995. Theory of mind and rule-based reasoning. *Cognitive Development* 10:483–527.

Gale, E., P. de Villiers, J. de Villiers, and J. Pyers. 1996. Language and theory of mind in oral deaf children. In *Proceedings of the Twentieth Annual Boston University Conference on Language Development*, vol. 1, ed. A. Stringfellow, D. Cahana-Amitay, E. Hughes, and A. Zukowski. Somerville, Mass.: Cascadilla Press.

Gopnik, A., and J. W. Astington. 1988. Children's understanding of representational change and its relation to the understanding of false belief and the appearance-reality distinction. *Child Development* 59:26–37.

Gopnik, A., and A. N. Meltzoff. 1997. *Words, thoughts, and theories.* Cambridge, Mass.: MIT Press.

Gopnik, A., and H. M. Wellman. 1994. The theory theory. In *Mapping the mind: Domain specificity in cognition and culture*, ed. L. A. Hirschfeld and S. A. Gelman, 257–93. Cambridge, U.K.: Cambridge University Press.

Gray, C. D., and J. A. Hosie. 1996. Deafness, story understanding, and theory of mind. *Journal of Deaf Studies and Deaf Education* 1:217–33.

Happe, F. G. E. 1995. The role of age and verbal ability in the theory of mind task performance of subjects with autism. *Child Development* 66:843–55.

Heider, F. 1958. *The psychology of interpersonal relations.* New York: Wiley.

Hoff-Ginsberg, E. 1997. *Language development*. Pacific Grove, Calif.: Brooks/Cole.

Holmes, H. A., C. Black, and S. A. Miller. 1996. A cross-task comparison of false-belief understanding in a Head Start population. *Journal of Experimental Child Psychology* 63:263–85.

Jenkins, J. M., and J. W. Astington. 1996. Cognitive factors and family structure associated with theory of mind development in young children. *Developmental Psychology* 32:70–78.

Kusché, C. A., and M. T. Greenberg. 1983. Evaluative understanding and role-taking ability: A comparison of deaf and hearing children. *Child Development* 54:141–47.

Leslie, A. M. 1994. Pretending and believing: Issues in the theory of ToMM. *Cognition* 50:211–38.

Lewis, C. 1994. Episodes, events, and narratives in the child's understanding of mind. In *Children's early understanding of mind: Origins and development*, ed. C. Lewis and P. Mitchell, 457–80. Hillsdale, N.J.: Lawrence Erlbaum.

Lillard, A. 1998. Ethnopsychologies: Cultural variations in theories of mind. *Psychological Bulletin* 123:3–32.

MacKay-Soroka, S., S. E. Trehub, and L. A. Thorpe. 1987. Deaf children's referential messages to mother. *Child Development* 58:385–94.

Marschark, M. 1993. *Psychological development of deaf children*. New York: Oxford University Press.

Meadow, K. P. 1975. The development of deaf children. In *Review of child development research*, Vol. 5, ed. E. M. Hetherington, 441–508. Chicago: University of Chicago Press.

Meadow, K. P., M. T. Greenberg, C. Erting, and H. Carmichael. 1981. Interactions of deaf mothers and deaf preschool children: Comparison with three other groups of deaf and hearing dyads. *American Annals of the Deaf* 126: 454–68.

O'Neill, D. K., J. W. Astington, and J. H. Flavell. 1992. Young children's understanding of the role that sensory experiences play in knowledge acquisition. *Child Development* 63:474–90.

Parasnis, I., ed. 1996. *Cultural and language diversity and the deaf experience*. Cambridge, U.K.: Cambridge University Press.

Perner, J. 1991. *Understanding the representational mind*. Cambridge, Mass.: MIT Press.

Peterson, C. C., and M. Siegal. 1995. Deafness, conversation, and theory of mind. *Journal of Child Psychology and Psychiatry* 36:459–74.

———. 1997. Domain specificity and everyday biological, physical, and psychological thinking in normal, autistic, and deaf children. In *The emergence of core domains of thought*, ed. H. M. Wellman and K. Inagaki, 55–70. San Francisco: Jossey-Bass.

———. 1998. Changing focus on the representational mind: Deaf, autistic, and normal children's concepts of false photos, false drawings, and false beliefs. *British Journal of Developmental Psychology* 16:301–20.

———. 1999. Representing inner worlds: Theory of mind in autistic, deaf, and normal hearing children. *Psychological Science* 10:126–29.

Pillow, B. H. 1993. Preschool children's understanding of the relationship between modality of perceptual access and knowledge of perceptual properties. *British Journal of Developmental Psychology* 11:371–89.

Poulin, C. 1996. Manipulation of discourse spaces in American Sign Language. In *Conceptual structure, discourse, and language,* ed. A. Goldberg, 421–33. Stanford, Calif.: CSLI Publications.

Povinelli, D. J., and S. deBlois. 1992. Young children's (Homo sapiens) understanding of knowledge formation in themselves and others. *Journal of Comparative Psychology* 106:228–38.

Remmel, E. 1999. Source memory and source knowledge in preschool children: Understanding of aspectuality develops around age 3½. Poster presented at the biennial meeting of the Society for Research in Child Development, April 15–18, Albuquerque, N.M.

Remmel, E., J. G. Bettger, A. M. Weinberg, S. Novotny, and A. A. Eberwein. 2000. The relationships between theory of mind, executive function, and parental hearing status in signing deaf children. Manuscript submitted for publication.

Ross, L. 1977. The intuitive psychologist and his shortcomings: Distortions in the attribution process. In *Advances in experimental social psychology,* ed. L. Berkowitz, 10:173–220. New York: Academic Press.

Ross, L., and A. Ward. 1996. Naive realism in everyday life: Implications for social conflict and misunderstanding. In *Values and knowledge,* ed. T. Brown, E. Reed, and E. Turiel, 103–35. Hillsdale, N.J.: Lawrence Erlbaum.

Ruffman, T., J. Perner, and L. Parkin. 1999. How parenting style affects false-belief development. *Social Development* 8:395–411.

Russell, P. A., J. A. Hosie, C. D. Gray, C. Scott, N. Hunter, J. S. Banks, and M. C. Macaulay. 1998. The development of theory of mind in deaf children. *Journal of Child Psychology and Psychiatry* 39:903–10.

Scholl, B. J., and A. M. Leslie. 1999. Modularity, development, and "theory of mind." *Mind and Language* 4:131–53.

Siegal, M. 1999. Language and thought: The fundamental significance of conversational awareness for cognitive development. *Developmental Science* 2:1–14.

Spencer, P. E. 1996. The association between language and symbolic play at two years: Evidence from deaf toddlers. *Child Development* 67:867–76.

Steeds, L., K. Rowe, and A. Dowker. 1997. Deaf children's understanding of beliefs and desires. *Journal of Deaf Studies and Deaf Education* 2:185–95.

Stich, S. P. 1983. *From folk psychology to cognitive science: The case against belief.* Cambridge, Mass.: MIT Press.

Stich, S., and S. Nichols. 1998. Theory theory to the max: A critical notice of Gopnik and Meltzoff's *Words, thoughts, and theories. Mind and Language* 13:421–49.

Watson, A. C., C. L. Nixon, A. Wilson, and L. Capage. 1999. Social interaction skills and theory of mind in young children. *Developmental Psychology* 35:386–91.

Wellman, H. M. 1990. *The child's theory of mind.* Cambridge, Mass.: MIT Press.

Wellman, H. M., and S. A. Gelman.1998. Knowledge acquisition in foundational domains. In *Handbook of child psychology: Cognition, perception, and language,* Vol. 2, 5th ed., ed. D. Kuhn and R. S. Siegler, 523–73. New York: Wiley.

Wimmer, H., and J. Perner. 1983. Beliefs about beliefs: Representation and constraining function of wrong beliefs in young children's understanding of deception. *Cognition* 13:103–28.

Zaitchik, D. 1990. When representations conflict with reality: The preschooler's problem with false beliefs and "false" photographs. *Cognition* 35:41–68.

9

EMOTIONAL DEVELOPMENT IN DEAF CHILDREN: FACIAL EXPRESSIONS, DISPLAY RULES, AND THEORY OF MIND

Colin D. Gray, Judith A. Hosie,

Phil A. Russell, and Ellen A. Ormel

Little is known about emotional development in deaf children. The psychology of deafness has been comparatively slow to benefit from the vigorous research programs on emotional development that, in recent years, have transformed mainstream developmental psychology. Since the fifties, there have been reports that prelingually deaf children raised in a spoken language environment have difficulties with their emotional and social development. The real nature of these difficulties, however, is unclear, and there are many potential confounding variables, both contextual and methodological. There are, however, some recurring themes. Problems with empathy and impulsive control, for example, have frequently been reported (Bachara, Raphael, and Phelan 1980; Greenberg and Kusché 1993; Levine 1956, 1960; Levine and Wagner 1974; Odom, Blanton, and Laukhuf 1973). Later work has set the emotional life of deaf children in the broader contexts of communication and parent–child interaction. For example, Calderon and Greenberg (1993) have studied their emotional development within families. To date, however, there have been few controlled investigations of emotional development in deaf children, and it is the purpose of this chapter to present some recent experimental work.

The question of how deaf children acquire emotional understanding is one of some urgency. The recognition and labeling of those emotions that are most clearly reflected in facial expressions are correlated with measures of social competence (Custrini and Feldman 1989), as well as with popularity and social likeability (Denham and Burton 1996; Denham et al. 1990; Nowicki and Duke 1992). In hearing children, emotional understanding, social development, and intellectual growth have all been shown to be closely linked (Nowicki and Duke 1992). The attention paid to emotional understanding in intervention programs designed to

The research described in this chapter was funded by the Economic and Social Research Council grant #R000236273. The authors wish to thank William P. Brown, Diane Clark, Michael Karchmer, and Marc Marschark for reading the manuscript and making so many helpful comments. We are grateful to Christeen Scott and Norma Hunter for gathering the data with such care and thoroughness. We also wish to thank Mairi Macaulay, Margaret Falconer, Joan Grant, and the other teachers at the Aberdeen School for the Deaf for their unfailing support and encouragement.

facilitate social adjustment (Denham and Burton 1996; Greenberg and Kusché 1993) is further testimony to its importance for success in school.

In the United Kingdom, following the strong endorsement of "mainstreaming" by the Warnock Committee (1978), the emphasis has been moving away from the specialized school for the deaf toward the provision of extra help for deaf children in ordinary schools. With deaf children, however, the success of mainstreaming is likely to depend at least partly upon the extent to which they adjust emotionally and socially to their new environment.

THE COMPLEX NATURE OF EMOTIONAL UNDERSTANDING

The development of emotional understanding is, as stated earlier, an integral part of a child's personal, social, and intellectual development (Barrett 1993; Barrett and Campos 1987; Campos, Campos, and Barrett 1989; Goleman 1995; Jenkins, Oatley, and Stein 1998; Salovey and Mayer 1990). However, emotional understanding has several components. Some, such as the identification of facial expressions of emotion and the interpretation of voice tone, are perceptual, in the sense that they require the presence of a physical stimulus (a real or pictured face, the sound of a voice). Others, however, are inferential in nature and do not depend on the presence of any particular physical stimulus. Empathy, for example, can be achieved through various channels of communication: direct conversation, watching a film or play, reading a story, or correspondence by letter or e-mail. Many other aspects of emotional life are similarly nonspecific to any particular medium.

The authors examined those aspects of children's emotional understanding that involve the identification of emotional expressions, the understanding of the causes of different expressions, and the knowledge and use of display rules. The children's understanding, however, was also considered in the wider context of social cognition. For this reason, we also decided to explore the children's performance on tests of theory of mind and related functions, such as the ability to ascertain another person's mental state from their line of regard.

LINGUISTIC BACKGROUND AND EDUCATION: AN IMPORTANT DISTINCTION

The education of deaf children is a field fraught with controversy, with no general agreement on the best strategy. In different parts of the same country, deaf children may experience quite different school regimes, according to the prevailing philosophy of the local authority. This heterogeneity makes it difficult to generalize from a study with deaf children from any particular school because what is true of them may not be true of deaf children elsewhere. Another crucial consideration is the child's linguistic background. The experience of a deaf child of deaf parents (DD), particularly signing deaf parents, differs in many important respects from that of a deaf child with hearing parents (DH).[1] A growing body of ev-

---

1. Following convention, the term *DD* here denotes a deaf child of deaf parents, and *DH* a deaf child of hearing parents.

idence indicates that this distinction is an important one, with profound implications for a deaf child's development. There is also good reason to think that early access to language, whether sign language or the prevailing spoken language of the community, is of crucial importance for development. Some approaches may promote this access more effectively than others. The authors' own experience has largely been with DH children, educated according to the total communication philosophy. Our findings do not always agree with those of studies that have used DD children or those educated in bilingual schools, in which natural sign language is the official school medium.

IDENTIFICATION AND INTERPRETATION OF FACIAL EXPRESSIONS OF EMOTION

Studies of the face-processing abilities of hearing infants indicate that, from an early age, they can discriminate among faces with different emotional expressions. By the age of 3 months, they can distinguish among photographs of expressions of surprise, anger, and sadness (Young-Browne, Rosenfeld, and Horowitz 1977). Additionally, they can distinguish smiling from frowning expressions (Barrerra and Maurer 1981) and can discriminate among expressions of happiness with different intensities (Kuchuk, Vibbert, and Bornstein 1986). Although the infants' performance at this age is impressive, it is believed that the emotional significance of different expressions is not fully understood until about the age of 7 months (Kestenbaum and Nelson 1990). Moreover, it is not until approximately 9 months of age that the infant begins to use the emotional expressions of others as social signals, a phenomenon known as *social referencing* (Feinman 1992).

The fact that infants can discriminate among different facial expressions within the first year of life by no means implies that their understanding of facial expressions is fully developed. On the contrary, children's understanding of expressions, as reflected in their ability to comprehend and produce labels for them and to match them to emotive situations, improves throughout childhood (Borke 1971, 1973; Brody and Harrison 1987; Gross and Ballif 1991; Michalson and Lewis 1985; Mood, Johnson, and Shantz 1978). For example, although hearing children as young as 2 years of age can, to some extent, sort photographs of facial expressions of emotion into different categories (Bullock and Russell 1984, 1985; Russell and Bullock 1986), they find some emotions, particularly anger, more difficult to identify than others, such as joy and sadness (Carlson, Felleman, and Masters 1983; Denham 1986a, 1986b; Ireson and Shields 1982; Michalson and Lewis 1985; Reichenbach and Masters 1983; Walden 1991). Tests of the ability to name different facial expressions have also shown that children have difficulty in producing and comprehending labels for the emotions of disgust, surprise, and fear (Harrigan 1984; Markham and Adams 1992; Michalson and Lewis 1985). The remainder of this section describes studies of DH children's perception of facial expressions of emotion and the extent to which they can match such expressions appropriately to emotive situations.

Deaf Children's Identification and Labeling of Emotional Facial Expressions

Considering first the identification of emotional facial expressions, two contradictory hypotheses can be advanced. On the one hand, one might argue that because they rely heavily upon visual information, deaf children develop a heightened sensitivity to the meanings of facial expressions. Another consideration is that during their school years, DH children acquire natural sign language, in which stylized facial expressions of emotion have a phonemic (or cheremic) function, as when the eyebrows are used to mark questions or to denote attitude (Deuchar 1984; Kyle and Woll 1985). It is possible that this use of facial expressions as linguistic markers may refine and enhance deaf children's knowledge and understanding of the emotions concerned. Thus, one might predict that in tests involving the discrimination of facial expressions of emotion, deaf children would perform better than hearing children.

An alternative argument is that although the interpretation of facial expressions of emotion is considered to be a nonverbal skill, it usually develops within an auditory, linguistic context. Therefore an alternative hypothesis, diametrically opposed to the first, is that loss of auditory input during infancy has a detrimental effect upon DH children's ability to identify facial expressions of emotion. Research suggests that the voice and the human face may be inextricably linked during early mother–infant communication (Locke 1993). Not only do hearing infants prefer to look at faces that make speechlike vocalizations (Kuhl and Meltzhoff 1982), but their understanding of static facial expressions (e.g., joy and anger) is also facilitated by the presence of auditory information that matches the expressions in emotional tone (Phillips et al. 1990; Walker-Andrews and Lennon 1991). Toward the end of the second year of development, dyadic exchanges between young children and their parents, other adults, siblings, and peers enable them to observe others' expressions and listen to how such expressions are interpreted. Thus, early social interactions play a vital role in facilitating children's acquisition and use of vocabulary relating to emotional states (Bretherton et al. 1986; Dunn, Bretherton, and Munn 1987).

There is little doubt that lack of auditory input causes difficulties in communication between hearing mothers and their deaf infants. The natural reciprocity of mother–infant interaction is more difficult to achieve, and the synchronization of behavior is often problematic because deaf infants must shift their attention from the environment to their mother in order to receive her communications (Wood et al. 1986). These difficulties may account for the relatively low frequency and duration of the interactions observed between deaf infants and their hearing mothers (Lederberg and Mobley 1990; Wedell-Monnig and Lumley 1980). It is also likely that during the preschool years, DH children will have less exposure to emotional language simply through being unable to overhear other people talk. They probably also receive fewer and less complex explanations of their own and other people's emotional displays, at least until a common language has developed. Hearing members of deaf children's families rarely have sufficient fluency in sign language to instruct them on the need for emotional dissembling or to engage in conversations about abstract mental states (Marschark 1993).

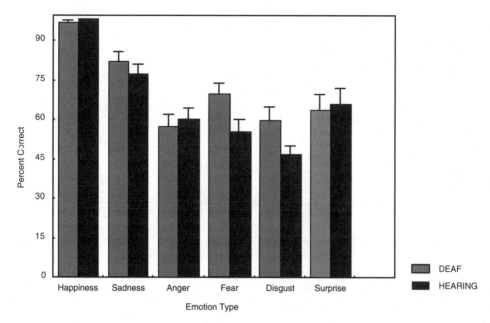

Figure 1. Percentage Correct Performance of Deaf and Hearing Children on Tasks Measuring Understanding of Emotional Expressions. (The vertical error bars represent one standard error of the mean.)

Producing and Comprehending Emotional Labels

The authors asked two groups of hearing and DH children of elementary school age (of mean ages 6 years and 11 years, respectively) to match photographs of facial expressions of happiness, sadness, anger, fear, disgust, and surprise and to produce and explain labels for them. Accuracy data showed comparable mean overall levels of performance for deaf and hearing children of the same age. Figure 1 shows that in both the deaf and hearing groups, happiness and sadness were the most accurately perceived emotions: The children achieved markedly lower levels of accuracy with anger, disgust, and surprise.

Error data revealed that children in both groups confused anger with disgust, and fear with surprise. The younger groups of deaf and hearing children, however, also showed a tendency to confuse the negative expressions of anger, disgust, and fear with sadness. These results suggest that the understanding of facial expressions of emotion is closely similar in deaf and hearing children.

This study's most important finding was that despite their early sensory loss, DH children are able to match photographs of expressions, as well as produce and comprehend labels for pictures of expressions, as well as hearing children. Moreover, although it is clear from figure 1 that the children in either group found some emotional expressions more difficult to comprehend than others, the order of difficulty was similar for both groups, with happiness and sadness being the easiest and disgust and surprise the most difficult.

The patterns of the errors that the children made were especially revealing because they suggest that DH children and hearing children have much the same conceptual understanding of these emotions. For example, the youngest deaf and hearing children often used "sadness" as a label for expressions of disgust and anger. This finding is consistent with the view that young children tend to use sadness as a catch-all or default category until they have learned to discriminate among the unique elicitors and distinctive features of the different negative expressions (Russell and Bullock 1986).

Identification of Emotions Experienced by Story Characters

Although facial expressions are often studied in isolation, they are generated and transmitted in a social context. For this reason, we decided to study the same children's ability to link the primary expressions of emotion to the feelings of a protagonist in various emotive situations arising in stories. This method of studying emotional response and understanding has been widely used with hearing children (Gross and Ballif 1991). However, some DH children have difficulty in understanding stories, whether written or signed (Banks, Gray, and Fyfe 1990; Gray et al.1992; Gray and Hosie 1996).[2] Rather than proper "stories," therefore, simple scenarios, or vignettes, were used; these were compiled after careful consultation with the teachers at the Aberdeen School for the Deaf to ensure that all vocabulary, settings, and events were familiar to the children in the study.

Previous studies examining deaf children's ability to match facial expressions of emotion to short emotion-arousing scenarios present a rather disappointing picture of the empathic abilities of DH children (Bachara et al. 1980; Odom et al. 1973). Odom et al. (1973) asked 7- to 8-year-old deaf and hearing children to identify the emotional states of cartoon characters depicted in various emotive situations by making selections from an array of photographs of faces bearing emotional expressions. The deaf children found it more difficult to select the right photographs. On the other hand, the deaf and hearing children were equally good at sorting photographs into a given set of emotion categories.

Odom et al. (1973) studied only the incidence of *correct* responses. Arguably, the kinds of *errors* that children make also offer insight into the categories they are using when they are making their assignments (Bullock and Russell 1984; Russell 1980; Russell and Bullock 1985, 1986; Russell, Suzuki, and Ishida 1993). With the exception of Bullock and Russell (1984) and Russell and Bullock (1986), few studies have examined children's errors in detail. According to Russell and Bullock's (1986) model, children should tend to confuse emotions that are similar in the levels of arousal and pleasure with which they are associated. Their experiments

---

2. It is not, of course, claimed that this is true of all deaf children, among whom, as with hearing children, there is great variation.

confirmed this prediction: Surprise was confused with fear, and anger was confused with disgust.

Given the similar levels of performance of the hearing and deaf children in the study of facial expressions, we decided to compare their ability to link expressions to emotive stories. This experiment differed from previous work in several important respects:

1.   The youngest deaf (and hearing) children (5- to 7-year-olds) were younger than those in previous studies: Bachara et al. (1980) used preadolescents who were at least 9 years old; the children in Odom et al. (1973) were 7 to 8 years old.

2.   The deaf and hearing children's performance was compared on six different emotions considered separately.

3.   Photographs of children's faces were taken especially for the study.

Two groups of hearing and deaf children of elementary school age (7 years and 11 years) took part in the study. The children were asked to match facial expressions of happiness, sadness, anger, fear, disgust, and surprise to the feelings of a protagonist in a series of emotion-arousing vignettes. In one story, for example, Mary has gone outside to play with her new balloon, but the wind has whipped it away from her.

A story consisted of four events, each illustrated with a drawing. In the balloon story, the first drawing showed Mary's father giving her the balloon. The second showed her playing with the balloon in the yard, while the third showed her running with the balloon on a string. The fourth showed her looking on helplessly as the balloon was being carried away.

Each episode was signed to the child, and the illustrative picture was then presented. After the final picture had been presented, the child was asked to show what the protagonist's face would look like by selecting one of six photographs. The child was then asked to label the chosen face. Finally, the child was asked to explain why that face had been chosen.

The hearing children assigned appropriate facial expressions to the story characters significantly more accurately than did the deaf children, in agreement with the findings of Odom et al. (1973). The results also showed that the performance of both deaf and hearing children improved with age and that some facial expressions (happiness, sadness, and disgust) were more accurately assigned than others (surprise, fear, and anger).

Sometimes a child interpreted a story as evoking a different emotion from the one intended. For example, the child, on receiving what was supposed to be an anger-evoking story, might point to the face with the sad expression, label it as "sad," and explain this choice by saying, "Because it's a sad story." (This happened most frequently with the youngest deaf children.) Both deaf and hearing children, however, showed a tendency to interpret anger-eliciting stories as evoking sadness. The younger groups of deaf and hearing children also showed a tendency to associate sadness with fear-eliciting stories and happiness with surprise-eliciting stories. Although the deaf children were less accurate than hearing children at assigning facial expressions, the similarity of the score profiles of the two groups of children suggests that their interpretations of the emotions aroused by the stories were also similar.

The most interesting outcome of the research reported in this section is that, despite probable differences in their early socialization of emotion, DH children and hearing children are strikingly similar in their understanding of the facial expressions of happiness, sadness, anger, fear, disgust, and surprise. Specifically, deaf and hearing children share a common understanding of the features that distinguish these expressions, the labels associated with them, and the events that give rise to them.

The close parallel in performance between the deaf and hearing children raises several questions. The first relates to the selection of facial expressions used. Happiness, sadness, anger, fear, disgust, and surprise are all emotions for which clear and unambiguous facial expressions exist (Ekman 1984; Ekman and Friesen 1976; Ekman and Oster 1979; Izard 1971). On this basis, one might take the view that children's initial understanding of emotion is anchored to these expressions, which may be part of a biologically based signalling system (Buck 1988; Ekman 1984; Izard and Malatesta 1987). Assuming this interpretation is correct, experience may still play a role in a child's acquisition of emotional understanding, even at the perceptual level. The role of such experience, however, may be to activate an existing system rather than to build a new one. Therefore, quite different experiential histories may have exactly the same effect, explaining how the supposedly different experiences of DH and hearing children could result in similar performance profiles in the children of both groups.

Another interpretation, however, is that because all children produce (and recognize) certain basic facial expressions of emotion during the first year of life, these expressions are likely to be labeled and discussed. Thus, even if deaf children raised in a spoken language environment are deprived of opportunities to engage in many conversations about emotion, the conversations that do take place are likely to revolve around those emotions for which there are distinctive facial expressions. This may be the reason why deaf and hearing children share a common understanding of these expressions and the events that give rise to them.

UNDERSTANDING AND USE OF DISPLAY RULES

During the elementary school years, hearing children's emotional development moves rapidly beyond an understanding of the facial expressions of happiness, sadness, anger, fear, disgust, and surprise. Specifically, children begin to demonstrate an appreciation of *display rules* (Ekman, Friesen, and Ellsworth 1972)—that is, the principles governing the circumstances in which emotions may (or may not) be expressed and the correct ways of expressing them. For example, although one may be disappointed (even annoyed) by a loss in a competitive game, one is expected to be gracious in defeat, to avoid expressing one's disappointment, and to congratulate the winner in a pleasant manner. The winner, on the other hand, is expected to refrain from unseemly exultation and to try to sweeten the pill of defeat for the loser by intoning some phrase such as "Close game" or "I was really lucky."

There is evidence that the degree to which children have acquired display rules is a good indicator of their general level of social maturity. Garner (1996) observed that the prosocial behavior of a group of third- and fourth-grade hearing children, as measured by the Prosocial Behaviour Questionnaire (Weir and Duveen 1981), was positively correlated with their actual use of display rules (e.g., smiling and saying "thank you" on receiving an undesirable gift).

Development of Display Rules

The use of display rules presupposes an awareness of the difference between felt and expressed emotion (Saarni 1993). This awareness is evident even in very young hearing children who, at 3 or 4 years of age, inhibit the expression of emotion in certain social situations: For example, on receiving an unwanted present, they conceal their disappointment (Cole 1986).

Harris (1989) argues that although children's early use of display rules is neither deliberate nor strategic (Cole 1986), they begin to learn that their expressions can have a misleading effect by observing the impact of their facial expressions upon others' behavior. Thus, children's understanding of display rules entails a *cognitive discovery* involving an awareness of the distinction between actual (or felt) emotion and apparent emotion (i.e., the emotion that is apparent to an onlooker).

Nevertheless, it would appear that socialization processes are fundamental to this cognitive discovery. For example, through their own experiences, children learn that by modifying their behavior they can protect themselves and the feelings of others. It is also likely that children's initial attempts to simulate emotion are largely imitation and mimicry, as when a child, having tripped and fallen while among friends, feigns amusement by joining in with their laughter. Children also receive explicit instruction from parents and peers. For example, when children are about to receive a present, parents will often instruct them to smile and say "thank you" (see Saarni 1993).

As children grow older, they are exposed to more complex forms of reasoning about why certain emotions should be concealed in different situations. For example, adults provide children with practical reasons for regulating their expressive behavior (e.g., "if you behave like that, you won't be allowed to go out and play"). They also emphasize the impact of unregulated emotional behavior on the feelings of others (e.g., "Don't cry, because if Grandma sees that you're upset, she'll be sad, too"). The use of such emotionally charged statements is an effective means of disciplining children (Denham, Zoller, and Couchoud 1994; Dunn, Brown, and Beardsall 1988) and may also have a powerful effect upon their use and understanding of display rules.

We have already noted that DH children are reported to interact less frequently and more briefly with their mothers than do hearing children (Lederberg and Mobley 1990; Wedell-Monnig and Lumley 1980). It has also been observed that some DH children interact less frequently with their peers and spend less time in cooperative play (Higgenbotham and Baker 1981; Vandell and George 1981). The resulting lack of conversation and of experience with the vocabulary of emotions and mental states could affect the DH child's acquisition of display rules.

A Study of Deaf Children's Understanding of Display Rules

The authors (Hosie et al. 2000) examined DH and hearing children's reported use of display rules in story situations designed to require the regulation of anger, fear, or happiness. We also explored the children's reasons for choosing to conceal these emotions. Two samples of deaf and hearing children of both elementary and secondary school age (with means 8 and 14 years) participated in the experiment. Each story was signed to the children, and they were asked whether, in the same circumstances as the protagonist, they would conceal or hide their emotions. They were also asked to say why the protagonist concealed or showed their emotion.

The results showed high rates of reported display rule usage by both deaf and hearing children of elementary and secondary school age, with no significant difference between the groups. The deaf and hearing children differed, however, in the type of emotion they were most likely to conceal. Deaf children were significantly less likely to conceal happiness. They were also significantly less inclined to conceal anger.

In contrast with the similar rates of reported concealment by the deaf and hearing children, the latter were able to offer significantly fewer reasons for their decision to conceal. Whereas the hearing children in either age group were able to give reasons for concealing emotions on more than 95 percent of occasions, the deaf children were often unable to explain why they chose to conceal an emotion. The older deaf children offered explanations on 70 percent of occasions, and the younger deaf children, on average, explained their choice on fewer than 50 percent of occasions.

Analysis of the children's reasons for hiding their emotions indicated that self-protection was the primary motivation for concealing anger and fear. Some children also gave self-protective reasons for concealing happiness: "Because she would be angry with me if I didn't." Others gave other-protective (prosocial) reasons, such as, "Because she would be hurt if I showed I was too happy." Only the older deaf children gave prosocial reasons for concealing happiness, whereas hearing children of all ages did so. For happiness, nearly 90 percent of the hearing children's reasons were prosocial, compared with only 43 percent of the deaf children's. In the case of anger, the same trend was evident, although it was less marked.

Our study shows that, despite the possible paucity of their early interactive experiences and lack of opportunity to learn about the rules of social interaction, the DH children were as able as the hearing children to regulate their expressive behavior appropriately. This generalization must be qualified, however, by the fact that hearing category interacted with emotion type. The deaf children were significantly less likely than the hearing children to report concealing happiness and anger but no less likely to report concealing fear. One interpretation of these findings is that the deaf children are less likely to report emotion concealment in situations where it would usually take place, at least partly, for prosocial reasons. Prosocial reasons for concealment should figure more prominently in happiness and anger situations than in fear situations, where concealment is likely to be practiced almost entirely for self-protective reasons.

Prosocial reasoning clearly requires a relatively sophisticated awareness and understanding of other people's mental states. Perhaps the social circumstances of

DH children (alluded to earlier) delay the acquisition of mental-state knowledge in these children (Peterson and Siegal 1995; Russell et al. 1998). If that is true, deaf children's ability to regulate their emotional expression to protect the feelings of others may also develop more gradually. Also, certain aspects of emotional dissemblance—that is, knowledge of the misleading effects that the simulation of emotions can have upon the thoughts and feelings of others (and upon oneself)—may be especially difficult for DH children.

A developmental delay in deaf children's understanding of prosocial reasons is consistent with evidence that in hearing children the understanding of display rules is at first strongly associated with the protection of their own feelings rather than those of others (Zeman and Garber 1996). The understanding of prosocial rules emerges only later. The DH children, then, can be seen as displaying a pattern that is typical of younger hearing children.

There is, however, another possible interpretation of the results. Perhaps the pattern of the deaf children's responses reflects not a difficulty with mental states but an inability to *articulate* their reasons for concealment in these situations. Although the nature of the task was clearly understood by all of the children and illustrations were used to support the signed content of the stories, an answer to the second question "Why would you show/not show . . . ?" required the children to articulate a more complex statement than the simple "show/not show" response required by the first question. It is possible, then, that the deaf children were at a disadvantage when it came to producing reasons. Moreover, they may have found prosocial reasoning particularly difficult to convey. Harris (1989) argues that all display rules, both self-protective and prosocial, have a recursive structure and involve reasoning about mental states (e.g., "I don't want you to know how I feel"). He also suggests that prosocial reasoning is more complex because it carries this recursive structure further: "The child who adopts a display rule to protect another person's feelings is not just saying: 'I do not want you to know how I feel' but is anticipating the repercussions of that knowledge and effectively saying: 'I don't want you to be saddened by knowing how I feel' " (Harris 1989, 145).

It seems unlikely, however, that deaf children's tendency to supply fewer reasons and a smaller proportion of prosocial reasons for concealing emotion is purely a consequence of their difficulty in articulating their reasons. More plausibly, the ability to articulate awareness of the reasons for concealing emotion develops hand-in-hand with the awareness itself. Indeed, Harris (1989) argues that the ability to articulate the recursive structure of display rules actually facilitates children's appreciation of their function.

MIXED EMOTIONS

In addition to acquiring display rules, young schoolchildren also begin to appreciate the possibility of emotional ambivalence. The same person, event, or object can at once be the source of both negative and positive feelings. As with many other aspects of emotion, evidence suggests that, although infants express emotional ambivalence *behaviorally* (Campos et al. 1983), conscious awareness of mixed emotions emerges more gradually. It is not until the age of 8 years or older that children acknowledge the existence of simultaneous and contradictory emotional reactions in themselves and in other people (Donaldson and Westerman 1986; Harris 1983; Harter and Buddin 1987; Reissland 1985).

There is good reason to suppose that lack of awareness of emotional ambivalence, either in oneself or in other people, could lead to difficulties with interpersonal communication and self-regulation. Harter (1977) has shown that failure to recognize mixed feelings toward others (and, indeed, toward oneself) is common among children referred to clinicians with school and adjustment problems. She observed that during play therapy, such children expressed "all-or-none" reactions to events such as the birth of a new sibling or provocation by a friend. These children failed to recognize that these events could simultaneously arouse both positive and negative feelings.

Most studies of mixed emotions have stressed the importance of cognitive factors in the development of children's understanding of ambivalence (Harris 1983, 1989, 1993; Harter 1977; Kestenbaum and Gelman 1995). Harter and Buddin (1987), however, have investigated the extent to which understanding of mixed emotions is related to socialization. They suggest that when parents discuss and label their own mixed emotions, their children's understanding of such matters is facilitated. The results indicated that children under 8 years of age are unable to acknowledge the existence of simultaneous emotions at all. At about 8 years, however, they accept that one can simultaneously experience different emotions about different people or events. It is only after passing through this transition stage (and others) that the child eventually comes to accept that one may experience contradictory emotions about the same person.

If the understanding of mixed emotions does indeed depend upon socialization, the implications for DH children are clear. In hearing children, the subtleties of emotional understanding are mainly imparted through the medium of spoken and written language, and quite young hearing children acquire such expressions as "mixed feelings." DH children, on the other hand, who often find it difficult to acquire the dominant spoken language in their social milieu, may not have access to the sorts of explanations and conversational experiences that promote such insights. (The situation of native signers, who have early access to language and to the benefits it brings, is quite different.)

The authors studied DH children's understanding of mixed emotions by using short story scenarios designed to evoke two contradictory emotions (happiness and sadness). The study was modeled partly on an experiment by Harris (1983, experiment 2). Children were presented with six stories, each involving both a positive (happy) and a negative (sad) event. There were two kinds of stories. In *sequential* stories, a negative and a positive event were each contained in a substory. For example, the first substory might begin: Simon makes a little wooden house for his bicycle. A fire occurs. Now follows the happy component: His bicycle is all right. Next comes the second substory: Simon makes a little wooden house for this bicycle. A fire occurs. Now comes the sad component: The house burns down. In *simultaneous* stories, the negative and positive events were in the same story. For example, a story might begin: Simon makes a little wooden house for his bicycle. A fire occurs. Now the happy and sad components follow together: His bicycle is all right; but the house burns down. After the children had been told a story, they were asked whether the story protagonist felt happy, sad, or both.

If DH children's understanding of mixed emotions develops as in hearing children, deaf children of elementary school age (mean age: 8 years, 11 months) should acknowledge that the protagonist in the sequential stories will feel happiness and sadness in response to the positive and negative events, respectively. They cannot, however, be expected to do this with the simultaneous stories. The older children (mean age: 14 years, 5 months) should be able to acknowledge the existence of contradictory emotions in both the sequential and simultaneous stories. If, on the other hand, a developmental delay occurs, the DH children in the younger group may not only experience difficulty with contradictory emotions in the simultaneous stories but may also deny the possibility of contradictory emotions in the sequential stories as well.

The hearing children were indeed more inclined to accept the coexistence of opposing emotions than were the deaf children. Many of the deaf children did not report contradictory emotions, even with the sequential stories. However, although these results are interesting, no firm conclusions can be drawn from this preliminary work. In particular, deaf children are as likely as any other children not only to experience conflicting emotions in everyday life but also to accept and acknowledge their ambivalence. It may be that in the future, more sensitive paradigms will show that DH children have a greater knowledge and acceptance of emotional ambivalence than is reflected in the results outlined here.

EMOTIONAL DEVELOPMENT AND THEORY OF MIND

An understanding of emotional display rules entails the realization that the expression of one's own emotions can influence not only another person's behavior but also that person's *feelings*. Implicit in this idea is the ability to appreciate, first, that other people have emotional feelings and, second, that those feelings can be different from one's own.

Awareness of others' feelings is a specific aspect of a more general understanding of their mental states, which has become widely known as *theory of mind* (Premack and Woodruff 1978; Wellman 1990). Possession of a theory of mind involves imputing mental states to others, appreciating that these states can be different from one's own, and understanding that others' behavior is related to their mental states. Theory of mind has become one of the theoretical cornerstones of modern developmental psychology. Much of the extensive research into the development of theory of mind in children has been concerned with the cognitive mental states of believing and knowing (Lewis and Mitchell 1994; Wellman 1990). It is clear, however, that theory of mind and emotional understanding are developmentally intertwined. Part of the development of emotional understanding is the realization that how others behave is linked to how *they* feel and not necessarily to how *you* feel. For example, children come to understand that an event that brings them happiness, such as winning a game, may bring disappointment to an opponent and that the opponent's behavior may, as a result, be quite different from their own.

Although there is much debate about the exact nature of the developmental mechanisms underlying the emergence of theory of mind (Astington 1996), a number of theorists stress the importance of appropriate social experience, including conversational interactions with others that provide opportunities for learning about mental states (Dunn 1996; Harris 1996; Leekam 1993; Lillard 1997). Through this experience, children can learn that others can have mental states that differ from their own and that this difference has implications for how others behave.

If such experience is important, theory of mind development should be susceptible to variations in the quantity and quality of social opportunities for learning about mental states. Following this line of reasoning, Peterson and Siegal (1995) hypothesized that DH children, who are likely to experience some impoverishment of relevant conversational experience, might show delayed development of theory of mind. The Sally/Anne false-belief task (Baron-Cohen, Leslie, and Frith 1985) requires the participant to realize that another person's behavior reflects their belief, even if that belief is false. Basically, the Sally/Anne test is a puppet play in which one puppet, Sally, places a marble in a basket and then leaves the scene, whereupon puppet Anne (who stays) transfers the marble to a box. Sally returns. The question is: Where will Sally look for her marble? The correct answer requires the realization that Sally will act upon her false belief that the marble is still where she had put it before leaving. Very young children will point at the box, presumably because they cannot yet represent Sally's mind.

Employing a variant of the Sally/Anne test, Peterson and Siegal found that the majority (65 percent) of their group of DH children aged 8 to 13 years failed the test. (Most 4- to 5-year-old hearing children pass.) They were unable to detect any significant relationship between performance on the test and chronological age, suggesting that the accumulation of social experience over the school years, when signing and other communicative skills greatly improve, may actually have little impact on the development of theory of mind at this later stage.

Given the importance of theory of mind as a social tool for explaining, predicting, and manipulating the behavior of other people (Brown, Donelan-McCall, and Dunn 1996), the social and communication implications of theory of mind impairment in deaf children are considerable. With this in mind, the authors decided to repeat Peterson and Siegal's study with a sample of deaf (predominantly DH) children whose ages ranged more widely than those of the children in Peterson and Siegal's study (Russell et al. 1998). There were three age groups:

1.   4 years, 9 months to 7 years, 1 month

2.   8 years, 9 months to 12 years, 6 months

3.   13 years, 6 months to 16 years, 11 months

Although only 28 percent of the children passed the false-belief test, which is consistent with Peterson and Siegal (1995), performance *was* age-related, with a significantly higher proportion of the oldest age group passing. (The proportions of children from the three age groups passing the tests were 17 percent, 10 percent, and 60 percent for the youngest, middle, and oldest groups, respectively.) Some deaf children, therefore, are eventually able to pass false-belief tests.

A tension often exists between group trends and individual performance. Both the authors' results and those of Peterson and Siegal (1995) show that some DH children, even a few in the youngest age range, passed the false-belief test.

Why some DH children do this much earlier than others remains unexplained, although one might speculate that at least some of the variation is attributable to differences in the quantity or quality of mental-state learning opportunities in the home or general social environment. One specific prediction is that DD children, who would be expected to encounter greater conversational opportunities for learning about the mental states of others, should show little or no theory of mind delay.

Peterson and Siegal (1997) tested DD, DH, and hearing children (healthy 4-year-old children and high-functioning autistic children) in three knowledge domains: theory of mind, biology, and physics. The children ranged in age from 3 years, 9 months to 14 years, 8 months. The children were all tested on Baron-Cohen, Leslie, and Frith's (1985) Sally/Anne test of false belief. They also attempted two biological tests (the seeds test and animals reared by different species) that require a common-sense understanding of breeding. (Melon seeds grow into melon, not orange, plants, even if they are planted beside orange trees. Young animals reared by other species grow up to be members of their own species, not that of their foster-parents.) The children's understanding of the physical world was tested by the false-photo test (Zaitchik 1990). The ability to perceive that a photo is false requires the understanding that a photograph will depict what was in front of the camera when the photograph was taken, whatever may have happened since. Neither the biology test nor the false-photo test requires knowledge of mental states for successful performance.

All the children could pass the physics and biology tests without any difficulty. On the psychological false-belief test, however, the DH children had a significantly lower success rate. The DD children, on the other hand, performed better than any other group in the study. This result supports the hypothesis that language (in this case sign language) gives deaf children access to the experience that they need to acquire theory of mind.

Some might argue that the Sally/Anne false-belief task presents special difficulties for DH children, not because they have yet to acquire theory of mind, but because they do not understand what is required of them. Despite researchers' modifications of the basic Sally/Anne false-belief paradigm to minimize the linguistic demands it makes upon the participant, some of the children may have thought that they were being asked for the toy's present position. If so, it may be that some of the other tests of false belief that have been devised specify the child's task more clearly. In the United Kingdom, a popular candy known as "Smarties" were, until recently, always packaged in a unique cylindrical container that no child could fail to recognize. In the "Smarties test," (Perner, Leekam, and Wimmer 1987), a child is shown a Smarties cylinder and, expecting to find the candy inside it, discovers pencils instead. The false-belief question is: What will a new arrival on the scene think the cylinder contains? Because the Smarties test involves attractive, familiar objects, it may place children in a less threatening situation than the Sally/Anne test, in which they must "make the acquaintance" of the puppets and involve themselves in the story action.

Peterson and Siegal (1999) tested signing DD children, oral deaf children, DH children, hearing preschoolers, and autistic children with the Smarties test, the "changed appearance task" (Leekam and Perner 1991), and the Sally/Anne test. As in their earlier study (Peterson and Siegal 1997), the DD children outperformed the DH and younger hearing children. In contrast, the DH children had difficulty with the false-belief variants. This study broadens the evidential base for the conversational hypothesis not only by further sampling from the population but also by sampling more extensively from the domain of false-belief tasks. However, it is important to acknowledge that data based solely on false-belief tasks cannot provide an adequate basis for statements about mental-state knowledge in general. Researchers in this area now need to move beyond false-belief tests and consider other paradigms for the exploration of mental-state knowledge.

The Interpretation of Line of Regard in Prelingually Deaf Children

A person's line of regard is a rich potential source of information that can help us explore mental states. By showing the focus of another's attention, line of regard can indicate desire, fear, suspicion, and so on, depending on the context. Young hearing children are well aware of the significance of line of regard. For example, Baldwin (1991) showed that infants of 16 to 19 months can use an adult's line of regard to resolve labeling inconsistencies.

The ability to use line of regard to ascertain another's mental state may be an essential prerequisite for the acquisition of theory of mind. Baron-Cohen (1991; Baron-Cohen and Cross 1992) has argued that an important precursor of theory of mind is what Bruner (1983) has termed "the management of joint attention." Two important aspects of joint attentional skill are (a) the splitting of attention between what one is doing oneself and what another person is doing and (b) the monitoring of the other person's focus of attention. The utilization of line of regard plays a central role in joint attention and is a precursor of more advanced interactive behavior, such as turn-taking (Denham et al. 1994).

There is reason to suspect that a profoundly deaf child may find it difficult to make full use of line of regard (Scott et al. 1999). Because hearing babies who are only a few minutes old turn their heads toward an auditory source (Wertheimer 1961) and young hearing children orient their gaze toward a sound, it is likely that there is a biological coordination between line of regard and auditory localization. Although there is no reason to suppose that this predisposition is absent in profoundly deaf children, it is inaccessible because there is no auditory source to activate it. Profoundly deaf children, therefore, may be less attuned to line of regard and less able to use it to ascertain other people's mental states.

Baron-Cohen and his associates (1995) have developed a methodology for ascertaining hearing children's sensitivity to the significance of gaze and line of regard. Using cartoon faces, they established that a majority (typically 80 percent or more) of 4-year-old hearing children of normal intelligence attended to the eyes and were able to trace imaginary straight lines to identify the target of the gaze of a cartoon face. Moreover, they could also use line of regard to infer mental states such as desires and goals. Their methodology was adapted by the authors to make it suitable for use with prelingually profoundly deaf children.

The ability of severely and profoundly deaf children ages 5 to 12 to utilize and interpret another person's visual line of regard was studied in four experiments using cartoon faces (Scott et al. 1999). In the first experiment, each child was presented with pairs of cartoon faces and asked to say which one was looking at them. In the second experiment, each child was asked to say which of four pieces of candy a cartoon character, Charlie, who was eyeing one of them, wanted. (In a "desire" condition, the question was which piece of candy Charlie wanted; in the "intention" condition, the question was which piece of candy Charlie intended to take.) In the third experiment, the children were asked to trace an imaginary line from a directional indicator (a pointing finger or arrow) to an object at which the indicator was directed. In the fourth experiment, the object of the exercise was to see whether the children could ignore line of regard when it provided misleading information. The children were asked which of two boxes was the smaller. Because the cartoon character, Charlie, was always looking at the larger box, it was always a mistake to follow his line of regard.

Neither the hearing nor the deaf children had difficulty in determining whether a face was looking directly at them. However, both groups had more difficulty with tasks requiring them to infer mental states of desire and intention from line of regard and to ignore line of regard when it was inappropriate to attend to this cue. DH children appear to find the second group of tasks more difficult than do hearing children. The results of the line-of-regard experiment are consistent with the hypothesis that lack of conversational experience can delay not only the emergence of theory of mind itself but also the appearance of certain precursors of theory of mind that some might regard as innate.

Theory of Mind, Emotional Development, and Deaf Children

Emotional understanding, in its fullest sense, implies at least some of the essential features of theory of mind. For example, to have empathy is to be able to "read the minds" of others in social situations. The same is true, a fortiori, of the use of the more sophisticated display rules. The use of such rules implies awareness not only of another person's emotional response but also of what that person might do as a consequence. The effective use of display rules implies that the user appreciates that an event that is good news for the observer may (even by that very fact) not be so for another. The most elementary theory of mind tests require appreciation of another's belief, but the use of display rules requires not only this knowledge but also a plan for correct social action on the basis of another person's possible consequent view of one's own mental state. Far from being quite separate aspects of psychological development, emotional understanding and theory of mind are intimately linked.

Nor should the understanding of display rules be viewed as, at best, a crude precursor of theory of mind. More complex theory of mind tests have been devised (Stone, Baron-Cohen, and Knight 1998). Suppose that in the setting of the usual Sally/Anne test, the participant is told that Sally, who has left the room, is actually observing events through a keyhole. To ask where Anne thinks Sally will look for her marble when she comes back is to ask about the participant's representation of another person's belief about a third person's belief. In the original test, the participant is asked about another person's representation of a situation, but the new test asks about the representation of a representation and is therefore known as a *second-order false-belief task* (Perner and Wimmer 1985). Arguably, the use of the more sophisticated display rules demands a similar embedding of representations and so can be regarded as being at a level of complexity comparable to higher-order theory of mind tasks.

Whatever may be the respective origins of display rule use and theory of mind, the two functions are closely related. The difficulties that DH children have with both tests of display rule knowledge and theory of mind tasks attest to the intimacy of the link.

EMOTIONAL DEVELOPMENT, LANGUAGE, AND COMMUNICATION

If conversational experience is important in the development of emotional understanding, one would expect substantial positive correlations between measures of linguistic and communicational competence and the tests of emotional understanding that we have considered in this chapter.

The children's language proficiency was measured by an inventory specially constructed for use at the Aberdeen School for the Deaf. The teachers rated each child on a number of measures, which fell into the two general categories of production and comprehension. Among the productive and receptive skills tested were sign vocabulary and fingerspelling, speechreading, the use of nonmanual features, the use of English markers, and the use of speech with signing. The inventory also contains several items specifically aimed at tapping conversational skills. These include the ability to sustain conversation, pay attention to another person when they are signing, deploy attention appropriately, take turns, and make use of eye contact.

In the experiment on children's understanding of emotional facial expressions, three tasks were used: matching, comprehension, and labeling. The correlations between these three tasks and a composite measure of expressive language were 0.18, 0.48, and 0.51, respectively. (The first correlation is statistically insignificant; the second and third are significant.) However, while the activities of labeling and comprehension could be expected to load more heavily than matching on language ability, language skills are also likely to relate to the children's ability to understand the task.

We have argued that the ability to use display rules in prosocial ways requires a child to have had sufficient experience with conversation. One would therefore expect a substantial correlation between the children's ability to use display rules and language competence in general. In particular, conversational ability should correlate strongly with display rule usage. In fact, although a composite total receptive ability measure correlates 0.53 with use of display rules, neither the correlation between use of display rules and interactive skill nor the correlation with expressive ability is significant. (The correlations are 0.38 and 0.37, respectively.) The correlations, however, are in the expected direction, and the sample size of 24 permits only a low-powered test of the null hypothesis. Other tasks, such as the theory of mind false-belief test, correlate positively and significantly with several of the linguistic and communication measures. For example, theory of mind correlates 0.47 and 0.42 with the use of fingerspelling and English language production, respectively; moreover, on the receptive side, theory of mind correlates 0.44 and 0.42 with recognition of sign vocabulary and the reading of fingerspelling, respectively. In general, the findings of this preliminary work indicate that emotional understanding in its various aspects is related to the child's linguistic and communicational abilities, consistent with the view that conversational experience is of central importance in the acquisition of more sophisticated display rules and theory of mind.

SUMMARY

The research reported in this chapter explores the emotional development of deaf children in its perceptual and inferential aspects. Although the results are suggestive, they must be interpreted with considerable caution. The various studies reported here are at least consistent with the view that early conversational experience plays a crucial role in helping a child gain access to other people's mental states. But authors vary in their interpretations of "conversation." Some stress the importance of explicit discussions of mental-state terms (Peterson and Siegal 1995). However, because the foundations of mental-state knowledge may be laid even before a child acquires language, it seems more appropriate to take a broader view of conversation as any meaningful exchange between children, whether verbal or nonverbal (Gray and Hosie 1996; Harris 1996). If this hypothesis is correct, DH children, who arguably lack early conversational experience, can be expected to show a developmental delay not only in the more sophisticated aspects of emotional development but also in their acquisition of related functions such as theory of mind.

We must stress, however, that although circumstantial evidence exists to suggest that DH children do indeed lack conversational experience, this has not been directly established. It is certainly not always the case because much depends upon the attitude and actions of the child's parents and the point at which the hearing loss is discovered. If true, it is only a generalization and subject to many exceptions.

The pattern of the results, however, is what one would expect on the basis of the conversation hypothesis. The DH children equalled the performance of their hearing contemporaries on the more perceptual aspects of emotional understanding, such as the recognition and interpretation of facial expressions of emotion. However, they performed less well in their understanding of display rules and theory of mind, precisely the functions where conversational experience is likely to be most important.

FUTURE RESEARCH

We now consider some possible future lines of inquiry deriving from the research described here. In this area, a powerful methodological strategy is to make comparisons among groups of deaf children with different linguistic backgrounds. Some important pioneering work has already been carried out comparing DH with DD children and other groups in their performance of false-belief theory of mind tasks (Peterson and Siegal 1997, 1999; Steeds, Rowe, and Dowker 1997). This work has tended to confirm the importance of the role of early interactive experience on the emotional development of the deaf child. This comparative paradigm could profitably be extended to many aspects of emotional development, including use of display rules, understanding of mixed emotions, and precursors of theory of mind, such as the ability to infer mental states from line of regard. It would be of great interest to know how native-signing DD children perform on tests of display rule use and understanding of mixed emotions. Although the conversational hypothesis predicts that DD children should significantly outperform DH children on such tests, there is, as yet, no evidence available to confirm this.

The study of display rule use found that DH children produced fewer prosocial reasons than hearing children for concealing happiness. The possibility that prosocial display rules possess a more complex recursive structure than self-protective rules is interesting in light of the difficulties that DH children have in passing standard tests of false belief. Advances in theory of mind in hearing children between 3 and 5 years of age may depend on the ability to reason with embedded rules (Frye, Zelazo, and Palfai 1995). Future research, therefore, might benefit from closer examination of the links between deaf children's ability to engage in recursive reasoning and their performance on tests of mental-state reasoning. Comparisons among different linguistic groups should be highly informative.

Much of the research reviewed in this chapter has focused on DH children's *receptive* understanding of emotions:

- their identification of facial expressions
- their appreciation of the emotions felt by story characters
- their judgments about other people's use of display rules in story scenarios
- their representation of other people's false beliefs
- their ability to infer mental states from another person's line of regard

Future research might profitably explore the *expressive* aspects of emotion in DH and DD children. Specifically, the following questions might be addressed:

- How accurately are the emotional expressions of deaf children (both spontaneous and voluntary) understood by deaf and hearing peers and adults?
- How do the facial expressions of deaf children differ, if at all, from those of hearing children?
- What is the effect of the acquisition of natural sign language (such as British Sign Language, in which grammatical facial expressions play an integral role) on the development of deaf children's emotional expressive behavior?

In some preliminary work by the authors, deaf children have been asked to pose various facial expressions of emotion, and deaf and hearing people have rated their expressions for typicality. There has also been some pilot work on the spontaneous expressions that the deaf children produce in social and play situations.

Some of the more complex emotions, such as pride, shame, guilt, and embarrassment, have no unique facial expressions to which parents and other adults can refer. Lewis (1993) suggests that knowledge of such emotions may arise from an evaluation of one's own behavior in relation to accepted cultural standards and rules. There has been little investigation of these emotions, even in hearing children. Nevertheless, it is of paramount importance to know more about how deaf children experience and manage them. The comparison among groups of deaf children with different linguistic backgrounds would also be especially illuminating.

Natural language data and naturalistic observation of children's interactions have become increasingly important in studies of hearing children's social and emotional development (Astington and Jenkins 1995). Future research on deaf children's development in these areas might also benefit from analysis of the spontaneous use of language about emotions and mental states by DH and DD children in their interactions with their parents, other adults, and peers.

References

Astington, J. 1996. What is theoretical about the child's theory of mind? A Vygotskian view of its development. In *Theories of theories of mind*, ed. P. Carruthers and P. K. Smith, 184–99. Cambridge, U.K.: Cambridge University Press.

Astington, J. W., and J. M. Jenkins. 1995. Theory of mind development and social understanding. *Cognition and Emotion* 9:151–65.

Bachara, G. H., J. Raphael, and W. J. Phelan. 1980. Empathy development in deaf pre-adolescents. *American Annals of the Deaf* 125:38–41.

Baldwin, D. A. 1991. Infants' contribution to the achievement of joint reference. *Child Development* 62:875–90.

Banks, J., C. Gray, and R. Fyfe. 1990. The written recall of printed stories by severely deaf children. *British Journal of Educational Psychology* 60:192–206.

Baron-Cohen, S. 1991. Precursors to a theory of mind: Understanding attention in others. In *Natural theories of mind*, ed. A. Whiten, 233–51. Oxford: Basil Blackwell.

Baron-Cohen, S., R. Campbell, A. Karmiloff-Smith, J. Grant, and J. Walker. 1995. Are children with autism blind to the mentalistic significance of the eyes? *British Journal of Developmental Psychology* 13:379–98.

Baron-Cohen, S., and P. Cross. 1992. Reading the eyes: Evidence for the role of perception in the development of a theory of mind. *Mind and Language* 6:166–80.

Baron-Cohen, S., A. M. Leslie, and U. Frith. 1985. Does the autistic child have a "theory of mind"? *Cognition* 21:37–46.

Barrerra, M. E., and D. Maurer. 1981. The perception of facial expressions by the three-month-old. *Child Development* 52:945–54.

Barrett, K. C. 1993. The development of nonverbal communication of emotion: A functionalist perspective. *Journal of Nonverbal Behavior* 17(3):145–69.

Barrett, K. C., and J. J. Campos. 1987. Perspectives on emotional development II: A functionalist approach to emotions. In *Handbook of infant development*, 2d ed., ed. J. Osofsky, 555–78. New York: Wiley.

Borke, H. 1971. Interpersonal perception of young children: Egocentrism or empathy? *Developmental Psychology* 5(2):263–69.

———. 1973. The development of empathy in Chinese and American children between three and six years of age: A cross-cultural study. *Developmental Psychology* 9(1):102–8.

Bretherton, I., J. Fritz, C. Zahn-Waxler, and D. Ridgeway. 1986. Learning to talk about emotions: A functionalist perspective. *Child Development* 57:529–48.

Brody, L., and R. Harrison. 1987. Developmental changes in children's abilities to match and label emotionally laden situations. *Motivation and Emotion* 11:347–65.

Brown, J. R., N. Donelan-McCall, and J. Dunn. 1996. Why talk about mental states? The significance of children's conversations with friends, siblings, and mothers. *Child Development* 67:836–49.

Bruner, J. 1983. *Child's talk: Learning to use language*. Oxford: Oxford University Press.

Buck, R. 1988. Nonverbal communication. *American Behavioral Scientist* 31:341–54.

Bullock, M., and J. A. Russell. 1984. Preschool children's interpretation of facial expressions of emotion. *International Journal of Behavioral Development* 7:193–214.

———. 1985. Further evidence on preschoolers' interpretation of facial expressions. *International Journal of Behavioral Development* 8:15–38.

Calderon, R., and M. T. Greenberg. 1993. Considerations in the adaptation of families with school-aged deaf children. In *Psychological perspectives on deafness*, ed. M. Marschark and M. D. Clark, 27–47. Hillsdale, N.J.: Lawrence Erlbaum.

Campos, J. J., K. C. Barrett, M. E. Lamb, H. H. Goldsmith, and C. Sternberg. 1983. Socioemotional development. In *Handbook of child psychology*, vol. 2, ed. J. J. Campos and M. H. Haith, 783–915. New York: Wiley.

Campos, J. J., R. G. Campos, and K. C. Barrett. 1989. Emergent themes in the study of emotional development and emotion regulation. *Developmental Psychology* 25(3):394–402.

Carlson, C., E. Felleman, and J. Masters. 1983. Influence of children's emotional states on the recognition of emotion in peers and social motives to change another's emotional state. *Motivation and Emotion* 7:61–79.

Cole, P. M. 1986. Children's spontaneous control of facial expression. *Child Development* 57:1309–21.

Custrini, R. J., and R. S. Feldman. 1989. Children's social competence and nonverbal encoding and decoding of emotions. *Journal of Child Clinical Psychology* 18:336–42.

Denham, S. 1986a. Affective understanding in young preschoolers and reactions to peers' emotions. Paper presented at the American Psychological Association, Washington, D.C.

———. 1986b. Social cognition, prosocial behavior, and emotion in preschoolers: Contextual validation. *Child Development* 57:194–201.

Denham, S. A., and R. Burton. 1996. A social-emotional intervention for at-risk 4-year-olds. *Journal of School Psychology* 34(3):225–45.

Denham, S. A., M. McKinley, E. A. Couchoud, and R. Holt. 1990. Emotional and behavioral predictors of preschool peer ratings. *Child Development* 61:1145–52.

Denham, S. A., D. Zoller, and E. A. Couchoud. 1994. Socialization of preschoolers' emotion understanding. *Developmental Psychology* 30(6):928–36.

Deuchar, M. 1984. *British Sign Language*. London: Routledge and Kegan Paul.

Donaldson, S. K., and M. A. Westerman. 1986. Development of children's understanding of ambivalence and causal theories of emotion. *Developmental Psychology* 22(5):655–62.

Dunn, J. 1996. The Emanuel Miller Memorial Lecture 1995. Children's relationships: Bridging the divide between cognitive and social development. *Journal of Child Psychology and Psychiatry* 37(5):507–18.

Dunn, J., I. Bretherton, and P. Munn. 1987. Conversations about feeling states between mothers and their young children. *Developmental Psychology* 23:132–39.

Dunn, J., J. Brown, and L. Beardsall. 1988. Family talk about feeling states and children's later understanding of others' emotions. *Developmental Psychology* 27:448–55.

Ekman, P. 1984. Expression and the nature of emotion. In *Approaches to emotion,* ed. K. Scherer and P. Ekman, 319–44. Hillsdale, N.J.: Lawrence Erlbaum.

Ekman, P., and W. V. Friesen. 1976. *Pictures of facial affect.* Palo Alto, Calif.: Consulting Psychologists' Press.

Ekman, P., W. Friesen, and P. Ellsworth. 1972. *Emotion in the human face.* New York: Pergamon.

Ekman, P., and H. Oster. 1979. Facial expressions of emotion. *Annual Review of Psychology* 30:527–54.

Feinman, S. 1992. In the broad valley: An integrative look at social referencing. In *Social referencing and the social construction of reality in infancy,* ed. S. Feinman, 3–14. New York: Plenum.

Frye, D., P. D. Zelazo, and T. Palfai. 1995. Theory of mind and rule-based reasoning. *Cognitive Development* 10:483–527.

Garner, P. W. 1996. The relations of emotional role taking, affective/moral attributions, and emotional display rule knowledge to low-income school-age children's social competence. *Journal of Applied Developmental Psychology* 17:19–36.

Goleman, D. 1995. *Emotional intelligence.* London: Bloomsbury.

Gray, C., J. Banks, R. Fyfe, and A. Morris. 1992. The use of verbatim and schematic strategies in the recall of written stories by deaf and hearing children. *British Journal of Educational Psychology* 62:88–105.

Gray, C., and J. Hosie. 1996. Deafness, story understanding and theory of mind. *Journal of Deaf Studies and Deaf Education* 1:217–233.

Greenberg, M. T., and C. A. Kusché. 1993. *Promoting social and emotional development in deaf children: The PATHS Project.* Seattle: University of Washington Press.

Gross, A. L., and B. Ballif. 1991. Children's understanding of emotion from facial expressions and situations: A review. *Developmental Review* 11:368–98.

Harrigan, J. A. 1984. The effects of task order on children's identification of facial expressions. *Motivation and Emotion* 8(2):157–69.

Harris, P. L. 1983. Children's understanding of the link between situation and emotion. *Journal of Experimental Child Psychology* 36:490–509.

———. 1989. *Children and emotion: The development of psychological understanding.* Oxford: Basil Blackwell.

———. 1993. Understanding emotion. In *Handbook of emotions,* ed. M. Lewis and J. M. Haviland, 237–46. New York: Guilford Press.

———. 1996. Desires, beliefs, and language. In *Theories of theories of mind,* ed. P. Carruthers and P. K. Smith, 200–20. Cambridge, U.K.: Cambridge University Press.

Harris, P. L., C. N. Johnson, D. Hutton, G. Andrews, and T. Cooke. 1989. Young children's theory of mind and emotion. *Cognition and Emotion* 3(4):379–400.

Harter, S. 1977. A cognitive-developmental approach to children's expression of conflicting feelings and a technique to facilitate such expression in play therapy. *Journal of Consulting and Clinical Psychology* 45(3):417–32.

Harter, S., and B. J. Buddin. 1987. Children's understanding of the simultaneity of two emotions: A five-stage developmental acquisition sequence. *Developmental Psychology* 23(3):388–99.

Higgenbotham, D. J., and B. M. Baker. 1981. Social participation and cognitive play differences in hearing-impaired and normally hearing preschoolers. *Volta Review* 83:135–49.

Hosie, J. A., C. D. Gray, P. A. Russell, C. Scott, and N. Hunter. 1998. The matching of facial expressions by deaf and hearing children and their production and comprehension of emotion labels. *Motivation and Emotion* 22:293–313.

Hosie, J. A., P. A. Russell, C. D. Gray, C. Scott, N. Hunter, J. S. Banks, and M. C. Macaulay. 2000. Knowledge of display rules in prelingually deaf and hearing children. *Journal of Child Psychology and Psychiatry and Allied Disciplines* 41:389–98.

Ireson, J., and M. Shields. 1982. The development of the young child's representation of emotion. London: University of London Institute of Education. [ERIC Document Reproduction Service no. ED 263 983]

Izard, C. 1971. *The face of emotion*. New York: Appleton-Century-Crofts.

Izard, C., and C. Malatesta. 1987. Perspectives on emotional development I: Differential emotions theory of early emotional development. In *Handbook of infant development*, ed. J. Osofsky, 494–554. New York: Wiley.

Jenkins, J. M., K. Oatley, and N. L. Stein. 1998. *Human emotions: A reader*. Malden, Mass.: Basil Blackwell.

Kestenbaum, R., and S. A. Gelman. 1995. Preschool children's identification and understanding of mixed emotions. *Cognitive Development* 10:443–58.

Kestenbaum, R., and C. A. Nelson. 1990. The recognition and categorisation of upright and inverted emotional expressions by seven-month-old infants. *Infant Behaviour and Development* 13:497–511.

Kuchuk, A., M. Vibbert, and M. H. Bornstein. 1986. The perception of smiling and its experiential correlates in three-month-old infants. *Child Development* 57:1054–61.

Kuhl, P. K., and A. N. Meltzhoff. 1982. The bimodal perception of speech in infancy. *Science* 218:1138–41.

Kyle, J. G., and B. Woll. 1985. *Sign language: The study of deaf people and their language*. Cambridge, U.K.: Cambridge University Press.

Lederberg, A. R., and C. E. Mobley. 1990. The effect of hearing impairment on the quality of attachment and mother-toddler interaction. *Child Development* 61:1596–1604.

Leekam, S. 1993. Children's understanding of mind. In *The development of social cognition*, ed. M. Bennett, 26–61. New York: Guilford Press.

Leekam, S. R., and J. Perner. 1991. Do autistic children have a metarepresentational deficit? *Cognition* 40:203–18.

Levine, E. S. 1956. *Youth in a soundless world*. New York: New York University Press.

———. 1960. *The psychology of deafness*. New York: Columbia University Press.

Levine, E. S., and E. E. Wagner. 1974. Personality patterns of deaf persons: An interpretation based on research with the hand test. *Perceptual and Motor Skills Monographs* 39(4).

Lewis, C., and P. Mitchell. 1994. *Children's early understanding of mind: Origins and development*. Hillsdale, N.J.: Lawrence Erlbaum.

Lewis, M. 1993. Self-conscious emotions: Embarrassment, pride, shame, and guilt. In *Handbook of emotions*, ed. M. Lewis and J. M. Haviland, 563–73. New York: Guilford Press.

Lillard, A. S. 1997. Other folks' theories of mind and behavior. *Psychological Science* 8:268–74.

Locke, J. L. 1993. The role of the face in vocal learning and the development of spoken language. In *Developmental neurocognition: Speech and face processing in the first year of life*, ed. B. de Boysson-Bardies, S. de Schonen, P. Jusczyk, P. McNeilage, and J. Morton, 317–28. Dordrecht, Netherlands: Kluwer Academic Publishers.

Markham, R., and K. Adams. 1992. The effect of type of task on children's identification of facial expressions. *Journal of Nonverbal Behaviour* 16(1):21–39.

Marschark, M. 1993. *Psychological development of deaf children*. New York: Oxford University Press.

Michalson, L., and M. Lewis. 1985. What do children know about emotions and when do they know it? In *The socialization of emotions*, ed. M. Lewis and C. Saarni, 117–39. New York: Plenum.

Mood, D., J. Johnson, and C. Shantz. 1978. Social comprehension and affect-matching in young children. *Merrill-Palmer Quarterly* 24:63–66.

Nowicki, S., and M. P. Duke. 1992. The association of children's nonverbal decoding abilities with their popularity, locus of control, and academic achievement. *Journal of Genetic Psychology* 153(4):385–93.

Odom, P. B., R. L. Blanton, and C. Laukhuf. 1973. Facial expressions and interpretation of emotion-arousing situations in deaf and hearing children. *Journal of Abnormal Child Psychology* 1:139–51.

Perner, J., S. Leekam, and H. Wimmer. 1987. Three-year-olds' difficulty with false belief: The case for a conceptual deficit. *British Journal of Developmental Psychology* 5:125–37.

Perner, J., and H. Wimmer. 1985. "John thinks that Mary thinks that . . .": Attribution of second-order false beliefs by 5- to 10-year-old children. *Journal of Experimental Child Psychology* 39:437–71.

Peterson, C. C., and M. Siegal. 1995. Deafness, conversation and theory of mind. *Journal of Child Psychology and Psychiatry* 36:459–74.

———. 1997. Psychological, biological and physical thinking in normal, autistic, and deaf children. In *The emergence of core domains of thought*, ed. H. M. Wellman and K. Inagaki, 55–70. San Francisco: Jossey-Bass.

———. 1999. Representing inner worlds: Theory of mind in autistic, deaf, and normal hearing children. *Psychological Science* 10:126–29.

Phillips, R. D., S. H. Wagner, C. A. Fells, and M. Lynch. 1990. Do infants recognize emotion in facial expressions?: Categorical and "metaphorical" evidence. *Infant Behavior and Development* 13:71–84.

Premack, D., and G. Woodruff. 1978. Does the chimpanzee have a "theory of mind"? *Behavior and Brain Sciences* 4:515–26.

Reichenbach, L., and J. C. Masters. 1983. Children's use of expressive and contextual cues in judgements of emotion. *Child Development* 54:993–1004.

Reissland, N. 1985. The development of concepts of simultaneity in children's understanding of emotions. *Journal of Child Psychology and Psychiatry* 26(5):811–24.

Russell, J. A. 1980. A circumplex model of affect. *Journal of Personality and Social Psychology* 39:1161–78.

Russell, J. A., and M. Bullock. 1985. Multidimensional scaling of emotional facial expressions: Similarity from preschoolers to adults. *Journal of Personality and Social Psychology* 48:1290–98.

———. 1986. On the dimensions preschoolers use to interpret facial expressions of emotion. *Developmental Psychology* 22:97–102.

Russell, J. A., N. Suzuki, and N. Ishida. 1993. Canadian, Greek, and Japanese freely produced emotion labels for facial expressions. *Motivation and Emotion* 17:337–51.

Russell, P. A., J. A. Hosie, C. D. Gray, C. Scott, N. Hunter, J. S. Banks, and M. C. Macaulay. 1998. The development of theory of mind in deaf children. *Journal of Child Psychology and Psychiatry* 39:903–10.

Saarni, C. 1993. Socialization. In *Handbook of emotions*, ed. M. Lewis and J. M. Haviland, 435–46. New York: Guilford Press.

Salovey, P., and J. D. Mayer. 1990. Emotional intelligence. *Imagination, Cognition and Personality* 9(3):185–211.

Scott, C., P. Russell, C. Gray, J. Hosie, and N. Hunter. 1999. The interpretation of line of regard by prelingually deaf children. *Social Development* 8:412–25.

Steeds, I., K. Rowe, and A. Dowker. 1997. Deaf children's understanding of beliefs and desires. *Journal of Deaf Studies and Deaf Education* 2:185–95.

Stone, V. E., S. Baron-Cohen, and R. T. Knight. 1998. Frontal lobe contributions to theory of mind. *Journal of Cognitive Neuroscience* 10:640–56.

Vandell, D., and L. George. 1981. Social interaction in hearing and deaf preschoolers: Successes and failures in initiation. *Child Development* 52:627–35.

Walden, T. A. 1991. Infant social referencing. In *The development of emotion regulation and dysregulation*, ed. J. Garber and K. A. Dodge, 69–88. Cambridge, U.K.: Cambridge University Press.

Walker-Andrews, A. S., and E. Lennon. 1991. Infants' discrimination of vocal expressions: Contributions of auditory and visual information. *Infant Behavior and Development* 14:131–42.

Warnock, M. 1978. Meeting special educational needs: A brief guide to the report of the Committee of Enquiry into Education of Handicapped Children and Young People. London: Her Majesty's Stationery Office.

Wedell-Monnig, J., and J. M. Lumley. 1980. Child deafness and mother-child interaction. *Child Development* 51:766–74.

Weir, K., and G. Duveen. 1981. Further development and validation of the Prosocial Behavior Questionnaire for use by teachers. *Journal of Child Psychology and Psychiatry* 22:357–74.

Wellman, H. 1990. *The child's theory of mind*. Cambridge, Mass.: MIT Press/Bradford Books.

Wertheimer, M. 1961. Psychomotor coordination of auditory and visual space at birth. *Science* 134:1692.

Wood, D., H. Wood, A. Griffiths, and I. Howarth. 1986. *Teaching and talking with deaf children*. New York: Wiley.

Young-Browne, G., H. Rosenfeld, and F. Horowitz. 1977. Infant discrimination of facial expressions. *Child Development* 48:555–62.

Zaitchik, D. 1990. When representations conflict with reality. *Cognition* 35:41–68.

Zeman, J., and J. Garber. 1996. Display rules for anger, sadness, and pain: It depends on who is watching. *Child Development* 67:957–73.

10

SOCIAL CHANGE AND CONFLICT: CONTEXT FOR RESEARCH ON DEAFNESS

Kathryn P. Meadow-Orlans

Social change is an interactive process in which progress or regress in one area is felt in many other areas. Thus, in the past thirty years, legislation has improved the educational and occupational status of deaf people, increasing positive attitudes about deafness and sign language, stimulating linguistic and educational research, convincing more hearing parents to learn sign language, creating new advocates for the Deaf community, and pressing for additional legislation—thereby renewing the cycle.

Figure 1 illustrates this concept of social change as it might apply to deafness. Because this collection of papers focuses on research, this area is at the apex of the diagram. However, any subject might occupy that position. The double-headed arrows indicate that the direction of influence for social change is reciprocal. One could say that because research had a favorable effect on public attitudes toward deafness, more research was conducted and supported, reinforcing the favorable attitudes. Interactions of influence are not confined to those summarized in figure 1. Surely, change in any one area can influence change in any other. Thus, federal funds can help to improve the educational status of deaf persons, and activities in the Deaf community can help to increase sign language use. A survey of changes in each of these arenas is the focus of the first section of this chapter. The role of conflict among various segments of the deafness-related communities is considered in the final section. It is proposed that the interplay of social change and conflict provides a context for understanding the direction of research in deaf education during the past forty years and will guide the future direction of deafness-related research as well.

At the time this chapter was written, the author served as a scientific review administrator in the Center for Scientific Review, National Institutes of Health. However, the views expressed represent her personal opinions and agency agreement or endorsement should not be inferred. Thanks to Harold Orlans, Anita Sostek, and the three editors for helpful comments.

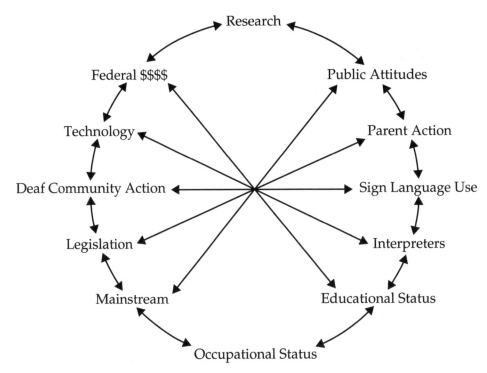

Figure 1. A Model of Social Change and Deafness

RECENT SOCIAL CHANGES AFFECTING DEAF PEOPLE

Linguistic and Behavioral Research

William Stokoe's linguistic research (1960) and his *Dictionary of American Sign Language* (Stokoe, Casterline, and Croneberg 1965) led to several significant changes in Deaf people's lives. The linguistic and academic credibility given a language formerly regarded as an inferior form of "pidgin" helped to remove a stigma from the Deaf community (Rée 1999) and to improve its members' self-respect. Sign language instruction and interpreter training increased, and American Sign Language (ASL) was accepted in fulfillment of language requirements for advanced academic degrees. Sign interpreting at public and professional meetings, religious services, TV addresses, and many other events increased enormously.

Stokoe's research on the linguistics of ASL was followed in the 1970s by that of Ursula Bellugi and Edward Klima at the Salk Institute, University of California, San Diego (Klima and Bellugi 1979). Whereas Stokoe, based at Gallaudet College (later, Gallaudet University), was interested in the practical applications of his research, Bellugi and Klima focused on the implications of their studies for the theoretical understanding of language acquisition and cerebral specialization. Two of Stokoe's protégés, Charlotte Baker Shenk and Dennis Cokely, developed ASL training materials (Baker and Cokely 1980). Two of his other students, Carol Ert-ing and Robert Johnson, have been linguistic and anthropology research advo-cates for the Deaf community (Erting 1994; Erting, Prezioso, and Hynes 1994; Johnson, Liddell, and Erting 1989). The National Institutes of Health (NIH) sup-ported the Bellugi/Klima laboratory for twenty years or more. Federal appropria-tions for Gallaudet, the National Science Foundation, and other sources supported Stokoe and his colleagues.

Behavioral research also influenced other areas included in figure 1. A series of studies compared the achievement, self-esteem, social adjustment, speech, and speechreading skill of deaf children with Deaf parents to those of deaf children with hearing parents (Brasel and Quigley 1977; Meadow 1967, 1968, 1969; Stuck-less and Birch 1966; Vernon and Koh 1970). These two groups created, in effect, a "natural experiment." All of the studies found that deaf children of Deaf parents performed at levels equal to or higher than children with hearing parents. Vernon and Koh (1970) limited their participants to deaf children with hearing parents who had deaf relatives. This made it more likely that the deafness of both groups was probably hereditary rather than due to a virus or illness that might affect cog-nitive functioning and depress educational achievement. The cumulative results of these studies supported the idea that sign language did not retard and might even enhance achievement (Marschark 1993).

Research with mothers and young deaf children in the mid 1960s showed that interactions were more positive when mothers used visually accessible communi-cation (Schlesinger and Meadow 1972). Thus, there was research evidence from several sources suggesting that the educational and behavioral lags of deaf chil-dren were related to the inability to communicate rather than to auditory depriva-tion. The U.S. Vocational Rehabilitation Administration (VRA) gave vital support and encouragement to this early behavioral research. VRA director Mary Switzer and Boyce Williams, a deaf man in charge of special programs related to deaf-ness, urged Hilde Schlesinger to apply for funds for research and clinical mental health services. In the 1960s, Schlesinger was the only psychiatrist in the United States who knew sign language. Thus, VRA supported non-oral approaches to deafness.

These streams of behavioral research encouraged hearing parents of deaf chil-dren to learn sign language and to lobby for the use of total communication in classrooms for young children, where heretofore only speech and speechreading had been allowed. Before 1965 virtually all deaf children younger than age 12 were taught by auditory/oral methods. By 1975 two-thirds of younger children and three-fourths of high-school-age students were said to be taught in total com-munication settings (Moores 1996). A difference of this magnitude might be called a "social revolution" rather than a "social change." Apparently, teachers and par-ents were ready to welcome non-oral communication and moved quickly when the dam was breached.

In the late 1960s, a deaf husband and wife were forced to go to court to estab-lish their competence to adopt children (Schlesinger and Meadow 1972). Today, re-searchers, teachers, and other professionals working with deaf children look to Deaf parents for successful strategies to create productive linguistic and educa-tional environments for deaf children (Erting, Thumann-Prezioso, and Benedict 2000; Mohay 2000; Swisher 2000).

This very brief discussion of some strands of linguistic and behavioral research illustrates the importance of research for social change as well as the dependence of research on a myriad of other factors. Funding support must be available for data collection and reporting; subjects must be willing to participate; researchers must have appropriate training if their work is to achieve credibility; and publication outlets must be in place with a receptive and knowledgeable audience of readers. In addition to all these components, it would seem that a confluence of nebulous attitudinal and atmospheric elements combine before a set of research results can start the snowball of social change.

Technology

Computer technology has opened new worlds for deaf people, changing their lives perhaps even more than those of hearing people. Closed-caption television provides access to mass culture as well as to middle-brow and high culture. Improved TTYs, video communication, visual techniques, real-time voice-to-print devices, and related technologies have hurtled onto the scene (Marschark 1997). Improved cochlear implants enable increasing numbers of deaf children and adults to hear to a greater or lesser extent (Clark, Cowan, and Dowell 1997; Spencer 2000). A 1996 survey of parents of 6- and 7-year-old deaf children found that a surprising 11 percent had received implants (Meadow-Orlans et al. 1997).

Technology has made earlier identification of deafness feasible. The average age of children identified with profound deafness decreased from about 36 months in 1970 to approximately 16 months in 1990 (Mace et al. 1991). Universal newborn-hearing screening, an unattainable dream less than a decade ago, is closer to reality. Almost half the states have legislation mandating screening at the time of birth with a goal of confirming hearing loss before the age of 3 months (American Speech-Language-Hearing Association 1999).

As the age of identification of hearing loss declined, it became feasible to study the early development of deaf infants and their families. The Gallaudet Infant Study was launched to study deaf infants with hearing parents with funding from the Maternal and Child Health Research Program, U.S. Public Health Service; the study later included deaf infants with Deaf parents with funding from the Office of Special Education and Rehabilitation, U.S. Department of Education (Koester 1995; Koester and Meadow-Orlans 1999; Meadow-Orlans 1997; Meadow-Orlans and Steinberg 1993; Spencer 1993; Spencer and Meadow-Orlans 1996). Technology also influenced research data collection and analysis: Video improvements and computer techniques for analyzing videotapes permitted many advances and refinements in deafness research.

Some of the improvements in assistive technology have direct relevance to parenting by Deaf adults, especially technology related to environmental awareness such as flashing lights or vibration signals for telephones and doorbells, child monitors, alarm clocks, and visual fire/security alarms (Harkins 1991; Meadow-Orlans 1995). These devices make deaf parents more independent, increasing their confidence and that of the wider community in their parenting skills.

The increasing importance of technology in the lives of deaf children and adults raises new issues while emphasizing old ones. The contributions to technology of professionals in varying fields relevant to deafness becomes more evident. Engineers who work on assistive devices, computer technicians who adapt software for uses specific to deafness, physicians who perform implant surgery—all join the periphery of various deaf communities. The efficacy of much of the new technology needs evaluation by competent researchers, and their results will in turn determine the future direction and use of many of the devices that are still under development.

Federal Support

Federal support for scholars and for projects related to deafness continues to influence the shape of the research enterprise. As more researchers become interested in theoretical and practical issues surrounding deafness, more grant requests are being submitted to federal agencies, whose priorities help to determine the thrust and direction of research.

In 1989 the National Institutes of Health funded 57 projects related to deafness, compared to 157 active in 1999 (table 1). Most were sponsored by the National Institute of Deafness and Other Communication Disorders (NIDCD). However, a broader range of institutes funded deafness-related work in 1999 (13 compared to 8 in 1989).

In 1989 regular research grants to individuals accounted for 75 percent of deafness-related projects; in 1999, when a greater range of mechanisms was available, that type of grant accounted for 54 percent of the total (table 2). Program projects and center grants, typically large-scale efforts, sometimes involving several institutions, accounted for 9 percent in 1989 and 14 percent in 1999. An example of a program project is titled "Cochlear implants in children." Individual career-development awards are mentored training and full-time research awards for researchers in early, mid, or late career; these are also called "K" awards and fall under the National Research Services Award program, together with fellowships. (Marc Marschark, author of numerous publications on deafness, completed several major projects under one of these grants.) Pre- and postdoctoral fellowships are designed to encourage young scientists. Recently, special fellowships were set aside specifically for minority students and those with disabilities. Small grants are meant for the collection of pilot data, with a maximum of $100,000 per year allowed for three years. Small Business Innovation Research grants were mandated by Congress so that each institute must earmark 1.5 percent of its budget to fund projects under this mechanism.

Table 3 shows the kinds of individual research grants supported by NIDCD. In 1989 and 1999 most grants were in the "hard sciences." Research in genetics rose sharply during the decade—from 0 to 20 percent of the grants, reflecting the burgeoning of the Human Genome Project.

As the country prospered economically and became more health conscious, the U.S. Congress allocated more funds to health-related research. These increases are reflected in the numbers of deafness-related proposals supported by NIH in the decade 1989–1999. The NIDCD, while relatively new, has sponsored widely publicized conferences highlighting the importance of universal hearing screening, thus having influence beyond monetary support of research.

Table 1. Deafness Research Supported by the National Institutes of Health, 1989 and 1999, by Institute, Percent, and Number of Grants

Institute	1989 % (N)	1999 % (N)
Deafness and Other Communication Disorders (NIDCD)	77.2 (44)	69.4 (109)
Child Health and Human Development (NICHD)	-0-	6.4 (10)
Neurology and Stroke (NINDS)	8.8 (5)	3.8 (6)
General Medical Science (NIGMS)	-0-	3.8 (6)
Cancer (NCI)	-0-	3.8 (6)
Mental Health (NIMH)	1.8 (1)	2.6 (4)
Diabetes, Digestive and Kidney Disease (NIDDK)	1.8 (1)	2.6 (4)
Aging (NIA)	1.8 (1)	2.6 (4)
Occupational Health (NIOSH)	-0-	1.9 (3)
Eye (NEI)	3.5 (2)	1.3 (2)
Arthritis and Musculoskeletal (NIAMS)	-0-	.6 (1)
Fogarty International Center	-0-	.6 (1)
Allergies and Infectious Diseases (NIAID)	-0-	.6 (1)
Environmental and Health Sciences (NIEHS)	1.8 (1)	-0-
Heart, Lung, and Blood (NHLBI)	3.5 (2)	-0-
Total	100.2 (57)	100.0 (157)

Source: National Institutes of Health (2000).

Legislation

In the last thirty years, several important legislative changes with implications for deaf children have occurred. Public Law 94–142 was passed in 1975, requiring all states to provide free appropriate education for children with disabilities between the ages of 5 and 18. Also required were nondiscriminatory testing, individualized education plans, and schooling in the "least restrictive environment." Public Law 101–476, the Individuals with Disabilities Education Act of 1990, is a revision of P.L. 94–142. It requires that services be provided from the time of identification until age 21 and the development of an individual family service plan (Moores 1996). The required "least restrictive environment" changed school enrollment patterns for deaf children. Between 1974 and 1994, the proportion of children enrolled in residential schools decreased from 40 percent to 22 percent. In the same

Table 2. Deafness Research Supported by the National Institutes of Health, 1989 and 1999, by Funding Mechanism, Percent, and Number of Grants

Mechanism	1989 % (N)	1999 % (N)
Regular research grant to individuals	75.4 (43)	53.5 (84)
Program projects and center grant	8.8 (5)	14.0 (22)
Individual career development awards	8.8 (5)	6.3 (10)
Pre- and postdoctoral fellowships	-0-	4.5 (7)
Small grant	-0-	5.7 (9)
First award to new investigators	3.5 (2)	3.8 (6)
Small Business Innovation Research	-0-	3.8 (6)
Intramural research	-0-	3.8 (6)
Pilot, conference, merit, and bridge grants	3.5 (2)	2.6 (4)
Contract	-0-	.6 (1)
Training	-0-	.6 (1)
Cooperative agreement	-0-	.6 (1)
Total	100.0 (57)	99.8 (157)

Source: National Institutes of Health (2000).

time period, proportions of deaf children enrolled in local public schools increased from 44 percent to 69 percent (Moores 1996). As this shift occurred, the need for trained interpreters in educational environments increased. This need spurred further growth in interpreter-training programs. Although much of the program content is focused on legal and medical interpreting, educational interpreting is increasing as deaf students are incorporated into classrooms with hearing students. In 1995 at least 500 educational programs were utilizing sign interpreters (Moores 1996).

The Americans with Disabilities Act (ADA) of 1990 generated far-reaching changes for deaf people. The act sought to remove unfair barriers to employment by asking employers to make "reasonable accommodations" for current or potential employees with disabilities (Emerton, Foster, and Gravitz 1996). Christiansen and Barnartt (1995) make a persuasive argument for the idea that it was necessary to "re-frame" public definitions of disability before the ADA could be enacted: "Disability had to be 'destigmatized' (Goffman 1963), so that persons with disabilities were not viewed as deviant, before there could be support for ideas about

Table 3. Regular Research Grants Supported by the National Institute of Deafness and Other Communication Disorders, 1989 and 1999, by Topic, Percent, and Number of Grants

Topic	1989 % (N)	1999 % (N)
Anatomy/physiology/chemistry	53.1 (17)	49.2 (29)
With genetic components	-0-	(1)
Involve animal subjects	(10)	(15)
Involve noise or other trauma	(1)	(3)
Genetics	-0-	20.3 (12)
Involve animal subjects	-0-	(9)
Language acquisition/processes	15.6 (5)	11.9 (7)
Include sign language	(5)	(2)
Cochlear implants	9.4 (3)	6.8 (4)
Noise or other trauma	3.1 (1)	1.7 (1)
Cytomegalovirus	6.3 (2)	3.4 (2)
Speech/speechreading	9.4 (3)	5.1 (3)
Tactile communication	3.1 (1)	1.7 (1)
Total	100.0 (32)	100.1 (59)

Source: National Institutes of Health (2000).

integration that are central to ADA" (Christiansen and Barnartt 1995, 214). They also suggest that the favorable media accounts generated by the Deaf President Now student movement at Gallaudet University in 1987–1988 contributed to this reframing that led to the ADA. Thus, in the figure 1 model, Deaf community action influenced new legislation resulting in greater participation in the mainstream and (it is hoped) in improved social and occupational status for deaf people.

Deaf adults and the hearing parents of deaf children have become increasingly politically sophisticated, contributing materially to the positive legislative outcomes of the past thirty years. The success of the student Deaf President Now movement provided positive nationwide exposure to deafness, serving as a springboard for many of the young activists and creating widespread public approval. As deaf people move into the mainstream, more and more opportunities are created, and the former stigma of deafness decreases with each forward movement.

Educational and Occupational Achievements

Barnartt and Christiansen (1996) show that the status of deaf people has improved a great deal from the 1970s to the 1990s. However, because the status of hearing people also improved, deaf people continue to lag behind. Nevertheless, their gains are impressive. In the 1970s, about 18 percent of hearing males and 8 percent of deaf males were college graduates; in the 1990s, those numbers rose to 25 and 13 percent, respectively. In the 1970s, 11 percent of hearing females and 5 percent of deaf females were college graduates; in the 1990s, it was 19 and 9 percent. Differences between hearing and deaf men were statistically significant in both time periods; those between hearing and deaf women were not significant at either time (Barnartt and Christiansen 1996).

In 1972, 40 percent of hearing men and 20 percent of deaf men held white-collar jobs. In 1990–1991, the respective proportions were 46 and 35 percent. In 1972, 61 percent of hearing women and 37 percent of deaf women had white-collar jobs; by 1990–1991, those numbers rose to 71 percent of hearing and 66 percent of deaf women. For both men and women, earlier differences were significant, and later ones were not (Barnartt and Christiansen 1996).

It is easy to see how higher educational attainment can lead to greater occupational success and how job requirements or employer benefits can spur educational attainment. As the occupational status of deaf people increases, so does their participation in the mainstream of community and national life—all of which contribute to a shifting of public attitudes about the attributes, qualifications, and achievements of deaf people.

Efforts to further positive change in all of the previously discussed areas are important in one central respect: improving the quality of life for deaf people. Occupational status may be the single best predictor of quality of life, and educational achievement the single best engine for improving job opportunities. If this is true, the advances reflected in the cited statistics merit cautious optimism about the effects of efforts toward social change.

THE ROLE OF CONFLICT IN THE SOCIAL CHANGE–RESEARCH EQUATION

The preceding analysis of social change has focused on positive changes in the lives of deaf people in recent decades. Despite many steps forward, there have been some steps back. Almost every positive change has been accompanied by bitter skirmishes and conflicts (although, happily, rarely by violence). Every discipline has opposing philosophical schools, and discourse is often less than polite. Are the intensity and longevity of disagreement greater in this field than in other disciplines? Is conflict a necessary or at least an expected corollary of change, a reflection of the strong commitment of parties to opposing views? The editors of a collection of essays on American education, entitled *Criticism, Conflict, and Change*, suggested that "just as 'all dogs need fleas,' . . . all educational systems need critics" (Hurwitz and Maidmont 1970, 1).

Another author suggests that conflict is endemic in American culture. Americans, Deborah Tannen declares, argue too much and "have created a pervasive

warlike atmosphere that makes us approach public dialogue, and just about any-
thing we need to accomplish, as if it were a fight" (Tannen 1998, 3). However, bitter conflicts about deafness are confined neither to our country nor to this century
(Plann 1997; Van Cleve 1993; Winefield 1987). Whatever the particular area of conflict, language mode looms as an element in either the foreground or background.
Language and identity are inextricably entwined, and, as someone has said, "My
language is me." Thus, an effort to understand the controversies and conflicts surrounding deafness, language mode, and identity are central to the discussion of
intellectual conflicts in the arena of deafness research.

Hearing Parents

In the 1960s, the oral versus manual education controversy was perhaps at its
height. Some hearing parents, against the advice and practice of educators, were
beginning to utilize sign language with their very young deaf children. Nearly
all professionals teaching children younger than age 12 were hearing by definition and decree. Persons with more than a certain decibel hearing loss were pro-
hibited, often by law, from teaching young deaf children in public institutions.
Professionals' proscriptions matched the desires of hearing parents who hoped,
sometimes against compelling evidence to the contrary, that their children
would acquire speech and language skills like their own. Thus, the idea that
"my language is me" resonated strongly for hearing parents, reinforcing the advice they received from professionals. The professionals were molded from the
training they received in graduate school. Rarely did teachers of young deaf
children know Deaf adults or hearing professionals (counselors and rehabilitation personnel) who had frequent contact with Deaf adults, least of all any who
had attended residential schools.

A community psychiatrist described the situation in the schools for deaf children during this period as follows:

> Most professionals in the school clearly aligned themselves on one side of the
> conflict or the other. Most saw the controversy as an either/or question. Belief
> in a methodology was invariably more than an intellectually held tenet; it be-
> came a strongly emotionally invested crusade. As in other crusades it was ac-
> companied by a dislike growing into hatred and devaluation of the opponent.
> (Schlesinger and Meadow 1972, 202–3)

Deaf Adults

The adult deaf children of hearing parents who experienced the rigid oral-
language training of that earlier period usually had first learned sign language
in their younger years from peers with Deaf parents. Those attending residential
schools were exposed to signing teachers (many of whom were Deaf) when they
reached middle school at age 12 or 13. Unable to communicate with family
members except in rudimentary ways, they felt themselves to be "outsiders in a

hearing world" (Higgins 1980). To become full-fledged members of a Deaf community, where pride of identity, language, and culture was growing, was exciting and rewarding (Meadow-Orlans and Erting 2000; Padden and Humphries 1988).

Like other groups who have been oppressed and excluded from the educational, occupational, and economic rewards of society, the changes that began to appear for Deaf people were sometimes accompanied by a backlash of anger and exclusionary reprisals. Deaf adults began to "speak out" (Jacobs 1989). The children of deaf adults (CODAs) organized an association and began to tell their own unique stories (Bull 1998; Davis 2000, Preston 1994; Sidransky 1990; Walker 1986).

Contemporary Controversies

The new conflicts and controversies pit subgroups against each other: those who are hard of hearing against those who are profoundly deaf (Brueggemann 2000) and people born deaf against those adventitiously deafened. Hearing parents who choose an oral education for a deaf child are termed "abusive" and "incompetent." Researchers whose results fail to support a particular position are labeled "audists," and accused of hiding "exploitative" motives behind a "mask of benevolence" (Lane 1992).

As the oral–manual controversy wound down, "total communication" became the most frequently cited method in educational settings. Usually indiscernible from the "simultaneous method" used in the past by many teachers, this consisted of speaking while signing a truncated or "pidgin" form of ASL. With the invention of artificial sign systems, such as Manual Codes for English (MCE) (Bornstein, Saulnier, and Hamilton 1983; Gustason, Pfetzing, and Zawolkow 1972), designed to follow English grammar and syntax more closely, new arguments arose regarding the efficacy of the new systems. These systems, too, came under attack as unnatural, slow, and difficult to use, with proponents who expected they would provide deaf children the basis for improved English language skills (Bornstein, Saulnier, and Hamilton 1980; Kluwin 1981a, 1981b). In addition to these communication options, other systems also had their staunch supporters: the Rochester Method (fingerspelling), Cued Speech (speech sounds captured by combining handshapes and positions), and the auditory–verbal method (a variant of speech-only training) (Marschark 1997; Moores 1996; Schwartz 1996).

In the late 1980s these debates faded and were replaced by those proposing that ASL should be the initial language used with young deaf children in classrooms, with the rationale that a firm grounding in a natural, easily acquired visual language would support the acquisition of written English as a second language (Johnson, Liddell, and Erting 1989). This approach was termed "bi-lingual/bi-cultural" or "bi-bi" and also became the center of raging arguments for and against (Bowe 1992; Mayer and Akamatsu 1999; Stewart 1993).

The sharp decline in numbers of residential school students noted earlier was accompanied by sometimes bitter controversies. For many years Deaf adults viewed the state residential schools as the point of dissemination for their language and culture. They identified themselves by schools attended rather than birthplace (Padden 1996). On the other hand, hearing parents were loath to send their children (especially their younger children) to boarding schools located many miles from some students' homes. For any low-incidence population with special educational needs, there are both pluses and minuses for integrated and segregated schooling. Some parents believe that the advantages of living at home and learning to manage with hearing peers outweigh the disadvantages of social isolation experienced by profoundly deaf students who communicate only through sign language. Some school districts are reluctant to spend the money necessary to provide interpreters and/or notetakers for the few deaf students who need them in public school classrooms, and parents must battle to provide these educational aids (Moores 1992).

Another current controversy surrounds the increasing use of cochlear implants with young deaf children. One Deaf researcher remarks that a new, frequently exclusionary deafness rhetoric has emerged since 1990, emphasizing "the most extreme of clashes, a debate between Deaf people, doctors, and hearing parents over cochlear implants. Deaf people are described as challenging the ulterior motives of doctors and hearing parents . . . [while] hearing parents . . . accuse Deaf people of unnatural and unnecessary claims to cultural rights" (Padden 1996, 79–80). Objections to this surgical procedure are often coupled by Deaf adults with objections to deafness-related genetic engineering and more generally to reliance on a "medical model" rather than a cultural one. Thus, any measures that would lead to the prevention or "cure" of deafness, thereby reducing its prevalence, are regarded by some as a threat to the Deaf community. A Deaf father of three deaf children illustrates these feelings:

> [We] are witnessing a very powerful movement through government funding and support from influential organizations and individuals for eliminating deafness. We have noted that serious investments have been made in genetic engineering and cochlear implants. . . . We cannot and will not support the genetic engineering research and development nor will we use the option of cochlear implants in our children. . . . If Deaf people make meaningful contributions, why are there some people trying to make this group extinct? Are Deaf people worthless? (Mowl 1996, 233–34)

One advocate for the Deaf community summarized the two opposing positions:

> A modern miracle of biotechnology, the media suggest, and yet the National Association of the Deaf has called the FDA approval [of cochlear implants for young children] "unsound scientifically, procedurally, and ethically." Audiologists and otologists proclaim the implant is a dramatic advance; yet the American deaf community proclaims it a dangerous setback to their interests. (Lane 1993, 273)

In addition to opposing views between segments of the several deaf communities and with hearing professionals, there are occasional philosophical clashes between the Deaf community and the broader disability movement. The disability rights movement generally is fragmented into groups representing different disabilities, and the movement for deaf rights has been called one of the most glaring examples of this fragmentation (Christiansen and Barnartt 1995, 217). In 1994 an open split developed between representatives of the two groups when Judy Heumann, Assistant Secretary for the Office of Special Education and Rehabilitation Services, U.S. Department of Education, remarked that separate education for children with disabilities was "immoral" (Christiansen and Barnartt 1995, 207n). She angered and alienated Deaf advocates who had been working to strengthen state schools for the deaf (which they saw as transmitters of Deaf culture).

This climate of conflict can have unfortunate ramifications for research. Most researchers who work on deafness are hearing, although the number of deaf researchers is rising rapidly (Bowe 1992; Padden and Humphries 1988; Sheridan 2000; Stewart 1991, 1993; Supalla 1992). Hearing researchers are often challenged: What right do they have to conduct research in a community where they are outsiders? What are their credentials for research on a population whose condition they have not experienced? These are legitimate questions and the answers are not simple:

> Studying in someone else's backyard is [not] easy. . . . When the researcher does not share the culture of those she or he studies, there is the danger that the research will be conceived, conducted, and reported within a world view that seriously distorts the experience of informants. Strategies . . . to enhance . . . collaboration, feedback, and empowerment of research informants may help both insider and outsider researchers reduce distortion of findings and discover the perspectives of those they study. (Foster 1993–1994, 9–10)

These are insightful comments and wise suggestions. However, they mirror the insights from research strategies that thoughtful scholars observe when investigating any group to which they do not belong. Mertens (1998) states that the "emancipatory paradigm" is an increasingly accepted research approach: Scholars involved with disadvantaged groups, including those with disabilities, are more likely to involve members of those groups in the research process.

Research is exploring the transition from a cultural to a bicultural identity as more and more deaf people move back and forth between a "Deaf world" and a "hearing world." "A person who is bicultural . . . [has] the best of two or more social environments—the ability to participate in two cultures and the freedom to choose the best combination" (Emerton 1996, 37).

CONCLUSION

In this chapter an effort was made to document some of the major social changes occurring in the past thirty or forty years. During this period deaf people have made enormous strides toward matching the educational and occupational achievements of hearing people. Nevertheless, a gap remains, and research can help to close that gap.

One may expect that technology will continue to change everyone's lives, deaf as well as hearing, in ways that cannot be predicted or even imagined. As computers have an increasing impact on every person's life, those of all ages and resources will be affected. It is important that deaf people not be on the wrong side of the "digital divide." Medical advances, disease, health, and immigration patterns will change the demographic characteristics of the deaf population in the future. Even today, researchers neglect various subgroups, such as deaf children with disabilities. How do technological changes influence those lives? What kinds of adjustments do they make as adults? How does their status compare with that of hearing children and adults with similar disabilities? Another example is the lack of attention given to deaf people with emotional problems. One reason for this is the stigma attached to any suggestion that communication problems related to deafness might be a reason for an increased prevalence of adjustment or psychological difficulties for deaf children and youth. Other neglected subgroups include children from families where English is not spoken at home (an increasing proportion of those in special education classrooms), children who live in rural areas, and those from impoverished inner cities.

Social changes disrupt familiar social and cultural patterns. If, overall, these changes improve the condition of deaf people, their negative consequences may be welcomed as well as deplored. A reasoned compromise and a more harmonious acceptance of differences and similarities must eventually prevail. After all, certain enduring, essential facts will continue to govern the relationships of the Deaf and hearing communities: Most deaf children will grow up in hearing families; most deaf parents will produce hearing children. These facts may be immutable, but the attitudes and actions of the central and peripheral players in the continuing dramas may change. Research can document and evaluate the changes, thereby influencing the resulting attitudes and actions in the future as in the past.

REFERENCES

American Speech-Language-Hearing Association. 1999. Newborn Hearing Screening Grants for States Resulting from Title VI (the Walsh bill) of the FY2000 Labor-HHS-Education Appropriations Act of 1999. [Available: http://www.asha.org/infant_hearing/faq_infant_hearing.htm.]

Baker, C., and D. Cokely. 1980. *American Sign Language: A teacher's resource text on grammar and culture.* Silver Spring, Md.: T.J. Publishers.

Barnartt, S. N., and J. B. Christiansen. 1996. The educational and occupational attainment of prevocationally deaf adults: 1972–1991. In *Understanding deafness socially: Continuities in research and theory,* 2d ed., ed. P. C. Higgins and J. E. Nash, 60–70. Springfield, Ill.: Charles C. Thomas.

Bornstein, H., K. Saulnier, and L. Hamilton. 1980. Signed English: A first evaluation. *American Annals of the Deaf* 125:468–81.

———. 1983. *The Comprehensive Signed English Dictionary.* Washington, D.C.: Gallaudet College Press.

Bowe, F. 1992. Radicalism vs. reason: Directions in the educational use of ASL. In *A free hand: Enfranchising the education of deaf children,* ed. M. Walworth, D. F. Moores, and T. J. O'Rourke, 182–97. Silver Spring, Md.: T. J. Publishers.

Brasel, K. E., and S. P. Quigley. 1977. Influence of certain language and communication environments in early childhood on the development of language in deaf individuals. *Journal of Speech and Hearing Research* 20:81–94.

Brueggemann, B. J. 2000. *Lend me your ear: Rhetorical constructions of deafness.* Washington, D.C.: Gallaudet University Press.

Bull, T. 1998. *On the edge of Deaf culture: Hearing children/Deaf parents.* Alexandria, Va.: Deaf Family Research Press.

Christiansen, J. B., and S. N. Barnartt. 1995. *Deaf president now: The 1988 revolution at Gallaudet University.* Washington, D.C.: Gallaudet University Press.

Clark, G., R. Cowan, and R. Dowell, eds. 1997. *Cochlear implantation for infants and children: Advances.* San Diego: Singular Publishing.

Davis, L. J. 2000. *My sense of silence: Memoirs of a childhood with deafness.* Champagne, Ill.: University of Illinois Press.

Emerton, R. G. 1996. Marginality, biculturalism, and social identity of deaf people. In *Cultural and language diversity and the deaf experience,* ed. I. Parasnis, 136–45. New York: Cambridge University Press.

Emerton, R. G., S. Foster, and J. Gravitz. 1996. Deaf people in today's workplace: Use of the ADA and mediation processes in resolving barriers to participation. In *Understanding deafness socially: Continuities in research and theory,* 2d ed., ed. P. C. Higgins and J. E. Nash, 44–65. Springfield, Ill.: Charles C. Thomas.

Erting, C. J. 1994. *Deafness, communication, social identity: Ethnography in a preschool for deaf children.* Burtonsville, Md.: Linstok Press.

Erting, C. J., C. Prezioso, and M. Hynes. 1994. The interactional context of deaf mother–infant communication. In *From gesture to language in hearing and deaf children,* ed. V. Volterra and C. J. Erting, 97–106. Washington, D.C.: Gallaudet University Press.

Erting, C. J., C. Thumann-Prezioso, and B. S. Benedict. 2000. Bilingualism in a deaf family: Fingerspelling in early childhood. In *The deaf child in the family and at school: Essays in honor of Kathryn P. Meadow-Orlans,* ed. P. E. Spencer, C. J. Erting, and M. Marschark, 41–54. Mahwah, N.J.: Lawrence Erlbaum.

Foster, S. 1993–1994. Outsider in the deaf world: Reflections of an ethnographic researcher. *Journal of the Deafness and Rehabilitation Association* 27:1–10.

Goffman, E. 1963. *Stigma.* Englewood Cliffs, N.J.: Prentice-Hall.

Gustason, G., D. Pfetzing, and E. Zawolkow. 1972. *Signing Exact English.* Rossmoor, Calif.: Modern Signs Press.

Harkins, J. E. 1991. *Visual devices for deaf and hard of hearing people: State of the art.* GRI Monograph Series A, no. 3. Washington, D.C.: Gallaudet University.

Higgins, P. C. 1980. *Outsiders in a hearing world: A sociology of deafness.* Beverly Hills, Calif.: Sage Publications.

Hurwitz, E. Jr., and R. Maidmont, eds. 1970. *Criticism, conflict, and change: Readings in American education.* New York: Dodd, Mead, and Co.

Jacobs, L. M. 1989. *A deaf adult speaks out,* 3d ed. Washington D.C.: Gallaudet University Press.

Johnson, R. E., S. K. Liddell, and C. J. Erting. 1989. *Unlocking the curriculum: Principles for achieving success in deaf education.* Gallaudet Research Institute working paper 89–3. Washington, D.C.: Gallaudet University.

Klima E. S., and U. Bellugi. 1979. *The signs of language.* Cambridge: Harvard University Press.

Kluwin, T. 1981a. The grammaticality of manual representations of English in classroom settings. *American Annals of the Deaf* 125:417–21.

———. 1981b. A rationale for modifying classroom signing systems. *Sign Language Studies* 31:179–88.

Koester, L. S. 1995. Face-to-face interactions between hearing mothers and their deaf infants. *Early Development and Parenting* 18:145–53.

Koester, L. S., and K. P. Meadow-Orlans. 1999. Responses to interactive stress: Infants who are deaf or hearing. *American Annals of the Deaf* 144:395–403.

Lane, H. 1992. *The mask of benevolence: Disabling the deaf community.* New York: Knopf.

———. 1993. Cochlear implants: Their cultural and historical meaning. In *Deaf history unveiled: Interpretations from the new scholarship,* ed. J. V. Van Cleve, 272–91. Washington, D.C.: Gallaudet University Press.

Mace, A. L., K. L. Wallace, M. Q. Whan, and P. G. Stelmachowicz. 1991. Relevant factors in the identification of hearing loss. *Ear and Hearing* 12:287–93.

Marschark, M. 1993. *Psychological development of deaf children.* New York: Oxford University Press.

———. 1997. *Raising and educating a deaf child.* New York: Oxford University Press.

Mayer, C., and C. T. Akamatsu. 1999. Bilingual-bicultural models of literacy education for deaf students: Considering the claims. *Journal of Deaf Studies and Deaf Education* 4:1–8.

Meadow, K. P. 1967. *The effect of early manual communication and family climate on the deaf child's development.* Ph.D. diss., University of California, Berkeley.

———. 1968. Early manual communication in relation to the deaf child's intellectual, social, and communicative functioning. *American Annals of the Deaf* 113:29–41.

———. 1969. Self-image, family climate, and deafness. *Social Forces* 47:428–38.

Meadow-Orlans, K. P. 1995. Parenting with a sensory or physical disability. In *Handbook of parenting,* vol. 4, ed. M. H. Bornstein, 57–84. Mahwah, N.J.: Lawrence Erlbaum.

———. 1997. Effects of mother and infant hearing status on interactions at twelve and eighteen months. *Journal of Deaf Studies and Deaf Education* 2:27–36.

Meadow-Orlans, K. P., and C. Erting. 2000. Deaf people in society. In *Mental health and deafness,* ed. P. Hindley and N. Kitson, 3–24. London: Whurr Publishers.

Meadow-Orlans, K. P., D. M. Mertens, M. A. Sass-Lehrer, and K. Scott-Olson. 1997. Support services for parents and their children who are deaf or hard of hearing. *American Annals of the Deaf* 142:278–93.

Meadow-Orlans, K. P., and A. G. Steinberg. 1993. Effects of infant hearing loss and maternal support on mother–infant interactions at 18 months. *Journal of Applied Developmental Psychology* 14:407–26.

Mertens, D. M. 1998. *Research methods in education and psychology: Integrating diversity with quantitative and qualitative approaches.* Thousand Oaks, Calif.: Sage Publications.

Mohay, H. 2000. Language in sight: Mothers' strategies for making language visually accessible to deaf children. In *The deaf child in the family and at school: Essays in honor of Kathryn P. Meadow-Orlans,* ed. P. E. Spencer, C. J. Erting, and M. Marschark, 151–66. Mahwah, N.J.: Lawrence Erlbaum.

Moores, D. F. 1992. A historical perspective on school placement. In *Toward effective school programs for deaf students,* ed. T. Kluwin, D. F. Moores, and M. Gaustad, 7–29. New York: Teachers College Press.

———. 1996. *Educating the deaf, psychology, principles, and practices,* 4th ed. Boston: Houghton Mifflin.

Mowl, G. E. 1996. Raising deaf children in a hearing society: Struggles and challenges for deaf native ASL users. In *Cultural and language diversity and the deaf experience,* ed. I. Parasnis, 232–45. New York: Cambridge University Press.

National Institutes of Health. 2000. [Available: http://commons.cit.nih.gov/ crisp_lib.query.]

Padden, C. A. 1996. From the cultural to the bicultural: The modern deaf community. In *Cultural and language diversity and the deaf experience,* ed. I. Parasnis, 79–98. New York: Cambridge University Press.

Padden, C., and T. Humphries 1988. *Deaf in America.* Cambridge: Harvard University Press.

Plann, S. 1997. *A silent minority: Deaf education in Spain, 1550–1835.* Berkeley: University of California Press.

Preston, P. 1994. *Mother father deaf: Living between sound and silence.* Cambridge: Harvard University Press.

Rée, J. 1999. *I see a voice.* New York: Henry Holt.

Schlesinger, H. S., and K. P. Meadow. 1972. *Sound and sign: Childhood deafness and mental health.* Berkeley: University of California Press.

Schwartz, S. 1996. *Choices in deafness: A parents' guide to communication options,* 2d ed. Bethesda, Md.: Woodbine House.

Sheridan, M. A. 2000. Images of self and others: Stories from the children. In *The deaf child in the family and at school: Essays in honor of Kathryn P. Meadow-Orlans,* ed. P. E. Spencer, C. J. Erting, and M. Marschark, 5–20. Mahwah, N.J.: Lawrence Erlbaum.

Sidransky. R. 1990. *In silence: Growing up in a deaf world.* New York: St. Martin's Press.

Spencer, P. E. 1993. Communication behaviors of infants with hearing loss and their hearing mothers. *Child Development* 36:311–21.

———. 2000. Every opportunity: A case study of hearing parents and their deaf child. In *The deaf child in the family and at school: Essays in honor of Kathryn P. Meadow-Orlans,* ed. P. E. Spencer, C. J. Erting, and M. Marschark, 111–32. Mahwah, N.J.: Lawrence Erlbaum.

Spencer, P. E., and K. P. Meadow-Orlans. 1996. Play, language, and maternal responsiveness. *Child Development* 67:3176–91.

Stewart, D. A. 1991. *Deaf sport: The impact of sports within the deaf community.* Washington, D.C.: Gallaudet University Press.

———. 1993. Bi-bi to MCE? *American Annals of the Deaf* 138:331–37.

Stokoe, W. C. Jr. 1960. *Sign language structure: An outline of the visual communication systems of the American deaf.* Studies in linguistics, occasional papers 8. Department of Anthropology and Linguistics, University of Buffalo, New York.

Stokoe, W. C. Jr., D. C. Casterline, and C. G. Croneberg. 1965. *A dictionary of American Sign Language on linguistic principles.* Washington, D.C.: Gallaudet College Press.

Stuckless, E. R., and J. W. Birch. 1966. The influence of early manual communication on the linguistic development of deaf children. *American Annals of the Deaf* 111:452–60.

Supalla, S. J. 1992. *The book of name signs*. San Diego: DawnSignPress.

Swisher, M. V. 2000. Learning to converse: How deaf mothers support the development of attention and conversational skills in their young deaf children. In *The deaf child in the family and at school: Essays in honor of Kathryn P. Meadow-Orlans*, ed. P. E. Spencer, C. J. Erting, and M. Marschark, 21–40. Mahwah, N.J.: Lawrence Erlbaum.

Tannen, D. 1998. *The argument culture: Moving from debate to dialogue*. New York: Random House.

Van Cleve, J. V., ed. 1993. *Deaf history unveiled: Interpretations from the new scholarship*. Washington, D.C.: Gallaudet University Press.

Vernon, M., and S. D. Koh, 1970. Early manual communication and deaf children's achievement. *American Annals of the Deaf* 115:527–36.

Walker, L. A. 1986. *A loss for words: The story of deafness in a family*. New York: Harper and Row.

Winefield, R. 1987. *Never the twain shall meet*. Washington, D.C.: Gallaudet University Press.

11

CONTEXT, COGNITION, AND DEAFNESS: PLANNING THE RESEARCH AGENDA

Marc Marschark

A chapter on the future of research in deaf studies and deaf education or any other field could adopt either of two approaches.[1] One possibility would be to try to predict new topics and new directions based on previous and contemporary trends. Such an undertaking would be simple and straightforward, at least for short-term prognostication. It would be extremely difficult, however, to factor in advances in other fields or events in nonresearch areas (e.g., the economy, technology, politics). Further, without knowing the results of those studies, it would be difficult to foresee changes beyond the near future because the results of various investigations will create a very different context for research that comes after them. The farther one looks into the future, the more complex and difficult prediction would be, and the greater the probability that unforeseen findings and events would change everything.

An alternative approach, and the one adopted in this chapter, would be to address research *priorities*, rather than *predictions*, for the future. Based on assessments of the current state of the art and collected from appropriate audiences, this approach would still provide some predictive power for the near-term research agenda, but it also would have greater utility for those planning the agenda. The only hazards of the method include publicly putting ourselves on notice for our collective shortcomings and thereby necessarily committing to trying to remedy them in the future. We can live with that.

This chapter is divided into two parts. The first half concerns the current opportunities and challenges for research in deaf education and allied fields, together with some of the factors shaping the current and future research agendas.

A version of some of the material in this chapter was presented at the annual meeting of the Conference of Educational Administrators Serving the Deaf, Pittsburgh, May 1999.

---

1. The term *deaf education* here, as well as later references to "deaf children" and "deafness," follow the traditions in our field and are not meant in any pathological sense. The fact that such terms are now seen as insensitive or incorrect by some commentators (more than one of whom has seen fit to write to the author) is rather surprising in view of the continued use of "schools for the deaf," "deaf clubs," and so on by members of the culturally Deaf community. Interestingly, most such complaints come from hearing rather than deaf correspondents, suggesting that the issue may be more one of political correctness than of interpersonal sensitivity.

The second half of the chapter presents an informal study of priorities for investigation in the field, as seen by those most centrally involved in day-to-day educational and research activities. The order of these two sections is actually reversed from what was originally planned, simply by accident of the responses obtained in "data collection." Not coincidentally, the two parts mesh well, and it is useful first to set the historical and theoretical backgrounds for the discussion of what issues should be at the top of our research agenda in the coming years.

LAYING A FOUNDATION FOR THE FUTURE

In the context of considering future research priorities, it would be informative to track past changes in education and research in the field alongside changes in the Deaf community, civil rights and disability-related legislation, progress in related fields (e.g., psychology and linguistics), and the growth of technology in society.[2] Such an investigation would help to explain research trends in specific areas as well as the interplay between research and the needs and demands of those who directly or indirectly pay for that research. As interesting as it might be, such an exercise probably does not belong in this volume and could fill a book itself. Instead, this chapter will consider several more specific issues that go directly to the heart of what this field is all about. These topics, raised by researchers, teachers, and parents of deaf children, constitute the research agenda for the near future.

Underlying this discussion is the belief that our entry into the new millennium coincides with a new urgency and new opportunities concerning the development and education of deaf learners. It is not only a situation born of legal requirements and political will, but also a linking of practical needs and scientific progress. Despite tremendous progress in research over the past 25 years, a lot still remains to be done. Many deaf children and their hearing parents still lack effective communication and interaction at home and at school, and many deaf students still are not achieving in school at the level that is necessary for educational and vocational success. At the same time, we do appear to be at a threshold, at least if we approach the issue in a collaborative, broad-minded manner.

It is not my intention here to argue for a particular research agenda, although the collected research priorities of others offer some excellent alternatives. Rather, the goal is to provide an outline of research needs, as seen by those who are most closely involved in the development and education of deaf children. As a starting point, it seems important to get some misunderstandings out of the way. Until recently, for example, many people associated with deaf education assumed that something called "applied research" or "educational research" was the only kind of study we needed in order to improve the academic process for deaf students. The situation is never so simple or clear-cut, of course, and it is now clear that a combination of applied and basic investigation can provide much more progress than either alone.

---

2. Unbeknownst to the author, a meeting had already been planned to address some of these issues at the time this chapter was written. The conference, "The American Deaf Community: Diversity and Change," was held at Gallaudet University in July 2000.

Contrary to what many people seem to expect, advances relating to the education of deaf children have often been led by scientific studies on related topics rather than by educational studies per se. Included among these areas are the social-psychological and later academic benefits of early intervention programs (Calderon and Greenberg 1997; Moores and Meadow-Orlans 1990), the linguistics and psycholinguistics of acquiring ASL as a first language and English as a second language (Marschark et al. 1998; Siple 1978), memory for verbal and nonverbal information (Marschark and Lukomski, this volume; Wilson, this volume), and the reading strategies employed—or not employed—by deaf students (Gaustad 2000; Musselman 2000; Wilbur 2000). Most of these basic studies have been driven by the need to understand the complex learning processes that are necessary for educational, social, and personal success of deaf individuals, even if the applied questions were not primary. Recent studies of teaching and learning processes among deaf students thus have brought basic and applied research closer together, but there is still a divide.

If there is a rift between basic and applied research, it is an artificial one—or at least an accidental one. Most researchers involved in deaf education per se started out in this field and have focused specifically on deaf students in school. Until recently they have been more concerned with the dynamics of the classroom, student characteristics, and curriculum issues than cognitive processes presumed to underlie learning. In contrast, most researchers involved in related basic research on topics such as social processes, problem solving, or reading started out in other fields such as psychology, linguistics, or child development. Until recently, they have generally been more concerned with understanding the basic mechanisms of learning, language, and cognition than with the practical implications of their findings. Given these different backgrounds and aims, it is not surprising that investigators in these two schools have tended to use different methodologies and focus on different levels of analysis. They also frequently publish in different journals, attend different conferences, and have different audiences. Ultimately, however, they all share some underlying goals: wanting to understand learning and the ways in which characteristics of teachers and learners (or information and information-processors) might influence outcomes.

THE THORNIEST OF ISSUES

In the current climate of competition for resources and pressure from our constituencies to demonstrate the impact of our investigations, both basic and applied investigators are feeling pressure. This situation presents an opportunity, but also a potential trap. One educational administrator recently complained that researchers have been trying to understand and improve the reading abilities of deaf students for 100 years with little progress. "Maybe it's time to just move on," he suggested. Little progress?! Forty years ago we did not know that deaf students who signed rather than spoke "had language" (Furth 1966; cf. Stokoe, this volume). Twenty years ago, we did not know that deaf readers could acquire the phonological skills (apparently) necessary for optimal reading (Conrad 1979; cf. Leybaert, Content, and Alegria 1987; Lang and Stokoe 2000). And ten years ago we did not know that mentally representing text as sign language required more memory capacity than representing it as spoken language (Waters and Doehring 1990; Wilson, this volume). Although these findings in themselves do not directly provide for improved reading abilities among deaf students, they are all central to understanding the challenges faced by young deaf readers and have fundamentally changed the ways we go about educating deaf children—or they should (Marschark and Lukomski, this volume). True, the reading skills of deaf students have not increased as dramatically as we might like, but they have shown some improvement in the past few years (Traxler 2000).

The fact that we have had only modest success in improving literacy and other academic skills of deaf students is taken by some observers as an indicator that "something is wrong somewhere." Administrators might point a finger at research that does not answer or even ask the "right" questions, but more often they point to their own lack of funding. Parents, meanwhile, tend to point their fingers at teachers and schools (i.e., administrators), whereas teachers complain that the problem is a lack of time and resources. But there is a basic error here. Assuming that our inability to resolve the literacy issue is an indicator of some foundational problem in education is like saying that there is something wrong with medicine because we have not yet cured cancer or the common cold. Simply put, it ignores the fact that there is no one "cause" of deaf children's reading difficulties, and the variables that we know are involved are exceedingly difficult if not impossible to change. These include factors as diverse as most deaf children not sharing an accessible first language with their hearing parents, the fact that natural sign languages do not directly parallel natural spoken languages, and the relatively low level of sign language skills required by many teacher-training programs. Still, print literacy is an essential skill in western culture, and the pressure to "solve the problem" of lower literacy skills among many deaf students cannot be taken off the agenda or ignored, no matter how many false starts and shortfalls there may have been in the past. Rather, we should use the past to help plan for the future (Power and Leigh 2000).

As we pursue the literacy agenda and plot its trajectory, we are all well aware of the fact that we are in the midst of some subtle and not-so-subtle changes that are likely to influence work in that area. Two such changes are particularly worthy of mention insofar as they will have major pragmatic and scientific implications for our field: the acceleration of educationally relevant technology and changes in the priorities of our audiences. Let us consider each of these in turn.

TECHNOLOGY AND THE DEAF LEARNER

In a discussion such as this one, it is impossible to ignore the rapidly changing worlds of wireless communication, digital imaging, and computing. All of these promise to change education as we know it, even as other technologies, such as distance learning, cochlear implants, and speech-to-print technologies, promise to change the ability of deaf learners to access instruction and communication in a variety of different ways.

Information Technology

Computers, the Internet, and related information technologies have the potential to fundamentally transform the way that students who are deaf and hard of hearing are educated. The graphics and animation capabilities of computers present the opportunity for multimedia and visually based presentations specifically oriented toward their visuospatial strengths, and the Internet offers a valuable and almost limitless resource for teachers and students on almost any topic. At present, however, most computing remains heavily text-dependent, thus placing even greater demands on the reading skills of deaf students. Waters and Dochring (1990) argued that the demands of the "information age" made an eleventh- or twelfth-grade reading level the minimum necessary for functional literacy.[3] Our dependence on computers has increased considerably in the decade since, and yet reading abilities of deaf students have increased only up to the point where 18-year-olds are reading, on average, at about a fifth-grade level (Traxler 2000). Further, there is little substantive evidence so far to support the assumption that learning is enhanced by Internet resources even for hearing students (Owston 1997).

The situation is much the same with regard to the possibility of any educational impact from increased availability of captioning. Over the past decade, captioning technology has greatly improved access to information for deaf students both in the classroom and at home. Most obviously, there is now easier access to educational media through either open or closed captions. There are also many more opportunities for incidental learning of world knowledge outside the classroom through closed captioning on television. Beyond the content of the shows themselves, reading captions would appear to provide avenues for deaf students to improve their English language skills, insofar as more reading leads to improved reading skill (Stanovich 1986). Few empirical evaluations on this issue are available, however, and how much students gain from watching captioned films and television is unclear. Captioning is usually quite fast, suggesting the possibility that only better deaf readers will benefit significantly from captions the way they are produced now (Hertzog, Stinson, and Keiffer 1989).

Cochlear Implants

While the jury is still out on the Internet and captioning, we also await evidence concerning cochlear implants and other speech- and hearing-related technologies, as well as speech-to-print hardware and software.[4] Looking ahead, the role and

---

3. Third- to fourth-grade reading and writing levels are generally accepted as the level of functional literacy.

4. Voice recognition software is now commercially available and was used in the preparation of this chapter. Users' success with the technology varies widely, and it is not yet at a point where it can be used efficiently in classrooms, public lectures, the media, or in a portable communication device.

potential of cochlear implants is a major one for teachers and researchers alike, a concern made clear in the informal study described next.

As much as we might think of cochlear implants being the province of medical researchers, the rapidly increasing number of deaf children who are receiving implants raises a variety of issues beyond the extent to which they affect hearing: their support for language development, their impact on interpersonal communication and self-esteem, and so on. Research concerning these broader questions is just beginning, and so the long-term implications for development and education remain unclear. A study by Francis et al. (1999), however, found that the length of cochlear implant experience accounted for only one percent of the variability in whether K–12 students were enrolled in mainstream classrooms or special programs for deaf children.

Most broadly, implants generally do improve the perception of speech-related sound and support spoken language in individuals who have been selected as appropriate candidates. Adults who have lost their hearing typically show more rapid benefits following implantation compared to young children with congenital or early-onset hearing losses, whereas children show more continued improvement over time. Contrary to what some parents of deaf children believe (Kampfe et al. 1993), cochlear implants do not restore normal hearing even if they do help in the understanding of speech and the perception of sounds in the environment (National Institute on Deafness and Other Communication Disorders 1998). Some children with implants are extremely successful in spoken communication. Most function more like hard of hearing children, however, and for many it appears that sign language may be an important accompaniment to spoken language (Tomblin et al.1999). Unfortunately, we are not yet able to tell which children will fall into which group.

Why have developmental and educational researchers been so slow off the mark in conducting studies with children who have cochlear implants? First, funding for cochlear implants comes primarily from medical sources, and the reality is that continued funding for related research largely depends on demonstrating improved auditory reception at frequencies relevant for speech perception. Although preliminary evidence is encouraging (Geers and Moog 1994; Robbins et al. 1995; Tomblin et al. 1999; Waltzman et al. 1997), issues relating to language, learning, and literacy have not been part of the medical research agenda and are just now reaching ours (discussed later). Second, but not unrelated, is the fact that most candidates for implantation are drawn from mainstream programs or others emphasizing spoken language, and parents have often been required to enroll their children in such programs if their children are to receive the implants. This situation is changing, and many total communication programs now serve children who have implants. Nevertheless, such restrictions mean that previous evaluations of cochlear implants have not included unbiased samples of deaf children, thus limiting the generality of their conclusions.

For now, the debate about cochlear implants will continue, often focusing on the potential social, emotional, and cultural implications of cochlear implants rather than their actual impact on deaf children (Crouch 1997; Lane 1992; Rose, Vernon, and Pool 1996). Advances in implant technology and the increasing frequency of children receiving implants will also continue. These changes will not remove literacy from the research agenda, but they likely will join it as one of the most pressing issues.

In short, a variety of technologies have the potential to change the educational opportunities for individuals who are deaf and hard of hearing. Access to communication through computers, captioning, TTYs, and digital information transfer has already improved the lives of deaf people. The degree to which they have enhanced the education of deaf learners remains to be determined. In the meantime, cochlear implants, speech-to-print technology, and visual and vibrotactile speech-supporting devices (Becker and Artelt 1998; Rönnberg et al. 1998) are offering deaf and hard of hearing individuals new communication alternatives that also merit educational evaluation. Not surprisingly, exploration of these technologies has become more prominent in research funding, and the chapter now turns to consideration of recent changes in funding priorities.

RESEARCH FUNDING AGENDAS

For many people, including those doing research in this field, the ways of federal funding for research are often obscure. Such funding is often essential for high-quality investigations into the more complex questions confronting us, but it sometimes seems elusive. In part, this situation occurs because investigators often see only the priorities for individual competitions and not the full context of the research funding agenda. That information is publicly available, however, and provides an interesting indicator of research to come. Regardless of whether any particular constituent group believes that designated priorities are the most important, these are areas that *will* receive broad research attention. As an example, we can examine differences between the National Strategic Research Plans of the National Institute on Deafness and Other Communication Disorders (NIDCD) for the years 1991–1993 and the years 2000–2002.[5]

In the 1991–1993 NIDCD *National Research Strategic Plan*, "Hearing and Hearing Impairment," "Speech and Speech Disorders," and "Language and Language Impairments" constituted three of the six separate sections (NIDCD 1991, 1992, 1993). In the "Language and Language Impairments" section, there were four major categories of "major scientific opportunities." Those categories and their subcategories are listed in table 1, where it can be seen that they were led by "Multicultural Issues" and "Language and Deaf People," both categories that implicitly recognize Deaf individuals as a linguistic, cultural minority. A full reading of the plan reveals a broader research agenda that also includes research relating to congenital and acquired hearing losses, auditory perception, and speech.

The listing in table 1 is selective, and I have provided details for only a few of the "opportunities" listed for each category. These topics still clearly reflect the call for rigorous study of signed and spoken languages, language development among deaf children, literacy, and, perhaps most importantly, interactions among these and related variables. At least for the 1990s, the NIH funding priorities

---

5. At the same time, it will be useful to keep in mind several other events that are part of the relevant context for these agendas: the Deaf President Now protest at Gallaudet University in 1988, the Americans with Disabilities Act of 1990, the conservative shift that took place in the U.S. Congress in 1994, and the designation of the 1990s as the "decade of the brain."

Table 1. Major Scientific Opportunities Identified within the "Language and Language Impairments" Section of the 1991–1993 NIDCD National Strategic Research Plan

Major Scientific Opportunities Identified	Specific Areas of Research Discussed
Multicultural Issues	1. simultaneous or consecutive acquisition of two or more linguistic systems
	2. normative studies for different languages or social dialects
	3. differences in cognitive development were learning styles and cultural systems of belief
Language and Deaf People	1. language development of deaf children
	2. studies of literacy in deaf children and adults
	3. basic research on sign language structure and function
Language and Its Disorders and Children	1. basis of language disorders in children
	2. assessment
	3. academic social, and vocational impact
	4. intervention
Language and Its Disorders and Adults	1. brain-language relations
	2. analyses of processes underlying language disorders
	3. assessment, intervention, and recovery
	4. comparative language studies

related to deafness were clearly supportive of attempts to enhance social, academic, and career opportunities for deaf and hard of hearing individuals.

In contrast to those more socially oriented areas of investigation, many of them held dear by those interested in the education and development of deaf learners, the strategic plan for the NIDCD for the years 2000–2002 (NIDCD 1999) looks very different. The "extraordinary scientific opportunities" listed in that plan are listed in table 2; those priorities that seem to resonate with the 1991–1993 plan are in italics.

The 2000–2002 document emphasizes, "Effective communication is central for the functioning of modern society. Although science and technology have greatly improved our capacity for communication, many aspects of contemporary life remain profoundly difficult for those with communication disorders. Such disorders often compromise social, emotional, educational, and vocational aspects of an individual's life" (1). Nonetheless, it is clear from the agenda of "extraordinary opportunities" that the emphasis in NIDCD funding, or at least the focus of its description of important questions, has shifted toward biological and medical investigations. Undoubtedly, this shift has resulted in part from increasing pressure from the U.S. Congress, which has generously augmented the NIH and National Science Foundation budgets while calling for greater accountability and more obvious advances in "hard" science. The shift is also consistent with what seems to be the mood of American taxpayers to look to medical science and technology to improve life.

These observations are not to suggest that federal agencies have stopped funding research relating to sign language, literacy, or cognitive functioning among deaf learners. NIDCD certainly is doing so, as is the U.S. Department of Education, which continues to seek improvement in communication and educational access for individuals who are deaf or hard of hearing. Nevertheless, such funding has become more competitive, and many members of the research community feel that they should be more involved in proactively shaping the research agenda rather than reacting to it. The reauthorization of the Individuals with Disabilities Education Act in 1999 called for greater public accountability in research relating to deafness, and it may be that this will provide such opportunities. Establishment of research agendas without researcher participation is something that would not happen in fields like medicine, physics, or astronomy. The fact that it happens in education suggests that many policymakers either believe "we understand it, because we have been through it" or that "it's not rocket science." Again, this is not to say that priorities established without broader input are necessarily inappropriate or off-target. Rather, the point is much more general: At a time when there is tremendous opportunity for enhancing our understanding of the *three Ls* of learning, language, and literacy in deaf students, we need to bring all parties together to establish a research agenda that will meet both immediate and long-term goals while being scientifically and financially realistic. So far, this has not happened.

SEEKING EFFECTIVE COMMUNICATION AND COLLABORATION

One could list a number of possible reasons for what appears to be a lack of interchange among researchers, policymakers/administrators, parents, and teachers in

Table 2. "Extraordinary Scientific Opportunities" within the 2000–2002 NIDCD National Strategic Research Plan. (Italics added to show research areas that resonate with the 1991–1993 plan.)

Extraordinary Scientific Opportunities Identified	Specific Areas of Research Discussed
Determine the Molecular and Epidemiological Bases of Normal and Disordered Communication	1. utilizing molecular biologic and genetic approaches to study human communication 2. applying emerging technologies in genetics and molecular biology to the clinical setting 3. developing animal models to identify specific disease gene loci 4. developing in vitro systems to facilitate the study of function at the molecular level
Study the Development, Deterioration, Regeneration, and Plasticity of Processes Mediating Communication	1. characterizing age-related changes in structural and functional plasticity 2. determining cellular and molecular mechanisms underlying sensory cell regeneration

Extraordinary Scientific Opportunities Identified	Specific Areas of Research Discussed
Study Perceptual and Cognitive Processing in Normal and Disordered Communication	1. investigating the molecular mechanisms of neurotransmission
	2. application of physiologic approaches, such as functional neuroimaging, in animal models
	3. *development of quantitative methods to analyze sensory, sensori-motor, and cognitive processing in humans, in particular, those processes not readily studied in animal models*
	4. *investigation of the perceptual and cognitive consequences of disor-dered communication and determining how these processes change with treatment*
Develop and Improve Devices, Pharmacologic Agents, and Strategies for Habilitation and Rehabilitation of Human Communication Disorders	1. *capitalizing on emerging technologies to design and improve devices that enhance communication*
	2. using clinical trials and other clinical studies to evaluate the efficacy of newly developed devices, drugs, and other therapies for individuals with communication disorders
	3. *developing cost-effective techniques for the assessment of speech/language development and disorders in the broad range of languages currently used by residents of the United States, taking into account all cultural and ethnic groups*
	4. using molecular genetic, electrophysiological imaging, and other approaches to precisely define the phenotypes of commu-nication disorders as a basis for optimizing clinical diagnosis and intervention

our field. Most of these have at least some historical bases related to the apparent "laboratory versus classroom" or "basic versus applied" perspectives alluded to earlier. In part, this situation has resulted from the fact that expectations are very different for university faculty who conduct research and teachers who would like to be involved in or benefit from research. Many collaborations have been sought or planned with the best intentions, only to meet lukewarm receptions from educational administrators who have other priorities, or to have teachers drop out due to lack of time, or to see researchers focus on "academic" questions that seem to have little payoff with regard to day-to-day educational issues.

Unfortunately, these are the realities of the situation. Administrators often feel they have more immediate needs than supporting research by "outsiders," and relatively few of them see the value in establishing internal or collaborative research groups. Teachers of deaf children typically are enthusiastic about research collaborations, but limited resources, limited time, and school demands do not leave them much opportunity for meaningful participation. And much of the payoff in research relating to education development is not short-term. Although we might try to design studies that have both immediate implications for practice and longer-term impact on theory, completing such studies takes time, and there is a long history of people collecting data in applied settings without ever reporting on the findings and the implications. There is no one direction to point a finger here—other than forward.

At the same time, there is also a "red herring" that continues to surface on a regular basis: that those who claim to be conducting research concerning deaf learners are out of touch with the real needs of the field and are really just "talking to each other."[6] This assumption appears to stifle enthusiasm within schools and may be responsible for the tendency not to include researchers in administrative discussions of the research agendas for our field. Generalizations of this sort appear to be as unsubstantiated as those suggesting that deaf children are concrete and literal in their thinking or that cochlear implants will destroy the Deaf community. Like many stereotypes, however, this attribution is difficult to shed. Also, like many stereotypes, it may well have some basis in truth. In keeping with my own orientation, it seemed that the best way to get to the truth was to collect some data. So I did. The study has little that would recommend it for publication in a scholarly journal. Nevertheless, it yielded some enlightening information that bears directly on the present discussion.

AN INFORMAL STUDY

This study had two purposes. One was to determine the extent to which university faculty who are engaged in research related to deafness and deaf education see the research agenda any differently than do teachers and educational administrators. The second purpose was equally pragmatic: It provided an opportunity to collect candidates for the research agenda from a relatively diverse group of indi-

---

6. This particular herring has been thrown at the author twice during preparation of this chapter, the second time including the quoted complaint.

viduals, all of whom have a vested interest in the research enterprise relating to the development and education of deaf students.

For the purposes of this informal investigation, three groups were selected: university-based researchers, teachers of deaf students, and educational administrators involved in programming for deaf students or at various levels of government. Some of the individuals I knew personally, some by reputation, and a few were referred by other participants. In all cases, I told the participants that I was collecting information concerning the research agenda in deafness for the next five to ten years. Conceding that I might have my own biases in that regard, each person was requested to provide up to three "big questions" that, given their areas of interest and expertise, they thought "will be on our agenda or should be on our agenda in the next decade." Participants were contacted through e-mail or in person, and approximately twenty individuals in each group were queried. They included deaf, hearing, and hard of hearing individuals drawn from seven different countries, but the results may be skewed by the fact that all were from "western" countries. Unless otherwise noted, all and only those priorities agreed upon by a simple majority of respondents are reported, in the order of the frequency of responses. Some "also rans" (defined by quantity, not quality) are also reported.

An important aside: To be true to my call for broad collaboration in decision making about research agendas, a more rigorous study would have included a survey of parents as well. Most parents of deaf children appear highly supportive of the research enterprise, and I have yet to encounter one who suggested that we are headed in the wrong direction. In order to allow them at least some "voice" in this context, let me list (in my own words) several of the questions brought up to me most frequently, all of which involve extensive research efforts:

- What is better for my child, sign language or spoken language?
- How does sign language (versus spoken language) affect English literacy?
- Does learning sign language impede or prevent a child's learning spoken language?
- What about cochlear implants?
- How can I get fair assessments of my child's academic skills (and avoid "labeling")?

To be fair, I have not asked parents of deaf children the same questions I asked the other three groups, and so I do not claim that this list would necessarily correspond to parents' answers. Nonetheless, I am confident that the top three priorities of most parents are in the list somewhere. If I ever do this study "for real," I will be sure to include not only deaf and hearing parents but also other professionals serving deaf individuals and the Deaf community.

Let us now consider the research priorities suggested by teachers of deaf students. First, I have to confess to some surprise at the level of enthusiasm in the responses received. All of the teachers responded to my query, often offering to be involved in the research and expressing a willingness to discuss the implications of alternative outcomes even before the research was designed. This was not the "eye-rolling" and tolerating, if not downright patronizing, behavior I expected based on the calumnies that led to this research. Not so surprisingly perhaps, the primary research concern of both deaf and hearing teachers was English literacy.

Topics included ways to bridge from ASL to English, to improve reading, and to overcome "the abysmal language skills" of deaf students in mainstream programs. There was also a broad desire, expressed in different ways, to characterize a priori differences between high-literacy and low-literacy deaf students in hopes of finding something in the former group that could help the latter group (Toscano, McKee, and Lepoutre n.d.).

A second priority for the teachers, following closely behind literacy, was evaluating the viability of bilingual education, especially in terms of its long-term impact. In part, this issue was linked to English literacy, and teachers expressed some concern that the value of ASL notwithstanding, the hoped-for transition from ASL to English was proving more elusive than expected. The third consensus priority among teachers was technology and particularly cochlear implants. Realistically, teachers are more frequently finding children with cochlear implants in their classrooms, and they often feel ill prepared to deal with them. Cochlear implants were not in the curriculum when most currently active teachers received their educations, and there is some trepidation concerning the best ways to take advantage of the benefits of implants while ensuring that those benefits are not overestimated. Concerns about ensuring appropriate socialization for children with implants were also raised.

Among the "also rans" in the teachers' priorities, perhaps most noteworthy was the concern about measuring up to state-mandated performance standards and exit examinations. Although the topic was clearly a priority for them, it appeared that most teachers saw performance standards as more of a school issue than a research issue. Interestingly, there was no apparent interest in research concerning teaching methods, broadly defined.

Next let us consider responses from the researchers, whose response rate was almost 100 percent. When I asked other university faculty the "next decade" question, the greatest number predicted the need for research on new technologies and especially cochlear implants. Second place went to evaluation of bilingual education and early intervention programs. English literacy came in a close third, followed by a number of "also rans." In the researcher sample, one person mentioned the need for research on teachers and teaching.

Finally, consider the responses from the educational administrators. These results should be interpreted with some caution because fewer than half of the administrators I contacted sent responses. In any case, there were only two consensus priorities on the research agenda from this limited group. First on the list was the need for research on the potential impact of various technologies. Cochlear implants again took the lead, but the administrators also mentioned unfulfilled expectations, both educationally and in research, concerning captioning, teleconferencing, and computing. The second point of consensus concerned "the demise of traditional programs" (i.e., schools for the deaf) and ways that they might be continued in the future. Research on teaching again did not come close to making the list, although two of the administrators raised the issue of state performance standards.

Taken together, the most informative aspect of these findings is that the teachers and the researchers agreed on the need to focus on English literacy, both in its own right and in the context of bilingual programs, and that the administrators, teachers, and researchers agreed on the need to focus on the impact of new technologies. In particular, the results of this informal experiment indicated that diverse researchers in the field—the international sample was drawn from a variety of settings—were clearly in agreement with teachers and educational administrators with regard to the issues of greatest concern to those involved in the day-to-day challenges of educating deaf students.

Beyond research questions to be put on the agenda in this new millennium, several respondents offered comments that seemed particularly thought provoking, and some caught me by surprise. I do not have room for all of them here, but a few are especially relevant as they relate to the other issues under discussion.

First, an issue that often comes up, but not always publicly, concerns "sensitivity" in research, sometimes confused with "political correctness." Jeffrey Braden put the issue very well:

> Will the research community be able to pursue topics that some may construe as unpleasant (e.g., the possibility that deaf people may have less-developed verbal reasoning skills, or the issue of how a deaf person growing up with normal hearing parents can be declared fluent in ASL as an adult)? I think this is a "big question" in the context of scientific research. I see too much of our time spent on thought policing and less time asking the tough questions and following them up with rigorous research.

The question is a good one, and one for which I simply do not have an answer. My impression is that more hearing people than deaf people become uncomfortable when I talk about the future of cochlear implants or discuss differences in cognitive abilities in deaf and hearing children (see Marschark and Lukomski, this volume). A hearing member in one audience even stood up and told me that it was inappropriate for me to talk about such things because they were not respectful of deaf individuals. Yes, there certainly is the need for sensitivity in the questions that we ask, especially when hearing people are doing the asking (Clark and Hoemann 1991). As I have argued in several places, however, to ignore some of these difficult questions or to leave them to someone else simply because they make us uncomfortable does an even greater disservice to deaf children.

One respondent, Rosemary Calderon, raised another general question about research in our field, expressing her concern about "the decentralization of specific education programs for deaf and hard of hearing children." Calderon wrote,

> Not only is deaf residential school enrollment diminishing, but there also seems to be a trend toward fewer local, centralized school programs specifically for kids with hearing loss. . . . Either parents are insisting more on mainstreaming, or schools are unwilling to contract out to other programs that previously provided appropriate programs. Education dollars are shrinking and schools are more reluctant to see their dollars go out of district. This puts much more demands on the child, family, and educators. This continued progression toward keeping deaf children in their homes and in their immediate neighborhood schools . . . can be far reaching (with both positive and negative consequences). It just seems that families, children, and educators need more support now than ever, but not much thought is being given to what would be of most benefit.

When I first read this comment, I interpreted "support" in terms of research and the need to take what we have learned in the laboratory and share it with the broader audience. Calderon meant more than that: Her call was for a variety of resources to be brought to bear where they will do the most good for deaf students, not to where they will be most politically or administratively expedient. The issue is an important one in the present context primarily as it relates to the need to bring all relevant parties to the table in order to make the best use of our limited resources in optimizing educational opportunities for deaf youngsters. It is one of those cases where we all seem to recognize the need, but it just does not happen.

A third observation of interest was made by Richard Johnson in the context of advocating for research about educational interpreting, an issue mentioned by only two other respondents. It is surprising how little research there is on how interpreting influences the teaching–learning process. But Johnson's comment was specifically directed to the challenge encountered by deaf children who enter programs that emphasize sign language when they have little or no experience with it. He noted,

> There seems to remain the myth that deaf children are born knowing sign language. There are no legal requirements that schools teach this to children. . . . They now require that schools beef up braille instruction for blind kids—but nothing similar for sign language and deaf kids.

With all of the excellent research concerning the acquisition of sign language by young children in deaf families, it is surprising how little we know about the growth of sign language fluency during the school years. There is a constant search for means of evaluating deaf children's sign language skills (Maller et al. 1999), but we have not yet tackled the question of how young deaf children just entering school are able to learn through sign language (or any other language) when they do not have a firm foundation in a first language. Clearly, this is a challenge for teachers in the classroom who find themselves having to teach content and language at the same time. Bowe (1998) and others have argued that language is not something that can be taught but must be learned. Bowe suggested that teaching language "is something better suited to middle- and high-school levels, as a supplement to active learning. For the preschool and elementary levels, I suspect the emphasis must be on supporting the 'learning' of language rather than on its teaching." The problem is that, at least at the elementary level, there are curricula to be followed that will have a direct impact on subsequent courses and on state-mandated performance measures. How much class content can a teacher expect children to acquire when they are not fluent in the language of instruction? Complaints in this regard are common when it is spoken or written English that the deaf child is somehow expected to handle. Surely, the issue is no less serious when sign language is the hurdle. At least in that situation, there is potential access to information in the classroom, but the issue has not even surfaced on the research horizon.

Two final observations from one respondent should be offered here because they resonate well with both the letter and spirit of this chapter. In reflecting on my query, Robert Davila of the National Technical Institute for the Deaf noted, "It's amazing how much we don't know . . ." and called for finding ways to "bridge research findings and practical applications (i.e., we need to know how deaf children learn so that we can teach 'to them')." In these comments, Davila provides implicit recognition of the fact that research and application must go hand-in-hand if we are to achieve our millennium agendas. In order to best fit our instructional methods with the skills and fluencies of deaf students, it is essential that we understand their cognitive structures and strategies. Coupled with many of the suggestions offered by participants in my informal study, and especially the enthusiasm of teachers, researchers, and some administrators, this perspective augurs well for the future of collaborative research in our field. The question now is how we pursue these goals.

MOVING AHEAD

Clearly, one of the greatest difficulties for research on the education of deaf students is the sheer complexity of the matter. Most deaf children come from families in which effective early communication is a challenge, where there is limited exposure to competent language models, and a variety of social and experiential hurdles have to be overcome. I have argued elsewhere that these issues are tightly intertwined, and they undoubtedly have subtle and not-so-subtle influences on educational achievement (Marschark 2000). Beyond the content matter itself, we need to keep in mind that *good* studies take time, patience, and effort. They do not always provide "politically correct" answers, but when done properly they can provide valid answers. Research in our field has made incredible strides in the last two decades, even if we continue to be frustrated with a need for even faster progress. And what are our alternatives? There probably is no other segment of our educational system in which research and teaching have as much to offer each other or are in as much need of each other. Previous studies of language, learning, and literacy of deaf learners have now put researchers in a much better position to contribute to education than ever before. Advances in educational theory, methodology, and technology give us new avenues for the enhancement of academic success for deaf and hard of hearing students—opportunities that cannot be missed.

Barriers between research and application were not built overnight, and they will not be dismantled overnight—and they certainly will not be dismantled by demanding their abolition. What we need is more than dialogues among teachers, researchers, parents, and educational administrators. We need multisided collaborations with clear, commonly-agreed-upon, and realistic agendas, not ones dictated by a single constituent group while ignoring the realities of the others. Alas, we are not yet there, but we have seen significant progress as motivated teachers, parents, and investigators have torn down or gone around barriers to help deaf children succeed. Maybe not everyone feels this way, but there are enough of us. All we ask is that, as Lee Iacocca is reputed to have said, please, "lead, follow, or get out of the way."

SUMMARY

This chapter has argued that, armed with better tools and better knowledge of how to use them, we are in a much better position than ever before to make progress in research concerning deaf learners. Although research priorities and research accomplishments are in the eyes of the beholder, basic and applied research over the past 25 years has made great strides in elucidating psychological and situational factors influencing the development and educational success of individuals who were deaf or hard of hearing. Changes in society and technology may influence the precise nature of our research questions but do not make them any less interesting. No one who understood the full complexity of the question ever promised easy or fast solutions to the challenge of literacy among deaf students. No one is going to resolve the issue alone. This is not a time for giving up, retrenchment, or rhetoric. It is a time to roll up our sleeves, set clear goals, and set to work collaboratively. A coincidence of the calendar has given us the feeling of the beginning. Let's all take advantage of it.

REFERENCES

Becker, R., and C. Artelt. 1998. Evaluation of a training program using visible speech in German schools for the deaf. *Journal of Deaf Studies and Deaf Education* 3:157–72.

Bowe, F. 1998. Language development in deaf children. *Journal of Deaf Studies and Deaf Education* 3:73–77.

Calderon, R., and M. Greenberg. 1997. The effectiveness of early intervention for deaf children and children with hearing loss. In *The effectiveness of early intervention*, ed. M. J. Guralnik, 455–82. Baltimore: Paul H. Brookes.

Clark, M. D., and H. W. Hoemann. 1991. Methodological issues in deafness research. In *Advances in cognition, education, and deafness*, ed. S. Martin, 423–28. Washington D.C.: Gallaudet University Press.

Conrad, R. 1979. *The deaf school child: Language and cognition*. London: Harper and Row.

Crouch, R. A. 1997. Letting the deaf be deaf: Reconsidering the use of cochlear implants in prelingually deaf children. *Hastings Center Report* 27:14–21.

Francis, H. W., M. E. Koch, J. R. Wyatt, and J. K. Niparko. 1999. Trends in educational placement and cost-benefit considerations in children with cochlear implants. *Archives of Otolaryngology and Head and Neck Surgery* 125:499–503.

Furth, H. G. 1966. *Thinking without language*. New York: Free Press.

Gaustad, M. G. 2000. Morphographic analysis as a word identification strategy for deaf readers. *Journal of Deaf Studies and Deaf Education* 5:60–81.

Geers, A. E., and J. S. Moog, eds. 1994. Effectiveness of cochlear implants and tactile aids for deaf children: The sensory aids study at Central Institute for the Deaf. *Volta Review* 96:1–231.

Hertzog, M., M. S. Stinson, and R. Keiffer. 1989. Effects of caption modification and instructor intervention on comprehension of a technical film. *Educational Technology Research and Development* 37:59–68.

Kampfe, C. M., M. Harrison, T. Oettinger, J. Ludington, C. McDonald-Bell, and H. C. Pillsbury III. 1993. Parental expectations as a factor in evaluating children for the multichannel cochlear implant. *American Annals of the Deaf* 138: 297–303.

Lane, H. 1992. *The mask of benevolence.* New York: Alfred A. Knopf.

Lang, H. G., and W. Stokoe. 2000. A treatise on signed and spoken language in early 19th century deaf education in America. *Journal of Deaf Studies and Deaf Education* 5:196–216.

Leybaert, J., A. Content, and J. Alegria. 1987. The development of written word processing: The case of deaf children. Workshop presentation, ISPL Congress, University of Kassel.

Maller, S. J., J. L. Singleton, S. J. Supalla, and T. Wax. 1999. The development and psychometric properties of the American Sign Language Proficiency Assessments (ASL-PA). *Journal of Deaf Studies and Deaf Education* 4:249–69.

Marschark, M. 2000. Education and development of deaf children—or is it development and education? In *Development in context: The deaf children in the family and at school,* ed. P. Spencer, C. Erting, and M. Marschark, 275–92. Mahwah, N.J.: Lawrence Erlbaum.

Marschark, M., P. Siple, D. Lillo-Martin, and V. Everhart. 1997. *Relations of language and thought: The view from sign language and deaf children.* New York: Oxford University Press.

Moores, D. F., and K. P. Meadow-Orlans, eds. 1990. *Educational and developmental aspects of deafness.* Washington D.C.: Gallaudet University Press.

Musselman, C. 2000. How do children who can't hear learn to read an alphabetic script? A review of the literature on reading and deafness. *Journal of Deaf Studies and Deaf Education* 5:9–31.

National Institute on Deafness and Other Communication Disorders. 1991, 1992, 1993. *National Strategic Research Plan* (NIH Publication no. 95–3711). Washington D.C.: U.S. Department of Health and Human Services. [Available: http://www.nih.gov/nidcd/about/director/strategic.htm.]

National Institute on Deafness and Other Communication Disorders. 1999. *NIDCD strategic plan: FY2000–FY2002.* [Available: http://www.nih.gov/nidcd/about/director/strategic.htm]

Owston, R. D. 1997. The World Wide Web: A technology to enhance teaching and learning? *Educational Researcher* 27:27–33.

Power, D., and G. R. Leigh. 2000. Principles and practices of literacy development for deaf learners: A historical overview. *Journal of Deaf Studies and Deaf Education* 5:3–8.

Robbins, A. M., M. J. Osberger, R. T. Miyamoto, and K. S. Kessler. 1995. Language development in young children with cochlear implants. *Advances in Oto-Rhino-Laryngology* 50:160–65.

Rönnberg, J., U. Andersson, B. Lyxell, and K.-E. Spens. 1998. Vibrotactile speech tracking support: Cognitive prerequisites. *Journal of Deaf Studies and Deaf Education* 3:143–56.

Rose, D. E., M. Vernon, and A. E. Pool. 1996. Cochlear implants in prelingually deaf children. *American Annals of the Deaf* 141:258–61.

Siple, P., ed. 1978. *Understanding language through sign language research.* New York: Academic Press.

Spencer, P., C. Erting, and M. Marschark, eds. 2000. *Development in context: The deaf child in the family and a school.* Mahwah, N.J.: Lawrence Erlbaum.

Stanovich, K. 1986. Matthew effects. *Reading Research Quarterly* 4:360–406.

Tomblin, J. B., L. Spencer, S. Flock, R. Tyler, and B. Gantz. 1999. A comparison of language achievement in children with cochlear implants and children using hearing aids. *Journal of Speech, Language, and Hearing Research* 42:497–511.

Toscano, R. M., B. McKee, and D. Lepoutre. n.d. *Success with written English: Reflections of D/deaf college students: A pilot study.* Manuscript submitted for publication.

Traxler, C. B. 2000. The Stanford Achievement Test, 9th Edition: National norming and performance standards for deaf and hard-of-hearing students. *Journal of Deaf Studies and Deaf Education* 5:337–48.

Waltzman, S., N. Cohen, R. Gomolin, J. Green, W. Shapiro, D. Brackett, and C. Zara. 1997. Perception and production results in children implanted between 2 and 5 years of age. *Advances in Oto-Rhino-Laryngology* 52:177–80.

Waters, G. S., and D. G. Doehring. 1990. Reading acquisition in congenitally deaf children who communicate orally: Insights from an analysis of component reading, language, and memory skills. In *Reading and its development,* ed. T. H. Carr and B. A. Levy, 323–73. San Diego: Academic Press.

Wilbur, R. B. 2000. The use of ASL to support the development of English and literacy. *Journal of Deaf Studies and Deaf Education* 8:81–104.

INDEX

Note: Page numbers followed by a *t* refer to tables.

academic achievement tests, 30
accommodations, in cognitive assessments, 23–26
adaptive behavior, assessing, 21–22
American Sign Language
  apparent motion phenomenon and, 42–47
  linguistic research on, 162–63
  phonological structure, 42n
  in total communication, 171
  visual-spatial skills and, 74
Americans with Disabilities Act (ADA), 167–68
apparent motion
  for American Sign Language stimuli, 42–47
  for human movement, 40–41
applied research, 180–81. *See also* deafness research; educational research
articulatory loop, 76
aspectuality, 128–29
assessment accommodations, 23–26
assessment modifications, 26
assistive technology, 164
auditory perception, 38–39
  emotional development and, 138
  phonemic restoration effects, 39–40, 47
autism, 118

Baker Shenk, Charlotte, 162–63
basic research, 180–81. *See also* deafness research
behavioral genetics, 29
behavioral research, 163–64
belief-desire psychology, 115
Bellugi, Ursula, 162, 163
bilingual education, 12, 171
Braden, Jeffrey, 193
brain development, 12–13

Calderon, Rosemary, 193–94
captioning, 183
career-development awards, 165

Carolina Picture Vocabulary Test, 92
CDI. *See* Communicative Development Inventory
Central Institute for the Deaf Preschool Performance Scale, 27
children (*see also* deaf children of deaf parents; deaf children of hearing parents; deaf preschoolers)
  of deaf adults, 171
  hearing, sign language iconicity and, 67–68
civil proceedings, cognitive assessments and, 18–19
Clark, Andy, 11
Clark, Herb, 8–10
classifier morphemes, 56
clinical cognitive assessments (*see also* intelligence tests)
  accommodations, 23–26
  challenges of, 31
  contexts for, 14–19
    educational, 15–17
    forensic, 18–19
    medical, 18
    social services, 17–18
  controversies with
    deficit vs. difference, 28–29
    signed vs. interpreted administration, 30
    special vs. general norms, 29–30
    verbal vs. nonverbal testing, 30, 72–73
  differential diagnosis, 15–16
  formal tests, 23–28
  informal tests, 22–23
  interviews and record reviews, 20–22
  observations, 20
  purpose and importance of, 14–15, 19
  relationship to experimental assessments, 32
cochlear implants, 164, 172, 183–84, 192
cognitive abilities
  differences between deaf and hearing students, 71, 83
  environmental influences and, 29
  of Italian preschoolers, 57–59

cognitive abilities *(continued):*
language and, 71, 72, 73–75
low performance levels by deaf students, 71–72
memory abilities and, 75–77
organization of knowledge and, 77–79
problem-solving skills, 79–81
cognitive assessments *(see also* clinical cognitive assessments; intelligence tests)
of adaptive behavior, 21–22
cultural fairness issue, 73
issues with problem-solving skills, 79–81
of Italian preschoolers, 53
mental status exams, 21
of prior functioning and history, 22
verbal vs. nonverbal, 30, 72–73
cognitive development
brain development and, 12, 13
issues of appropriate development for deaf persons, 22
prelinguistic, 7–13
sign language acquisition and, 6–7, 12, 72
social constructs of deafness and, 6
use of hands and, 12–13
vocabulary development and, 88
Cokely, Dennis, 162–63
Communicative Development Inventory (CDI), 95–97, 107–8
complementation, syntactic, 127–28
completion effects, 39–40, 47. *See also* apparent motion
complex emotions, 154
computer technology, 164, 173–74, 183
construct-irrelevant variance, 24–25
construct underrepresentation, 24, 25, 30
conversational experience
emotional development and, 152–53
display rules, 143
facial expression identification, 138
mixed emotions, 146
mental state talk, 126–27, 138
theory of mind development and, 147–50, 151
criminal proceedings, cognitive assessments and, 18–19

Davila, Robert, 195
deaf children of deaf parents
behavioral research on, 163
Italian study of cognitive and language abilities in, 49–68
theory of mind development in, 119–21, 125, 128–29, 130, 149
vocabulary development in, 86, 98, 107
deaf children of hearing parents
behavioral research on, 163
early language experience and, 74
emotional development in, 153, 154
display rules, 143–45
identification and interpretation of facial expressions, 138–42
mixed emotions, 146–47
Italian study of cognitive and language abilities in, 49–68
theory of mind development in, 119, 120
aspectuality and, 128–29
critical period hypothesis and, 123–24
developmental delays, 129–30
educational environment and, 121–23
language and, 125–27
performance on false-belief tasks, 124–25, 148–50
vocabulary development in, 95–96, 99–100
deaf community
bicultural identity and, 173
cochlear implants and, 172
disability rights movement and, 172–73
neglected subgroups in, 174
oral vs. manual controversy and, 170–71
residential schools and, 171–72
total communication concept and, 171
deafness
paradigms for, 2
as socially constructed abstraction, 6
visual perception and, 38
deafness research, 179, 196
application issues, 195
collaborations and, 187, 190, 195
combining applied and basic investigations, 180–81
complexity of issues in, 195
factors affecting, 164
federally designated priorities, 185–87, 188–89*t*
federal support, 165, 166*t*, 167*t*, 168*t*
informally collected research agenda, 190–93
interdisciplinary approach, 1–4
linguistic and behavioral, 162–64
pressures for improving reading abilities and, 181–82

resource allocation in education and, 193–94
sensitivity and, 193
social conflict and, 173
on technology and education, 182–85
deaf preschoolers, Italian
language background and abilities, 50–51
study of cognitive and language abilities in, 49–68
assessment methodology and methodological problems, 53–57
cognitive ability, 57–59, 65–66
collection of normative data, 57
description of study children and families, 51–53
grammatical comprehension, 62–65, 66, 67
lexical comprehension, 59–62, 66
observation methodology, 53
Deaf President Now movement, 168
Department of Education, 187
desire psychology, 114–15, 119
developmental-interactive model, 2
Developmental Test of Visual Motor Integration (VMI), 53, 57–59
diaries, parental, 93–94
differential diagnosis, 15–16
Dimensional Change Card Sort task, 125
disabilities
Americans with Disabilities Act, 167–68
developmental, vocabulary growth and, 98
learning, 16
disability rights movement, 172–73
display rules
overview of, 142–43
social maturity and, 143
study of deaf children, 144–45
theory of mind and, 151–52
Down syndrome, 98
dynamic testing, 22–23

education
attainment levels, improvements in, 169
bilingual/bicultural, 12, 171
least restrictive environment requirement, 166–67
oral vs. manual controversy in, 170–71
role of cognitive assessments in, 15–17
total communication concept, 171
educational research (*see also* deafness research)

application issues, 195
collaborations, 187, 190, 195
combining with basic research, 180–81
complexity of issues in, 195
on educational interpreting, 194
federally designated priorities, 185–87, 188–89t
future of, 196
pressures for success and, 181–82
research agenda informally collected from diverse groups, 190–93
resource allocation in education and, 193–94
sensitivity and, 193
on sign language acquisition, 194
technology-related areas, 182–85
egalitarian fallacy, 24
emotional ambivalence, 145–47
emotional development
complex emotions and, 154
display rules, 142–45
identification and interpretation of facial expressions, 137–42
mixed emotions, 145–47
research areas, 135, 153–55
role of language and conversational experience in, 136–37, 138, 143, 146, 152–53
significance of, 135–36
theory of mind and, 147–52
emotional understanding, 136
environment, 29. *See also* language environment
experimental cognitive assessments, 32

facial expressions, identification and interpretation, 137–42
factor analysis, 28–29
false-belief tasks
deaf children and, 117–18, 124–25, 148–50
description of, 114–15
second-order, 151–52
syntactic complementation and, 127
verbal ability and, 116–17
false photograph test, 124, 149
fast-mapping, 101, 103–7
federal government
deafness research priorities and, 185–87, 188–89t
legislation affecting deaf persons, 166–68

federal government *(continued):*
  support for deafness research and proj-
    ects, 165, 166t, 167t, 168t
fellowships, 165
folk psychology, 114. *See also* theory of
  mind
forensics, cognitive assessments and,
  18–19
formal cognitive tests. *See* intelligence
  tests

GAEL-P. *See* Grammatical Analysis of
  Elicited Language-Presentence
  Level
Gallaudet Infant Study, 164
Gallaudet University, 168
gestures, prelinguistic, 7, 8–13
grammatical ability, of Italian preschool-
  ers, 62–65, 66, 67
  assessment tools, 53, 54–55
Grammatical Analysis of Elicited Lan-
  guage-Presentence Level (GAEL-
  P), 91, 97

hands, brain development and, 12–13
Heumann, Judy, 173

iconicity, 55, 67–68
Individual with Disabilities Education
  Act, 16, 166, 187
informal cognitive tests, 22–23
information technology, 183
intelligence. *See* cognitive abilities
intelligence tests
  accommodations, 23–26
  batteries, 25, 28–29
  construct-irrelevant variance and con-
    struct underrepresentation in,
    24–25
  controversies with
    deficit vs. difference, 28–29
    signed vs. interpreted administra-
      tion, 30
    special vs. general norms, 29–30
    verbal vs. nonverbal, 30, 72–73
  types of, 27–28
interdisciplinary research
  concerns and issues with, 2–3
  dialogues in, 3, 4
  integrating research paradigms in, 1–2
  value of, 1, 4
Internet, 183
interpreters, 167

administration of intelligence tests and,
  30, 31
in education, need for research on, 194
interviews, 20–22
intuitive psychology, 114. *See also* theory
  of mind
Italian, spoken
  grammatical comprehension in
    preschoolers, 62–63, 66
  lexical comprehension in preschoolers,
    59–60, 66
Italian Sign Language (LIS), 49
  classifier morphemes, 56
  grammatical comprehension in
    preschoolers, 63–65, 67
  iconicity and, 55, 67–68
  lexical comprehension in preschoolers,
    60–62, 66
  methodological issues with language
    tests and, 55–57
  used by hearing parents, 50–51

joint attention, 150
judicial proceedings, cognitive assessments and, 18–19

'K' awards, 165
key-word strategy, 82
Klima, Edward, 162, 163
knowledge, organization in long-term
  memory, 77–79

language assessments, of Italian
  preschoolers, 53–57
language environment
  cognitive development and, 6–7, 12,
    74–75
  parental hearing status and, 50–51, 74,
    136–37
  social-cognitive competence and,
    126–27
  vocabulary development and, 94
language-loaded tests
  arguments for and against, 30
  defined, 15n
  inappropriate assessment of mental re-
    tardation, 15
  problems with, 23, 24–25
  vs. nonverbal testing, 30, 72–73
language-reduced tests, 23, 27, 30, 72
language sampling, 92–93
language skills/development (*see also*
  conversational experience)

cognitive abilities and, 71, 72, 73–75
emotional development and, 136–37
of Italian preschoolers, 50–51, 66–68
    grammatical comprehension, 62–65
    lexical comprehension, 59–62, 66
    sign language iconicity and, 67–68
parental hearing status and, 50–51, 74,
    136–37
prelinguistic, 7–13
as research priority, 191–92
social-cognitive competence and,
    126–27
theory of mind and, 116–17, 125–28
visual-spatial skills and, 74
language space, 8–12
language time, 10, 12
learning disabilities, 16
least restrictive environment, 166–67
Leiter International Performance Scale
    (LIPS), 53, 58, 59
lexical comprehension, of Italian
    preschoolers, 59–62, 66
    assessment tools, 53, 54–55
lexicality constraints, 46–47
line of regard, 150–51
linguistic research, 162–63
LIPS. See Leiter International Performance
    Scale
LIS. See Italian Sign Language
literacy instruction, 81–82
long-term memory, organization of
    knowledge in, 77–79
L-space. See language-space
L-time. See language time

MacArthur Communicative Development
    Inventory. See Communicative De-
    velopment Inventory
manual (manifested) space, 11–13
"Master Mind" game, 80
Matrix Analogies Test, 27
medical services, cognitive assessments
    and, 18
memory
    articulatory loop, 76
    coding, 75–76
    organization and retrieval, 77–79
    strategies, 76–77
mental health problems, 174
mental health services, 31
mental retardation
    assessments of adaptive behavior and,
        21

assessments of prior cognitive function
    and, 22
misidentification of, 15
mental state talk, 126–27, 138
mental status exams, 21
Mirzoeff, Nicholas, 6
mixed emotions, 145–47
motion perception (see also apparent mo-
    tion; visual perception)
    constraints on, 40–41, 46–47
M-space. See manual space

National Institute of Deafness and Other
    Communication Disorders
    (NIDCD), 165, 166t, 167t, 168t,
    185–87, 188–89t
National Institutes of Health (NIH), 165,
    185, 187
National Research Services Awards, 165
National Science Foundation, 187
naturalistic language sampling, 92–93
NIDCD. See National Institute of Deaf-
    ness and Other Communication
    Disorders
NIH. See National Institutes of Health
nonverbal tests, 23, 27, 30, 72
novel words
    fast mapping strategy, 101, 103–7
    novel mapping strategy, 102–3, 104–5
    phonological encoding, 107

observations, in cognitive assessments, 20
occupational status, 169
oral deaf children, memory coding in,
    75–76
oral vs. manual education controversy,
    170–71

parent report instruments, 94–97. See also
    Communicative Development In-
    ventory
parents
    assessing child vocabulary knowledge,
        93–97
    hearing, use of sign language, 50–51,
        170
    hearing status
        child language development and,
            50–51, 74, 136–37
        child theory of mind development
            and, 119–21
        child vocabulary development and,
            95–96, 98–100

Peabody Picture Vocabulary Test-Form B (PPVT-B), 53–54, 55, 57, 59–62
Peabody Picture Vocabulary Test (PPVT), 91
Peabody Picture Vocabulary Test-Revised (PPVT-R), 55
perceptual space, 8–12
perceptual time, 10–11, 12
performance standards, 192
phonemic restoration effect, 39–40, 47
PPVT. *See* Peabody Picture Vocabulary Tests
prelinguistic cognitive development, 8–13
problem-solving skills, 79–81
Prosocial Behaviour Questionnaire, 143
prosocial reasoning, 144–45
P-space. *See* perceptual space
psychology of deafness, 4
P-time. *See* perceptual time
Public Law 94–142, 166
Public Law 101–476. *See* Individuals with Disabilities Education Act

Ravens Progressive Matrices tests, 27
reading instruction
    reading comprehension strategies, 82
    repeated readings methodology, 81–82
reading skills/comprehension
    expectations for research to improve, 181–82
    information technology and, 183
    as research priority, 191–92
    strategies for improving, 81–82
record reviews, 20–22
reduced-language tests, 23, 27, 30
referents, 101–2
rehearsal, 76–77
repeated readings strategy, 81–82
representational theory of mind
    in deaf children, 118–19, 129–30
    language and, 117
    overview of, 114–15
    syntactic complementation and, 127–28
residential schools, 166, 171–72
Reynell Developmental Language Scales, 95
rote memorization, 76–77

Schlesinger, Hilde, 163
schools
    least restrictive environment requirement, 166–67
    residential, 166, 171–72

semantic memory, 77–79
sensory compensation, 74
sign language interpreters. *See* interpreters
sign languages (*see also* American Sign Language; Italian Sign Language)
    early acquisition
        cognitive development and, 6–7, 12, 72
        as research area, 194
    iconicity and, 55, 67–68
    in memory coding, 76
    oral vs. manual controversy in education, 170–71
    phonological structure, 42n
    theory of mind and, 128
    total communication and, 163
    used by hearing parents, 50–51, 170
    visual perception and, 38, 39, 42–47, 74
Sign Supported Italian, 49, 51
Small Business Innovation Research grants, 165
Snidjer-Ooman Nonverbal Intelligence Tests, 27
social change
    conflict and, 161, 169–74
    federal legislation and, 166–68
    federal support for deafness research and projects, 165, 166t
    improvements in educational attainment and occupational status, 169
    as interactive process, 161
    from linguistic and behavioral research, 162–64
    technology and, 164–65, 173–74
social referencing, 137
social services, cognitive assessments and, 17–18
space
    language- and perceptual-space constructs, 8–12
    manual-space construct, 11–13
special education, 16–17
Stanford Achievement Test-9th edition, 30
state performance standards, 192
Stokoe, William, 162–63
Switzer, Mary, 163

Tannen, Deborah, 169
TCGB. *See* Test for Grammatical Comprehension in Children
teachers, research priorities and, 191–92
technology

and education, research areas in, 182–85
impact on deaf persons, 164–65, 173–74
test batteries, 25, 28–29
Test for Grammatical Comprehension in
    Children (TCGB), 54–57, 62–65
Test of Language Development, 91
test-teach-test assessments, 22–23
theory of mind
    defined and described, 113–14, 147
    emotional development and, 147–52
    language and, 116–17
    representational, 114–15
    sign language and, 128
    tests, control questions in, 125–26
theory of mind development
    domain-specific vs. domain-general
        knowledge, 116
    line of regard and, 150
    recent research in, 114
    social experience and, 147–48
    theory theory vs. module concept,
        115–16
theory of mind development in deaf chil-
    dren
    aspectuality, 128–29
    critical period hypothesis, 123–24
    developmental delays, 117–19, 148–50
    educational environment and, 121–23
    and language, 152–53
        conversational hypothesis, 147–50
        as data for theory of construction,
            126–27
        as representational structure, 127–28
        as task demand, 125–26
        line of regard and, 150–51
        new and future research areas, 128–29,
            130–31
        overview of, 129–30
        parental hearing status and, 119–21
        sign language and, 128
        theory theory vs. module concept,
            119–24
time, early conception of, 10–11
total communication, 163
"Tower of Hanoi" puzzle, 80
"Twenty Questions," 79

Universal Nonverbal Intelligence Test, 27

verbal ability, false-belief tasks and,
    116–17
verbal tests. See language-loaded tests
Vineland Adaptive Behavior Scale, 21

visual completion effects, 39–40. See also
    apparent motion
visual perception
    apparent motion, 40–41
        of American Sign Language stimuli,
            42–47
    completion effects, 39–40
    deafness and, 38
    of hearing persons, 38–39
    sign language and, 38, 39, 74
VMI. See Developmental Test of Visual
    Motor Integration
vocabulary assessments
    Communicative Development Inven-
        tory, 95–97, 107–8
    direct testing, 90–91
    naturalistic language sampling, 92–93
    parental diaries, 93–94
    parent report instruments, 94–97
    tests normed for deaf children, 91–92
    tests normed for hearing children, 91
vocabulary development
    cognitive development and, 88
    dimensions of, 89
    early vocabulary growth rate, 98–100
    factors affecting, 89
    findings from parent report instru-
        ments, 94–97
    level of vocabulary knowledge and,
        105–7, 108
    on-going research in, 89–90, 106–7
    phonological encoding of novel words,
        107
    vocabulary size assessments, 90–97
    word-learning processes, 100–7
vocabulary growth rate
    in deaf children of deaf parents,
        98–99
    in deaf children of hearing parents,
        99–100
    in hearing children, 98
Vocational Rehabilitation Administration,
    163

Wechsler Intelligence Scales, 27
Wechsler Performance Scales, 27, 31
Williams, Boyce, 163
word-learning processes
    based on knowledge of adults' social
        intentions, 102
    based on referents, 101–2
    fast-mapping, 101, 103–7
    in hearing children, 100–1

word-learning processes *(continued):*
  level of vocabulary knowledge and,
    105–7, 108
  novel mapping strategy, 102–3, 104–5
  phonological encoding, 107

working memory
  articulatory loop, 76
  coding, 75–76
  strategies, 76–77